The Standard Edition of the Complete Psychological Works of Sigmund Freud

Volume XVII

Sigmund Freud in 1916

THE STANDARD EDITION OF THE COMPLETE PSYCHOLOGICAL WORKS OF

Sigmund Freud

VOLUME XVII
(1917–1919)

AN INFANTILE NEUROSIS

and

OTHER WORKS

TRANSLATED FROM THE GERMAN
UNDER THE GENERAL EDITORSHIP OF
James Strachey

IN COLLABORATION WITH
Anna Freud

ASSISTED BY
Alix Strachey and Alan Tyson

VINTAGE
THE HOGARTH PRESS
AND THE INSTITUTE OF PSYCHO-ANALYSIS

Published by Vintage 2001

2 4 6 8 10 9 7 5 3 1

First published in Great Britain in 1955 by
The Hogarth Press

Vintage
Random House, 20 Vauxhall Bridge Road,
London SW1V 2SA

Random House Australia (Pty) Limited
20 Alfred Street, Milsons Point, Sydney
New South Wales 2061, Australia

Random House New Zealand Limited
18 Poland Road, Glenfield, Auckland 10,
New Zealand

Random House (Pty) Limited
Endulini, 5A Jubilee Road, Parktown 2193,
South Africa

The Random House Group Limited Reg. No. 954009
www.randomhouse.co.uk

A CIP catalogue record for this book
is available from the British Library

ISBN 0 09 942672 2

Papers used by Random House are natural, recyclable products made from wood grown in sustainable forests. The manufacturing processes conform to the environmental regulations of the country of origin

Printed and bound in Denmark by
Nørhaven A/S, Viborg

CONTENTS

VOLUME SEVENTEEN

FROM THE HISTORY OF AN INFANTILE NEUROSIS (1918[1914])

SHORTER WRITINGS (1919)

FROM THE HISTORY OF AN INFANTILE NEUROSIS
(1918 [1914])

EDITOR'S NOTE

AUS DER GESCHICHTE EINER INFANTILEN NEUROSE

(*a*) German Editions:
1918 *S.K.S.N.*, **4**, 578–717.
1922 *S.K.S.N.*, **5**, 1–140.
1924 Leipzig, Vienna and Zurich: Internationaler Psychoanalytischer Verlag. Pp. 132.
1924 *G.S.*, **8**, 439–567.
1931 *Neurosenlehre und Technik*, 37–171.
1947 *G.W.*, **12**, 29–157.

(*b*) English Translation:
'From the History of an Infantile Neurosis'
1925 *C.P.*, **3**, 473–605. (Tr. A. and J. Strachey.)

A few changes were introduced into the 1924 German edition, mainly in the matter of dates; and a long footnote was added at the end. The present translation is a revision of the one published in 1925.

This is the most elaborate and no doubt the most important of all Freud's case histories. It was in February, 1910, that the wealthy young Russian who is its subject came to Freud for analysis. His first course of treatment, which is the one reported on in this paper, lasted from then until July, 1914, when Freud regarded the case as completed. He began writing the case history in October of the same year and finished it in early November.[1] He held back its publication, however, for four years. No changes of moment, he tells us (p. 7*n*), were made in its final form, but two long passages were inserted. The later history of the case, after the conclusion of the first course of treatment, was described by Freud in the footnote which he added in the 1924 edition at the end of the paper (pp. 121–2).

[1] These dates are derived from Ernest Jones (1955, 312), based upon Freud's correspondence. In the footnote below, p. 7, he speaks of the winter of 1914–15.

Some still later information will also be found there, derived partly from material published subsequently by Freud himself and partly from data that have come to light since his death.

Freud made a number of references to the case of the 'Wolf Man' in works published both before and after the case history itself, and these may be worth enumerating. The first public evidence of Freud's interest in the case was a paragraph appearing over his signature in the early autumn of 1912 (*Zbl. Psychoanal.*, **2**, 680), and evidently stimulated by the wolf dream which is the central feature of the case history. It came out under the rubric 'Offener Sprechsaal' ('Open Forum') and ran as follows:

'I should be glad if those of my colleagues who are practising analysts would collect and analyse carefully any of their patients' dreams whose interpretation justifies the conclusion that *the dreamers had been witnesses of sexual intercourse in their early years*. A hint is no doubt enough to make it obvious that such dreams are in more than one respect of quite special value. Only those dreams can, of course, be regarded as evidential which themselves occurred in childhood and were remembered from that period.

Freud.'

A further paragraph on the subject appeared early in 1913 (*Int. Z. Psychoanal.*, **1**, 79):

'Children's Dreams with a Special Significance

'In the Open Forum of the *Zbl. Psychoanal.*, **2**, 680, I requested my colleagues to publish any dreams occurring in childhood "whose interpretation justifies the conclusion that the dreamers had been witnesses of sexual intercourse in their early years". I have now to thank Frau Dr. Mira Gincburg (of Breitenau-Schaffhausen) for a first contribution which seems to fulfil the conditions laid down. I prefer to postpone a critical consideration of this dream until more comparative material has been collected.

Freud.'

This note was followed by Dr. Gincburg's account of the dream in question. A similar dream was reported by Hitschmann later in the same year (*Int. Z. Psychoanal.*, **1**, 476), but there were no further communications on the subject by Freud. During the same summer, however, he published his paper on 'The Occurrence in Dreams of Material from Fairy

Tales' (1913*d*), which actually reported the wolf-dream and which was in part reprinted in the case history (p. 29 ff.); and early in the next year came the paper on '*Fausse Reconnaissance* in Psycho-Analytic Treatment' (1914*a*), describing another episode in the case. This, too, is partly reprinted here (p. 85). The metapsychological paper on 'Repression' (1915*d*), which was published before the present work though written after it, contains a paragraph referring to the patient's wolf phobia. Many years after the publication of the case history Freud returned to the case in the course of a discussion of children's animal phobias in *Inhibitions, Symptoms and Anxiety* (1926*d*). In Chapters IV and VII of that work the present patient's wolf phobia is compared with the horse phobia analysed in the case of 'Little Hans' (1909*b*). Finally, in one of his very last papers, 'Analysis Terminable and Interminable' (1937*c*), Freud made some critical comments on the technical innovation of setting a time-limit to the treatment, which he introduced in this case and describes on p. 11.

The primary significance of the case history in Freud's eyes at the time of its publication was clearly the support it provided for his criticisms of Adler and more especially of Jung. Here was conclusive evidence to refute any denial of infantile sexuality. But much else of high value emerged from the treatment, though some of it had already been given to the world during the four years' interval between the composition of the case history and its publication. There was, for instance, the relation between 'primal scenes' and 'primal phantasies', which led directly to the obscure problem of the possibility that the mental content of primal phantasies could be inherited. This was examined in Lecture XXIII of the *Introductory Lectures* (1916–17) but was further elaborated here in the additional passages on pp. 57 ff. and 95 ff. Again, the remarkable material in Section VII, dealing with the patient's anal erotism, was used by Freud in his paper 'On Transformations of Instinct' (1917*c*), p. 125 below.

Even more important was the light thrown by the present analysis on the earlier, oral, organization of the libido, which is discussed at some length on pp. 106–7 below. Freud's first *published* reference to this organization was in a paragraph added in 1915 to the third edition of his *Three Essays* (1905*d*), *Standard*

Ed., **7**, 198. The preface to this third edition bears the date 'October 1914'—the precise month during which he was writing his paper on the 'Wolf Man'. It seems likely that the 'cannibalistic' material revealed in this analysis played an important part in preparing the way for some of the most momentous of the theories with which Freud was occupied at this period: the interconnections between incorporation, identification, the formation of an ego-ideal, the sense of guilt and pathological states of depression. Some of these theories had already been expressed in the last essay of *Totem and Taboo* (written in the middle of 1913) and his paper on narcissism (finished early in 1914). Others were to appear in his 'Mourning and Melancholia'. This last was not published until 1917. But it was given its final shape at the beginning of May, 1915; and many of the views contained in it had been stated before the Vienna Psycho-Analytical Society on December 30, 1914, only a few weeks after the composition of this case history (Jones, 1955, 367).

Perhaps the chief clinical finding was the evidence revealed of the determining part played in the patient's neurosis by his *primary* feminine impulses. The very marked degree of his bisexuality was only a confirmation of views which had long been held by Freud and which dated back to the time of his friendship with Fliess. But in his subsequent writings Freud laid greater stress than before on the fact of the *universal* occurrence of bisexuality and on the existence of an 'inverted' or 'negative' Oedipus complex. This thesis was given its clearest expression in the passage on the 'complete' Oedipus complex in Chapter III of *The Ego and the Id* (1923*b*). On the other hand, a tempting theoretical inference to the effect that motives related to bisexuality are the invariable determinants of repression is strongly resisted (p. 110 f.)—a point to which Freud recurred at greater length soon afterwards in ' "A Child is Being Beaten" ' (1919*e*), p. 200 ff. below.

Finally, it is perhaps legitimate to draw attention to the extraordinary literary skill with which Freud has handled the case. He was faced with the pioneer's task of giving a scientific account of psychological events of undreamt-of novelty and complexity. The outcome is a work which not only avoids the dangers of confusion and obscurity but from first to last holds the reader's fascinated attention.

FROM THE HISTORY OF AN INFANTILE NEUROSIS[1]

I

INTRODUCTORY REMARKS

The case upon which I propose to report in the following pages (once again only in a fragmentary manner) is characterized by a number of peculiarities which require to be emphasized before I proceed to a description of the facts themselves. It is concerned with a young man whose health had broken down in his eighteenth year after a gonorrhoeal infection, and who was entirely incapacitated and completely dependent upon other people when he began his psycho-analytic treatment several years later. He had lived an approximately normal life during the ten years of his boyhood that preceded the date of his illness, and got through his studies at his secondary school

[1] This case history was written down shortly after the termination of the treatment, in the winter of 1914–15. At that time I was still freshly under the impression of the twisted re-interpretations which C. G. Jung and Alfred Adler were endeavouring to give to the findings of psycho-analysis. This paper is therefore connected with my essay 'On the History of the Psycho-Analytic Movement' which was published in the *Jahrbuch der Psychoanalyse* in 1914. It supplements the polemic contained in that essay, which is in its essence of a personal character, by an objective estimation of the analytic material. It was originally intended for the next volume of the *Jahrbuch*, the appearance of which was, howevers postponed indefinitely owing to the obstacles raised by the [first] Great War. I therefore decided to add it to the present collection of paper, [*S.K.S.N.*, 4] which was being issued by a new publisher [Heller, in place of Deuticke]. Meanwhile I had been obliged to deal in my *Introductory Lectures on Psycho-Analysis* (which I delivered in 1916 and 1917) with many points which should have been raised for the first time in this paper. No alterations of any importance have been made in the text of the first draft; additions are indicated by means of square brackets. [There are only two such additional passages, occurring on pp. 57 and 95. Elsewhere in this paper, as in the rest of the *Standard Edition*, square brackets indicate additions by the Editor. The words 'twisted re-interpretations' in this footnote stand for the German '*Umdeutungen*'. The English version was suggested by the author.]

without much trouble. But his earlier years were dominated by a severe neurotic disturbance, which began immediately before his fourth birthday as an anxiety-hysteria (in the shape of an animal phobia), then changed into an obsessional neurosis with a religious content, and lasted with its offshoots as far as into his tenth[1] year.

Only this infantile neurosis will be the subject of my communication. In spite of the patient's direct request, I have abstained from writing a complete history of his illness, of his treatment, and of his recovery, because I recognized that such a task was technically impracticable and socially impermissible. This at the same time removes the possibility of demonstrating the connection between his illness in childhood and his later and permanent one. As regards the latter I can only say that on account of it the patient spent a long time in German sanatoria, and was at that period classified in the most authoritative quarters[2] as a case of 'manic-depressive insanity'. This diagnosis was certainly applicable to the patient's father, whose life, with its wealth of activity and interests, was disturbed by repeated attacks of severe depression. But in the son I was never able, during an observation which lasted several years, to detect any changes of mood which were disproportionate to the manifest psychological situation either in their intensity or in the circumstances of their appearance. I have formed the opinion that this case, like many others which clinical psychiatry has labelled with the most multifarious and shifting diagnoses, is to be regarded as a condition following on an obsessional neurosis which has come to an end spontaneously, but has left a defect behind it after recovery.

My description will therefore deal with an infantile neurosis which was analysed not while it actually existed, but only fifteen years after its termination. This state of things has its advantages as well as its disadvantages in comparison with the alternative. An analysis which is conducted upon a neurotic child itself must, as a matter of course, appear to be more trustworthy, but it cannot be very rich in material; too many

[1] [In the editions before 1924 this read 'eighth'.]

[2] [We learn from Dr. Jones that among the psychiatrists consulted by the patient were such leaders of the profession as Ziehen in Berlin and Kraepelin in Munich.]

words and thoughts have to be lent to the child,[1] and even so the deepest strata may turn out to be impenetrable to consciousness. An analysis of a childhood disorder through the medium of recollection in an intellectually mature adult is free from these limitations; but it necessitates our taking into account the distortion and refurbishing to which a person's own past is subjected when it is looked back upon from a later period. The first alternative perhaps gives the more convincing results; the second is by far the more instructive.

In any case it may be maintained that analysis of children's neuroses can claim to possess a specially high theoretical interest. They afford us, roughly speaking, as much help towards a proper understanding of the neuroses of adults as do children's dreams in respect to the dreams of adults. Not, indeed, that they are more perspicuous or poorer in elements; in fact, the difficulty of feeling one's way into the mental life of a child makes them set the physician a particularly difficult task. But nevertheless, so many of the later deposits are wanting in them that the essence of the neurosis springs to the eyes with unmistakable distinctness. In the present phase of the battle which is raging round psycho-analysis the resistance to its findings has, as we know, taken on a new form. People were content formerly to dispute the reality of the facts which are asserted by analysis; and for this purpose the best technique seemed to be to avoid examining them. That procedure appears to be slowly exhausting itself; and people are now adopting another plan—of recognizing the facts, but of eliminating, by means of twisted interpretations, the consequences that follow from them, so that the critics can still ward off the objectionable novelties as efficiently as ever. The study of children's neuroses exposes the complete inadequacy of these shallow or high-handed attempts at re-interpretation. It shows the predominant part that is played in the formation of neuroses by those libidinal motive forces which are so eagerly disavowed, and reveals the absence of any aspirations towards remote cultural aims, of which the child still knows nothing, and which cannot therefore be of any significance for him.

Another characteristic which makes the present analysis

[1] [The evidential value of child-analysis had been discussed by Freud in the case history of 'Little Hans' (1909*b*), *Standard Ed.*, **10**, 6 and 101 ff.]

noteworthy is connected with the severity of the illness and the duration of the treatment. Analyses which lead to a favourable conclusion in a short time are of value in ministering to the therapeutist's self-esteem and substantiate the medical importance of psycho-analysis; but they remain for the most part insignificant as regards the advancement of scientific knowledge. Nothing new is learnt from them. In fact they only succeed so quickly because everything that was necessary for their accomplishment was already known. Something new can only be gained from analyses that present special difficulties, and to the overcoming of these a great deal of time has to be devoted. Only in such cases do we succeed in descending into the deepest and most primitive strata of mental development and in gaining from there solutions for the problems of the later formations. And we feel afterwards that, strictly speaking, only an analysis which has penetrated so far deserves the name. Naturally a single case does not give us all the information that we should like to have. Or, to put it more correctly, it might teach us everything, if we were only in a position to make everything out, and if we were not compelled by the inexperience of our own perception to content ourselves with a little.

As regards these fertile difficulties the case I am about to discuss left nothing to be desired. The first years of the treatment produced scarcely any change. Owing to a fortunate concatenation, all the external circumstances nevertheless combined to make it possible to proceed with the therapeutic experiment. I can easily believe that in less favourable circumstances the treatment would have been given up after a short time. Of the physician's point of view I can only declare that in a case of this kind he must behave as 'timelessly' as the unconscious itself,[1] if he wishes to learn anything or to achieve anything. And in the end he will succeed in doing so, if he has the strength to renounce any short-sighted therapeutic ambition. It is not to be expected that the amount of patience, adaptability, insight, and confidence demanded of the patient and his relatives will be forthcoming in many other cases. But the analyst has a right to feel that the results which he has attained from such lengthy work in one case will help substantially to reduce the length of the treatment in a subsequent case of equal severity, and that by submitting on a single occasion

[1] [See 'The Unconscious' (1915*e*), Part V.]

to the timelessness of the unconscious he will be brought nearer to vanquishing it in the end.[1]

The patient with whom I am here concerned remained for a long time unassailably entrenched behind an attitude of obliging apathy. He listened, understood, and remained unapproachable. His unimpeachable intelligence was, as it were, cut off from the instinctual forces which governed his behaviour in the few relations of life that remained to him. It required a long education to induce him to take an independent share in the work; and when as a result of this exertion he began for the first time to feel relief, he immediately gave up working in order to avoid any further changes, and in order to remain comfortably in the situation which had been thus established. His shrinking from a self-sufficient existence was so great as to outweigh all the vexations of his illness. Only one way was to be found of overcoming it. I was obliged to wait until his attachment to myself had become strong enough to counterbalance this shrinking, and then played off this one factor against the other. I determined—but not until trustworthy signs had led me to judge that the right moment had come—that the treatment must be brought to an end at a particular fixed date, no matter how far it had advanced. I was resolved to keep to the date; and eventually the patient came to see that I was in earnest. Under the inexorable pressure of this fixed limit his resistance and his fixation to the illness gave way, and now in a disproportionately short time the analysis produced all the material which made it possible to clear up his inhibitions and remove his symptoms. All the information, too, which enabled me to understand his infantile neurosis is derived from this last period of the work, during which resistance temporarily disappeared and the patient gave an impression of lucidity which is usually attainable only in hypnosis.[2]

Thus the course of this treatment illustrates a maxim whose truth has long been appreciated in the technique of analysis. The length of the road over which an analysis must travel with the patient, and the quantity of material which must be

[1] [The question of the length of analyses was discussed by Freud in 'Analysis Terminable and Interminable' (1937*c*).]

[2] [The effects of setting a time-limit to an analysis were considered by Freud in reference to this particular case in Section I of the paper quoted in the last footnote (1937 *c*).]

mastered on the way, are of no importance in comparison with the resistance which is met with in the course of the work, and are only of importance at all in so far as they are necessarily proportional to the resistance. The situation is the same as when to-day an enemy army needs weeks and months to make its way across a stretch of country which in times of peace was traversed by an express train in a few hours and which only a short time before had been passed over by the defending army in a few days.

A third peculiarity of the analysis which is to be described in these pages has only increased my difficulty in deciding to make a report upon it. On the whole its results have coincided in the most satisfactory manner with our previous knowledge, or have been easily embodied into it. Many details, however, seemed to me myself to be so extraordinary and incredible that I felt some hesitation in asking other people to believe them. I requested the patient to make the strictest criticism of his recollections, but he found nothing improbable in his statements and adhered closely to them. Readers may at all events rest assured that I myself am only reporting what I came upon as an independent experience, uninfluenced by my expectation. So that there was nothing left for me but to remember the wise saying that there are more things in heaven and earth than are dreamed of in our philosophy. Anyone who could succeed in eliminating his pre-existing convictions even more thoroughly could no doubt discover even more such things.[1]

[1] [The rather complicated chronology of the case will become clearer if reference is made to the footnote on p. 121 below.]

II

GENERAL SURVEY OF THE PATIENT'S ENVIRONMENT AND OF THE HISTORY OF THE CASE

I AM unable to give either a purely historical or a purely thematic account of my patient's story; I can write a history neither of the treatment nor of the illness, but I shall find myself obliged to combine the two methods of presentation. It is well known that no means has been found of in any way introducing into the reproduction of an analysis the sense of conviction which results from the analysis itself. Exhaustive verbatim reports of the proceedings during the hours of analysis would certainly be of no help at all; and in any case the technique of the treatment makes it impossible to draw them up. So analyses such as this are not published in order to produce conviction in the minds of those whose attitude has hitherto been recusant and sceptical. The intention is only to bring forward some new facts for investigators who have already been convinced by their own clinical experiences.

I shall begin, then, by giving a picture of the child's world, and by telling as much of the story of his childhood as could be learnt without any exertion; it was not, indeed, for several years that the story became any less incomplete and obscure.

His parents had been married young, and were still leading a happy married life, upon which their ill-health was soon to throw the first shadows. His mother began to suffer from abdominal disorders, and his father from his first attacks of depression, which led to his absence from home. Naturally the patient only came to understand his father's illness very much later on, but he was aware of his mother's weak health even in his early childhood. As a consequence of it she had relatively little to do with the children. One day, certainly before his fourth year,[1] while his mother was seeing off the doctor to the station and he himself was walking beside her, holding her hand,

[1] [See p. 76*n*. In the editions before 1924 this read 'perhaps in his sixth year'.]

he overheard her lamenting her condition. Her words made a deep impression upon him, and later on he applied them to himself [cf. p. 77]. He was not the only child; he had a sister, about two years his elder, lively, gifted, and precociously naughty, who was to play an important part in his life.

As far back as he could remember he was looked after by a nurse, an uneducated old woman of peasant birth, with an untiring affection for him. He served her as a substitute for a son of her own who had died young. The family lived on a country estate, from which they used to move to another for the summer. The two estates were not far from a large town. There was a break in his childhood when his parents sold the estates and moved into the town. Near relatives used often to pay them long visits upon one estate or the other—brothers of his father, sisters of his mother and their children, and his grandparents on his mother's side. During the summer his parents used to be away for a few weeks. In a screen memory he saw himself with his nurse looking after the carriage which was driving off with his father, mother and sister, and then going peaceably back into the house. He must have been very small at that time.[1] Next summer his sister was left at home, and an English governess was engaged, who became responsible for the supervision of the children.

In his later years he was told many stories about his childhood.[2] He knew a great deal himself, but it was naturally disconnected both as regards date and subject-matter. One of these traditions, which was repeated over and over again in his presence on the occasion of his later illness, introduces us to the problem with whose solution we shall be occupied. He seems at first to have been a very good-natured, tractable, and

[1] Two and a half years old. It was possible later on to determine almost all the dates with certainty.

[2] Information of this kind may, as a rule, be employed as absolutely authentic material. So it may seem tempting to take the easy course of filling up the gaps in a patient's memory by making enquiries from the older members of his family; but I cannot advise too strongly against such a technique. Any stories that may be told by relatives in reply to enquiries and requests are at the mercy of every critical misgiving that can come into play. One invariably regrets having made oneself dependent upon such information; at the same time confidence in the analysis is shaken and a court of appeal is set up over it. Whatever can be remembered at all will anyhow come to light in the further course of analysis.

even quiet child, so that they used to say of him that he ought to have been the girl and his elder sister the boy. But once, when his parents came back from their summer holiday, they found him transformed. He had become discontented, irritable and violent, took offence on every possible occasion, and then flew into a rage and screamed like a savage; so that, when this state of things continued, his parents expressed their misgivings as to whether it would be possible to send him to school later on. This happened during the summer while the English governess was with them. She turned out to be an eccentric and quarrelsome person, and, moreover, to be addicted to drink. The boy's mother was therefore inclined to ascribe the alteration in his character to the influence of this Englishwoman, and assumed that she had irritated him by her treatment. His sharp-sighted grandmother, who had spent the summer with the children, was of opinion that the boy's irritability had been provoked by the dissensions between the Englishwoman and the nurse. The Englishwoman had repeatedly called the nurse a witch, and had obliged her to leave the room; the little boy had openly taken the side of his beloved 'Nanya' and let the governess see his hatred. However it may have been, the Englishwoman was sent away soon after the parents' return, without there being any consequent change in the child's unbearable behaviour.

The patient had preserved his memory of this naughty period. According to his belief he made the first of his scenes one Christmas, when he was not given a double quantity of presents—which were his due, because Christmas Day was at the same time his birthday. He did not spare even his beloved Nanya with his importunity and touchiness, and even tormented her more remorselessly perhaps than any one. But the phase which brought with it his change in character was inextricably connected in his memory with many other strange and pathological phenomena which he was unable to arrange in chronological sequence. He threw all the incidents that I am now about to relate (which cannot possibly have been contemporaneous, and which are full of internal contradictions) into one and the same period of time, to which he gave the name 'still on the first estate'. He thought they must have left that estate by the time he was five years old.[1] Thus he could recollect how he had suffered

[1] [The patient probably had in mind the estate on which the family lived for most of the year (cf. p. 14). Some time after the two original

from a fear, which his sister exploited for the purpose of tormenting him. There was a particular picture-book, in which a wolf was represented, standing upright and striding along. Whenever he caught sight of this picture he began to scream like a lunatic that he was afraid of the wolf coming and eating him up. His sister, however, always succeeded in arranging so that he was obliged to see this picture, and was delighted at his terror. Meanwhile he was also frightened at other animals as well, big and little. Once he was running after a beautiful big butterfly, with striped yellow wings which ended in points, in the hope of catching it. (It was no doubt a 'swallow-tail'.[1]) He was suddenly seized with a terrible fear of the creature, and, screaming, gave up the chase. He also felt fear and loathing of beetles and caterpillars. Yet he could also remember that at this very time he used to torment beetles and cut caterpillars to pieces. Horses, too, gave him an uncanny feeling. If a horse was beaten he began to scream, and he was once obliged to leave a circus on that account. On other occasions he himself enjoyed beating horses. Whether these contradictory sorts of attitudes towards animals were really in operation simultaneously, or whether they did not more probably replace one another, but if so in what order and when—to all these questions his memory could offer no decisive reply. He was also unable to say whether his naughty period was *replaced* by a phase of illness or whether it persisted right through the latter. But, in any case, the statements of his that follow justified the assumption that during these years of his childhood he went through an easily recognizable attack of obsessional neurosis. He related how during a long period he was very pious. Before he went to sleep he was obliged to pray for a long time and to make an endless series of signs of the cross. In the evening, too, he used to make the round of all the holy pictures that hung in the room, taking a chair with him, upon which he climbed, and used to kiss each one of them devoutly. It was utterly inconsistent with this pious ceremonial—or, on the other hand, perhaps it was quite consistent with it—that he should recollect some blasphemous thoughts which used to come into his head like an inspiration

estates were sold, the family, as Freud informed the translators, bought a new one (cf. p. 93).]

[1] ['*Schwalbenschwanz*.' Here, and at the beginning of Section VIII below, the editions before 1924 read '*Admiral*'.]

from the devil. He was obliged to think 'God—swine' or 'God—shit'. Once while he was on a journey to a health-resort in Germany he was tormented by the obsession of having to think of the Holy Trinity whenever he saw three heaps of horse-dung or other excrement lying in the road. At that time he used to carry out another peculiar ceremonial when he saw people that he felt sorry for, such as beggars, cripples, or very old men. He had to breathe out noisily, so as not to become like them; and under certain conditions he had to draw in his breath vigorously. I naturally assumed that these obvious symptoms of an obsessional neurosis belonged to a somewhat later time and stage of development than the signs of anxiety and the cruel treatment of animals.

The patient's maturer years were marked by a very unsatisfactory relation to his father, who, after repeated attacks of depression, was no longer able to conceal the pathological features of his character. In the earliest years of the patient's childhood this relation had been a very affectionate one, and the recollection of it had remained in his memory. His father was very fond of him, and liked playing with him. From an early age he was proud of his father, and was always declaring that he would like to be a gentleman like him. His Nanya told him that his sister was his mother's child, but that he was his father's—which had very much pleased him. Towards the end of his childhood there was an estrangement between him and his father. His father had an unmistakable preference for his sister, and he felt very much slighted by this. Later on fear of his father became the dominating factor.

All of the phenomena which the patient associated with the phase of his life that began with his naughtiness disappeared in about his eighth year. They did not disappear at a single blow, and made occasional reappearances, but finally gave way, in the patient's opinion, before the influence of the masters and tutors, who then took the place of the women who had hitherto looked after him. Here, then, in the briefest outline, are the riddles for which the analysis had to find a solution. What was the origin of the sudden change in the boy's character? What was the significance of his phobia and of his perversities? How did he arrive at his obsessive piety? And how are all these phenomena interrelated? I will once more recall the fact that our therapeutic work was concerned with a subsequent and recent neurotic illness, and that light could only be thrown upon these earlier problems when the course of the analysis led away for a time from the present, and forced us to make a *détour* through the prehistoric period of childhood.

III

THE SEDUCTION AND ITS IMMEDIATE CONSEQUENCES

It is easy to understand that the first suspicion fell upon the English governess, for the change in the boy made its appearance while she was there. Two screen memories had persisted, which were incomprehensible in themselves, and which related to her. On one occasion, as she was walking along in front of them, she said: 'Do look at my little tail!' Another time, when they were on a drive, her hat flew away, to the two children's great satisfaction. This pointed to the castration complex, and might permit of a construction being made to the effect that a threat uttered by her against the boy had been largely responsible for originating his abnormal conduct. There is no danger at all in communicating constructions of this kind to the person under analysis; they never do any damage to the analysis if they are mistaken; but at the same time they are not put forward unless there is some prospect of reaching a nearer approximation to the truth by means of them.[1] The first effect of this supposition was the appearance of some dreams, which it was not possible to interpret completely, but all of which seemed to centre around the same material. As far as they could be understood, they were concerned with aggressive actions on the boy's part against his sister or against the governess and with energetic reproofs and punishments on account of them. It was as though . . . after her bath . . . he had tried . . . to undress his sister . . . to tear off her coverings . . . or veils—and so on. But it was not possible to get at any firm content from the interpretation; and since these dreams gave an impression of always working over the same material in various different ways, the correct reading of these ostensible reminiscences became assured: it could only be a question of phantasies, which the dreamer had made on the subject of his childhood at some time or other, probably at the age of puberty, and which had now come to the surface again in this unrecognizable form.

[1] [Freud entered into this at greater length in his paper 'Constructions in Analysis' (1937*d*), particularly in Section II.]

The explanation came at a single blow, when the patient suddenly called to mind the fact that, when he was still very small, 'on the first estate', his sister had seduced him into sexual practices. First came a recollection that in the lavatory, which the children used frequently to visit together, she had made this proposal: 'Let's show our bottoms', and had proceeded from words to deeds. Subsequently the more essential part of the seduction came to light, with full particulars as to time and place. It was in spring, at a time when his father was away; the children were in one room playing on the floor, while their mother was working in the next. His sister had taken hold of his penis and played with it, at the same time telling him incomprehensible stories about his Nanya, as though by way of explanation. His Nanya, she said, used to do the same thing with all kinds of people—for instance, with the gardener: she used to stand him on his head, and then take hold of his genitals.

Here, then, was the explanation of the phantasies whose existence we had already divined. They were meant to efface the memory of an event which later on seemed offensive to the patient's masculine self-esteem, and they reached this end by putting an imaginary and desirable converse in the place of the historical truth. According to these phantasies it was not he who had played the passive part towards his sister, but, on the contrary, he had been aggressive, had tried to see his sister undressed, had been rejected and punished, and had for that reason got into the rage which the family tradition talked of so much. It was also appropriate to weave the governess into this imaginative composition, since the chief responsibility for his fits of rage had been ascribed to her by his mother and grandmother. These phantasies, therefore, corresponded exactly to the legends by means of which a nation that has become great and proud tries to conceal the insignificance and failure of its beginnings.[1]

The governess can actually have had only a very remote share in the seduction and its consequences. The scenes with his sister took place in the early part of the same year in which, at the height of the summer, the Englishwoman arrived to take the place of his absent parents. The boy's hostility to the governess

[1] [See the longer discussion of this in Freud's study of Leonardo (1910*c*), near the beginning of Chapter II.]

came about, rather, in another way. By abusing the nurse and slandering her as a witch, she was in his eyes following in the footsteps of his sister, who had first told him such monstrous stories about the nurse; and in this way she enabled him to express openly against herself the aversion which, as we shall hear, he had developed against his sister as a result of his seduction.

But his seduction by his sister was certainly not a phantasy. Its credibility was increased by some information which had never been forgotten and which dated from a later part of his life, when he was grown up. A cousin who was more than ten years his elder told him in a conversation about his sister that he very well remembered what a forward and sensual little thing she had been: once, when she was a child of four or five, she had sat on his lap and opened his trousers to take hold of his penis.

I should like at this point to break off the story of my patient's childhood and say something of this sister, of her development and later fortunes, and of the influence she had on him. She was two years older than he was, and had always remained ahead of him. As a child she was boyish and unmanageable, but she then entered upon a brilliant intellectual development and distinguished herself by her acute and realistic powers of mind; she inclined in her studies to the natural sciences, but also produced imaginative writings of which her father had a high opinion. She was mentally far superior to her numerous early admirers, and used to make jokes at their expense. In her early twenties, however, she began to be depressed, complained that she was not good-looking enough, and withdrew from all society. She was sent to travel in the company of an acquaintance, an elderly lady, and after her return told a number of most improbable stories of how she had been ill-treated by her companion, but remained with her affections obviously fixed upon her alleged tormentor. While she was on a second journey, soon afterwards, she poisoned herself and died far away from her home. Her disorder is probably to be regarded as the beginning of a dementia praecox. She was one of the proofs of the conspicuously neuropathic heredity in her family, but by no means the only one. An uncle, her father's brother, died after long years of life as an eccentric, with indications pointing to the presence of a severe obsessional neurosis; while a good number of collateral relatives were and are afflicted with less serious nervous complaints.

Independently of the question of seduction, our patient, while he was a child, found in his sister an inconvenient competitor for the good opinion of his parents, and he felt very much oppressed by her merciless display of superiority. Later on he especially envied her the respect which his father showed for her mental capacity and intellectual achievements, while he, intellectually inhibited as he was since his obsessional neurosis, had to be content with a lower estimation. From his fourteenth year onwards the relations between the brother and sister began to improve; a similar disposition of mind and a common opposition to their parents brought them so close together that they got on with each other like the best of friends. During the tempestuous sexual excitement of his puberty he ventured upon an attempt at an intimate physical approach. She rejected him with equal decision and dexterity, and he at once turned away from her to a little peasant girl who was a servant in the house and had the same name as his sister. In doing so he was taking a step which had a determinant influence on his heterosexual choice of object, for all the girls with whom he subsequently fell in love—often with the clearest indications of compulsion—were also servants, whose education and intelligence were necessarily far inferior to his own. If all of these objects of his love were substitutes for the figure of the sister whom he had to forgo, then it could not be denied that an intention of debasing his sister and of putting an end to her intellectual superiority, which he had formerly found so oppressive, had obtained the decisive control over his object-choice.[1]

Human sexual conduct, as well as everything else, has been subordinated by Alfred Adler to motive forces of this kind, which spring from the will to power, from the individual's self-assertive instinct. Without ever denying the importance of these motives of power and prerogative, I have never been convinced that they play the dominating and exclusive part that has been ascribed to them. If I had not pursued my patient's analysis to the end, I should have been obliged, on account of my observation of this case, to correct my preconceived opinion in a direction favourable to Adler. The conclusion of the analysis unexpectedly brought up new material which, on the contrary,

[1] [Cf. Freud's earlier paper on this subject (1912*d*).]

showed that these motives of power (in this case the intention to debase) had determined the object-choice only in the sense of serving as a contributory cause and as a rationalization, whereas the true underlying determination enabled me to maintain my former convictions.[1]

When the news of his sister's death arrived, so the patient told me, he felt hardly a trace of grief. He had to force himself to show signs of sorrow, and was able quite coolly to rejoice at having now become the sole heir to the property. He had already been suffering from his recent illness for several years when this occurred. But I must confess that this one piece of information made me for a long time uncertain in my diagnostic judgement of the case. It was to be assumed, no doubt, that his grief over the loss of the most dearly loved member of his family would meet with an inhibition in its expression, as a result of the continued operation of his jealousy of her and of the added presence of his incestuous love for her which had now become unconscious. But I could not do without some substitute for the missing outbursts of grief. And this was at last found in another expression of feeling which had remained inexplicable to the patient. A few months after his sister's death he himself made a journey in the neighbourhood in which she had died. There he sought out the burial-place of a great poet, who was at that time his ideal, and shed bitter tears upon his grave. This reaction seemed strange to him himself, for he knew that more than two generations had passed by since the death of the poet he admired. He only understood it when he remembered that his father had been in the habit of comparing his dead sister's works with the great poet's. He gave me another indication of the correct way of interpreting the homage which he ostensibly paid to the poet, by a mistake in his story which I was able to detect at this point. He had repeatedly specified before that his sister had shot herself; but he was now obliged to make a correction and say that she had taken poison. The poet, however, had been shot in a duel.[2]

I now return to the brother's story, but from this point I must proceed for a little upon thematic lines. The boy's age at

[1] See below, p. 93. [For a fuller discussion of Adler's views, see Part III of 'On the History of the Psycho-Analytic Movement' (1914*d*).]

[2] [No doubt Pushkin.]

the time at which his sister began her seductions turned out to be three and a quarter years.[1] It happened, as has been mentioned, in the spring of the same year in whose summer the English governess arrived, and in whose autumn his parents, on their return, found him so fundamentally altered. It is very natural, then, to connect this transformation with the awakening of his sexual activity that had meanwhile taken place.

How did the boy react to the allurements of his elder sister? By a refusal, is the answer, but by a refusal which applied to the person and not to the thing. His sister was not agreeable to him as a sexual object, probably because his relation to her had already been determined in a hostile direction owing to their rivalry for their parents' love. He held aloof from her, and, moreover, her solicitations soon ceased. But he tried to win, instead of her, another person of whom he was fonder; and the information which his sister herself had given him, and in which she had claimed his Nanya as a model, turned his choice in that direction. He therefore began to play with his penis in his Nanya's presence, and this, like so many other instances in which children do not conceal their masturbation, must be regarded as an attempt at seduction. His Nanya disillusioned him; she made a serious face, and explained that that wasn't good; children who did that, she added, got a 'wound' in the place.

The effect of this intelligence, which amounted to a threat, is to be traced in various directions. His dependence upon his Nanya was diminished in consequence. He might well have been angry with her; and later on, when his fits of rage set in, it became clear that he really was embittered against her. But it was characteristic of him that every position of the libido which he found himself obliged to abandon was at first obstinately defended by him against the new development. When the governess came upon the scene and abused his Nanya, drove her out of the room, and tried to destroy her authority, he, on the contrary, exaggerated his love for the victim of these attacks and assumed a brusque and defiant attitude towards the aggressive governess. Nevertheless, in secret he began to look about for another sexual object. His seduction had given him the passive sexual aim of being touched on the genitals; we shall

[1] [In the editions before 1924 this read 'from three and a quarter to three and a half years'.]

presently hear in connection with whom it was that he tried to achieve this aim, and what paths led him to this choice.

It agrees entirely with our anticipations when we learn that, after his first genital excitations, his sexual researches began, and that he soon came upon the problem of castration. At this time he succeeded in observing two girls—his sister and a friend of hers—while they were micturating. His acumen might well have enabled him to gather the true facts from this spectacle, but he behaved as we know other male children behave in these circumstances. He rejected the idea that he saw before him a confirmation of the wound with which his Nanya had threatened him, and he explained to himself that this was the girls' 'front bottom'. The theme of castration was not settled by this decision; he found new allusions to it in everything that he heard. Once when the children were given some coloured sugar-sticks, the governess, who was inclined to disordered fancies, pronounced that they were pieces of chopped-up snakes. He remembered afterwards that his father had once met a snake while he was walking along a footpath, and had beaten it to pieces with his stick. He heard the story (out of *Reynard the Fox*) read aloud, of how the wolf wanted to go fishing in the winter, and used his tail as a bait, and how in that way his tail was broken off in the ice. He learned the different names by which horses are distinguished, according to whether their sexual organs are intact or not. Thus he was occupied with thoughts about castration, but as yet he had no belief in it and no dread of it. Other sexual problems arose for him out of the fairy tales with which he became familiar at this time. In 'Little Red Riding-Hood' and 'The Seven Little Goats' the children were taken out of the wolf's body. Was the wolf a female creature, then, or could men have children in their bodies as well? At this time the question was not yet settled. Moreover, at the time of these enquiries he had as yet no fear of wolves.

One of the patient's pieces of information will make it easier for us to understand the alteration in his character which appeared during his parents' absence as a somewhat indirect consequence of his seduction. He said that he gave up masturbating very soon after his Nanya's refusal and threat. *His sexual life, therefore, which was beginning to come under the sway of the genital zone, gave way before an external obstacle, and was thrown back by its influence into an earlier phase of pregenital organization.* As a result of the suppression of his masturbation, the boy's sexual life took on a sadistic-anal character. He became irritable and a tormentor, and gratified himself in this way at the expense of animals and humans. His principal object was his beloved Nanya, and he knew how to torment her till she burst into tears. In this way he revenged himself on her for the refusal he had met with, and at the same time gratified his sexual lust in the form which corresponded to his present regressive phase. He began to be cruel to small animals, to catch flies and pull off their wings, to crush beetles underfoot; in his imagination he liked beating large animals (horses) as well. All of these, then, were active and sadistic proceedings; we shall discuss his anal impulses at this period in a later connection.

It is a most important fact that some contemporary phantasies of quite another kind came up as well in the patient's memory. The content of these was of boys being chastised and beaten, and especially being beaten on the penis. And from other phantasies, which represented the heir to the throne being shut up in a narrow room and beaten, it was easy to guess for whom it was that the anonymous figures served as whipping-boys. The heir to the throne was evidently he himself; his sadism had therefore turned round in phantasy against himself, and had been converted into masochism. The detail of the sexual organ itself receiving the beating justified the conclusion that a sense of guilt, which related to his masturbation, was already concerned in this transformation.[1]

No doubt was left in the analysis that these passive trends had made their appearance at the same time as the active-sadistic ones, or very soon after them.[2] This is in accordance with the unusually clear, intense, and constant *ambivalence* [3] of the patient, which was shown here for the first time in the even development of both members of the pairs of contrary component instincts. Such behaviour was also characteristic of his later life, and so was this further trait: no position of the libido which had once

[1] [On the subject of beating-phantasies see Freud (1919*e*), below, p. 179 ff.]

[2] By passive trends I mean trends that have a passive sexual aim; but in saying this I have in mind a transformation not of the instinct but only of its aim.

[3] [This exceptional use of the term 'ambivalence' as referring to activity and passivity is discussed in an Editor's footnote in 'Instincts and their Vicissitudes' (1915*c*).]

been established was ever completely replaced by a later one. It was rather left in existence side by side with all the others, and this allowed him to maintain an incessant vacillation which proved to be incompatible with the acquisition of a stable character.

The boy's masochistic trends lead on to another point, which I have so far avoided mentioning, because it can only be confirmed by means of the analysis of the subsequent phase of his development. I have already mentioned that after his refusal by his Nanya his libidinal expectation detached itself from her and began to contemplate another person as a sexual object. This person was his father, at that time away from home. He was no doubt led to this choice by a number of convergent factors, including such fortuitous ones as the recollection of the snake being cut to pieces; but above all he was in this way able to renew his first and most primitive object-choice, which, in conformity with a small child's narcissism, had taken place along the path of identification.[1] We have heard already that his father had been his admired model, and that when he was asked what he wanted to be he used to reply: a gentleman like his father. This object of identification of his active current became the sexual object of a passive current in his present anal-sadistic phase. It looks as though his seduction by his sister had forced him into a passive role, and had given him a passive sexual aim. Under the persisting influence of this experience he pursued a path from his sister *via* his Nanya to his father—from a passive attitude towards women to the same attitude towards men—and had, nevertheless, by this means found a link with his earlier and spontaneous phase of development. His father was now his object once more; in conformity with his higher stage of development, identification was replaced by object-choice; while the transformation of his active attitude into a passive one was the consequence and the record of the seduction which had occurred meanwhile. It would naturally not have been so easy to achieve an active attitude in the sadistic phase towards his all-powerful father. When his father came home in the late summer or autumn the patient's fits of rage and scenes of fury were put to a new use. They had served for active-sadistic ends in relation to his Nanya; in relation to his father

[1] [For a fuller discussion of identification see Chapter VII of *Group Psychology* (1921*c*).]

their purpose was masochistic. By bringing his naughtiness forward he was trying to force punishments and beatings out of his father, and in that way to obtain from him the masochistic sexual satisfaction that he desired. His screaming fits were therefore simply attempts at seduction. In accordance, moreover, with the motives which underlie masochism, this beating would also have satisfied his sense of guilt. He had preserved a memory of how, during one of these scenes of naughtiness, he had redoubled his screams as soon as his father came towards him. His father did not beat him, however, but tried to pacify him by playing ball in front of him with the pillows of his cot.

I do not know how often parents and educators, faced with inexplicable naughtiness on the part of a child, might not have occasion to bear this typical state of affairs in mind. A child who behaves in this unmanageable way is making a confession and trying to provoke punishment. He hopes for a beating as a simultaneous means of setting his sense of guilt at rest and of satisfying his masochistic sexual trend.[1]

We owe the further explanation of the case to a recollection which emerged with great distinctness. This was to the effect that the signs of an alteration in the patient's character were not accompanied by any symptoms of anxiety until after the occurrence of a particular event. Previously, it seems, there was no anxiety, while directly after the event the anxiety expressed itself in the most tormenting shape. The date of this transformation can be stated with certainty; it was immediately before his fourth birthday. Taking this as a fixed point, we are able to divide the period of his childhood with which we are concerned into two phases: a first phase of naughtiness and perversity from his seduction at the age of three and a quarter up to his fourth birthday, and a longer subsequent phase in which the signs of neurosis predominated. But the event which makes this division possible was not an external trauma, but a dream, from which he awoke in a state of anxiety.

[1] [Cf. Freud's discussion of 'Criminals from a Sense of Guilt' which forms the third Section of his paper 'Some Character-Types Met with in Psycho-Analytic Work' (1916*d*).]

IV

THE DREAM AND THE PRIMAL SCENE

I HAVE already published this dream elsewhere,[1] on account of the quantity of material in it which is derived from fairy tales; and I will begin by repeating what I wrote on that occasion:

' "*I dreamt that it was night and that I was lying in my bed.* (*My bed stood with its foot towards the window; in front of the window there was a row of old walnut trees. I know it was winter when I had the dream, and night-time.*) *Suddenly the window opened of its own accord, and I was terrified to see that some white wolves were sitting on the big walnut tree in front of the window. There were six or seven of them. The wolves were quite white, and looked more like foxes or sheep-dogs, for they had big tails like foxes and they had their ears pricked like dogs when they pay attention to something. In great terror, evidently of being eaten up by the wolves, I screamed* and woke up. My nurse hurried to my bed, to see what had happened to me. It took quite a long while before I was convinced that it had only been a dream; I had had such a clear and life-like picture of the window opening and the wolves sitting on the tree. At last I grew quieter, felt as though I had escaped from some danger, and went to sleep again.

' "The only piece of action in the dream was the opening of the window; for the wolves sat quite still and without making any movement on the branches of the tree, to the right and left of the trunk, and looked at me. It seemed as though they had riveted their whole attention upon me.—I think this was my first anxiety-dream. I was three, four, or at most five years old at the time. From then until my eleventh or twelfth year I was always afraid of seeing something terrible in my dreams."

'He added a drawing of the tree with the wolves, which confirmed his description (Fig. 1). The analysis of the dream brought the following material to light.

'He had always connected this dream with the recollection that during these years of his childhood he was most tremendously afraid of the picture of a wolf in a book of fairy tales. His elder sister, who was very much his superior, used to tease him by holding up this particular picture in front of him on

[1] 'The Occurrence in Dreams of Material from Fairy Tales' (1913*d*).

some excuse or other, so that he was terrified and began to scream. In this picture the wolf was standing upright, striding out with one foot, with its claws stretched out and its ears pricked. He thought this picture must have been an illustration to the story of "Little Red Riding-Hood".

'Why were the wolves white? This made him think of the sheep, large flocks of which were kept in the neighbourhood of the estate. His father occasionally took him with him to visit these flocks, and every time this happened he felt very proud

Fig. 1.

and blissful. Later on—according to enquiries that were made it may easily have been shortly before the time of the dream—an epidemic broke out among the sheep. His father sent for a follower of Pasteur's, who inoculated the animals, but after the inoculation even more of them died than before.

'How did the wolves come to be on the tree? This reminded him of a story that he had heard his grandfather tell. He could not remember whether it was before or after the dream, but its subject is a decisive argument in favour of the former view. The story ran as follows. A tailor was sitting at work in his room, when the window opened and a wolf leapt in. The tailor hit after him with his yard—no (he corrected himself), caught him by his tail and pulled it off, so that the wolf ran away in terror. Some time later the tailor went into the forest, and suddenly saw a pack of wolves coming towards him; so he climbed up a tree to escape from them. At first the wolves were in perplexity; but the maimed one, which was among them and wanted to revenge himself on the tailor, proposed that they should climb one upon another till the last one could reach him. He himself —he was a vigorous old fellow—would be the base of the pyramid. The wolves did as he suggested, but the tailor had recognized the visitor whom he had punished, and suddenly called out as he had before: "Catch the grey one by his tail!" The tailless wolf, terrified by the recollection, ran away, and all the others tumbled down.

'In this story the tree appears, upon which the wolves were sitting in the dream. But it also contains an unmistakable allusion to the castration complex. The *old* wolf was docked of his tail by the tailor. The fox-tails of the wolves in the dream were probably compensations for this taillessness.

'Why were there six or seven wolves? There seemed to be no answer to this question, until I raised a doubt whether the picture that had frightened him could be connected with the story of "Little Red Riding-Hood". This fairy tale only offers an opportunity for two illustrations—Little Red Riding-Hood's meeting with the wolf in the wood, and the scene in which the wolf lies in bed in the grandmother's night-cap. There must therefore be some other fairy tale behind his recollection of the picture. He soon discovered that it could only be the story of "The Wolf and the Seven Little Goats". Here the number seven occurs, and also the number six, for the wolf only ate up six of the little goats, while the seventh hid itself in the clock-case. The white, too, comes into this story, for the wolf had his paw made white at the baker's after the little goats had recognized him on his first visit by his grey paw. Moreover, the two fairy tales have much in common. In both there is the eating up, the cutting open of the belly, the taking out of the people who have been eaten and their replacement by heavy stones, and finally in both of them the wicked wolf perishes. Besides all this, in the story of the little goats the tree appears. The wolf lay down under a tree after his meal and snored.

'I shall have, for a special reason, to deal with this dream again elsewhere, and interpret it and consider its significance in greater detail. For it is the earliest anxiety-dream that the dreamer remembered from his childhood, and its content, taken in connection with other dreams that followed it soon afterwards and with certain events in his earliest years, is of quite peculiar interest. We must confine ourselves here to the relation of the dream to the two fairy tales which have so much in common with each other, "Little Red Riding-Hood" and "The Wolf and the Seven Little Goats". The effect produced by these stories was shown in the little dreamer by a regular animal phobia. This phobia was only distinguished from other similar cases by the fact that the anxiety-animal was not an object easily accessible to observation (such as a horse or a dog), but was known to him only from stories and picture-books.

'I shall discuss on another occasion the explanation of these animal phobias and the significance attaching to them. I will only remark in anticipation that this explanation is in complete harmony with the principal characteristic shown by the neurosis from which the present dreamer suffered later in his life. His fear of his father was the strongest motive for his falling ill, and his ambivalent attitude towards every father-surrogate was the dominating feature of his life as well as of his behaviour during the treatment.

'If in my patient's case the wolf was merely a first father-surrogate, the question arises whether the hidden content in the fairy tales of the wolf that ate up the little goats and of "Little Red Riding-Hood" may not simply be infantile fear of the father.[1] Moreover, my patient's father had the characteristic, shown by so many people in relation to their children, of indulging in "affectionate abuse"; and it is possible that during the patient's earlier years his father (though he grew severe later on) may more than once, as he caressed the little boy or played with him, have threatened in fun to "gobble him up". One of my patients told me that her two children could never get to be fond of their grandfather, because in the course of his affectionate romping with them he used to frighten them by saying he would cut open their tummies.'

Leaving on one side everything in this quotation that antici-

[1] 'Compare the similarity between these two fairy tales and the myth of Kronos, which has been pointed out by Rank (1912).'

pates the dream's remoter implications, let us return to its immediate interpretation. I may remark that this interpretation was a task that dragged on over several years. The patient related the dream at a very early stage of the analysis and very soon came to share my conviction that the causes of his infantile neurosis lay concealed behind it. In the course of the treatment we often came back to the dream, but it was only during the last months of the analysis that it became possible to understand it completely, and only then thanks to spontaneous work on the patient's part. He had always emphasized the fact that two factors in the dream had made the greatest impression on him: first, the perfect stillness and immobility of the wolves, and secondly, the strained attention with which they all looked at him. The lasting sense of reality, too, which the dream left behind it, seemed to him to deserve notice.

Let us take this last remark as a starting-point. We know from our experience in interpreting dreams that this sense of reality carries a particular significance along with it. It assures us that some part of the latent material of the dream is claiming in the dreamer's memory to possess the quality of reality, that is, that the dream relates to an occurrence that really took place and was not merely imagined.[1] It can naturally only be a question of the reality of something unknown; for instance, the conviction that his grandfather really told him the story of the tailor and the wolf, or that the stories of 'Little Red Riding-Hood' and of 'The Seven Little Goats' were really read aloud to him, would not be of a nature to be replaced by this sense of reality that outlasted the dream. The dream seemed to point to an occurrence the reality of which was very strongly emphasized as being in marked contrast to the unreality of the fairy tales.

If it was to be assumed that behind the content of the dream there lay some such unknown scene—one, that is, which had already been forgotten at the time of the dream—then it must have taken place very early. The dreamer, it will be recalled, said: 'I was three, four, or at most five years old at the time I had the dream.' And we can add: 'And I was reminded by the dream of something that must have belonged to an even earlier period.'

The parts of the manifest content of the dream which were

[1] [See *The Interpretation of Dreams* (1900*a*), *Standard Ed.*, 5, 372.]

emphasized by the dreamer, the factors of attentive looking and of motionlessness, must lead to the content of this scene. We must naturally expect to find that this material reproduces the unknown material of the scene in some distorted form, perhaps even distorted into its opposite.

There were several conclusions, too, to be drawn from the raw material which had been produced by the patient's first analysis of the dream, and these had to be fitted into the collocation of which we were in search. Behind the mention of the sheep-breeding, evidence was to be expected of his sexual researches, his interest in which he was able to gratify during his visits with his father; but there must also have been allusions to a fear of death, since the greater part of the sheep had died of the epidemic. The most obtrusive thing in the dream, the wolves on the tree, led straight to his grandfather's story; and what was fascinating about this story and capable of provoking the dream can scarcely have been anything but its connection with the theme of castration.

We also concluded from the first incomplete analysis of the dream that the wolf may have been a father-surrogate; so that, in that case, this first anxiety-dream would have brought to light the fear of his father which from that time forward was to dominate his life. This conclusion, indeed, was in itself not yet binding. But if we put together as the result of the provisional analysis what can be derived from the material produced by the dreamer, we then find before us for reconstruction some such fragments as these:

A real occurrence—dating from a very early period—looking—immobility—sexual problems—castration—his father—something terrible.

One day the patient began to continue with the interpretation of the dream. He thought that the part of the dream which said that 'suddenly the window opened of its own accord' was not completely explained by its connection with the window at which the tailor was sitting and through which the wolf came into the room. 'It must mean: "My eyes suddenly opened." I was asleep, therefore, and suddenly woke up, and as I woke I saw something: the tree with the wolves.' No objection could be made to this; but the point could be developed further. He had woken up and had seen something. The attentive looking, which in the dream was ascribed to the wolves, should rather be shifted on to him. At a decisive point, therefore, a transposition has taken place; and moreover this is indicated by another transposition in the manifest content of the dream.[1] For the fact that the wolves were sitting on the tree was also a transposition, since in his grandfather's story they were underneath, and were unable to climb on to the tree.

What, then, if the other factor emphasized by the dreamer were also distorted by means of a transposition or reversal? In that case instead of immobility (the wolves sat there motionless; they looked at him, but did not move) the meaning would have to be: the most violent motion. That is to say, he suddenly woke up, and saw in front of him a scene of violent movement at which he looked with strained attention. In the one case the distortion would consist in an interchange of subject and object, of activity and passivity: being looked at instead of looking. In the other case it would consist in a transformation into the opposite; rest instead of motion.

On another occasion an association which suddenly occurred to him carried us another step forward in our understanding of the dream: 'The tree was a Christmas-tree.' He now knew that he had dreamt the dream shortly before Christmas and in expectation of it. Since Christmas Day was also his birthday, it now became possible to establish with certainty the date of the dream and of the change in him which proceeded from it. It was immediately before his fourth birthday. He had gone to sleep, then, in tense expectation of the day which ought to bring him a double quantity of presents. We know that in such circumstances a child may easily anticipate the fulfilment of his wishes. So it was already Christmas in his dream; the content of the dream showed him his Christmas box, the presents which were to be his were hanging on the tree. But instead of presents they had turned into—wolves, and the dream ended by his being overcome by fear of being eaten by the wolf (probably his father), and by his flying for refuge to his nurse. Our knowledge of his sexual development before the dream makes it possible for us to fill in the gaps in the dream and to explain the transformation of his satisfaction into anxiety. Of the wishes concerned in the formation of the dream the most powerful must have been the wish for the sexual satisfaction which he was at that time longing to obtain from his father. The strength of this wish

[1] [Cf. *The Interpretation of Dreams*, *Standard Ed.*, **4**, 288.]

made it possible to revive a long-forgotten trace in his memory of a scene which was able to show him what sexual satisfaction from his father was like; and the result was terror, horror of the fulfilment of the wish, the repression of the impulse which had manifested itself by means of the wish, and consequently a flight from his father to his less dangerous nurse.

The importance of this date of Christmas Day had been preserved in his supposed recollection of having had his first fit of rage because he was dissatisfied with his Christmas presents [p. 15]. The recollection combined elements of truth and of falsehood. It could not be entirely right, since according to the repeated declarations of his parents his naughtiness had already begun on their return in the autumn and it was not a fact that they had not come on till Christmas. But he had preserved the essential connection between his unsatisfied love, his rage, and Christmas.

But what picture can the nightly workings of his sexual desire have conjured up that could frighten him away so violently from the fulfilment for which he longed? The material of the analysis shows that there is one condition which this picture must satisfy. It must have been calculated to create a conviction of the reality of the existence of castration. Fear of castration could then become the motive power for the transformation of the affect.

I have now reached the point at which I must abandon the support I have hitherto had from the course of the analysis. I am afraid it will also be the point at which the reader's belief will abandon me.

What sprang into activity that night out of the chaos of the dreamer's unconscious memory-traces was the picture of copulation between his parents, copulation in circumstances which were not entirely usual and were especially favourable for observation. It gradually became possible to find satisfactory answers to all the questions that arose in connection with this scene; for in the course of the treatment the first dream returned in innumerable variations and new editions, in connection with which the analysis produced the information that was required. Thus in the first place the child's age at the date of the observation was established as being about one and a half years.[1] He

[1] The age of six months came under consideration as a far less probable, and indeed scarcely tenable, alternative.

was suffering at the time from malaria, an attack of which used to come on every day at a particular hour.[1] From his tenth year onwards he was from time to time subject to moods of depression, which used to come on in the afternoon and reached their height at about five o'clock. This symptom still existed at the time of the analytic treatment. The recurring fits of depression took the place of the earlier attacks of fever or languor; five o'clock was either the time of the highest fever or of the observation of the intercourse, unless the two times coincided.[2] Probably for the very reason of this illness, he was in his parents' bedroom. The illness, the occurrence of which is also corroborated by direct tradition, makes it reasonable to refer the event to the summer, and, since the child was born on Christmas Day, to assume that his age was $n + 1\frac{1}{2}$ years.[3] He had been sleeping in his cot, then, in his parents' bedroom, and woke up, perhaps because of his rising fever, in the afternoon, possibly at five o'clock, the hour which was later marked out by depression. It harmonizes with our assumption that it was a hot summer's day, if we suppose that his parents had retired, half undressed,[4] for an afternoon *siesta*. When he woke up, he witnessed a coitus *a tergo* [from behind], three times repeated;[5] he was able to see his mother's genitals as well as his father's organ; and he understood the process as well as its significance.[6] Lastly

[1] Compare the subsequent metamorphoses of this factor during the obsessional neurosis. In the patient's dreams during the treatment it was replaced by a violent wind. [Added 1924:] '*Aria*' = 'air'. ['*Mal-aria*' = 'bad air'.]

[2] We may remark in this connection that the patient drew only *five* wolves in his illustration to the dream, although the text mentioned six or seven.

[3] [It might perhaps be clearer to say '$n + \frac{1}{2}$'. The point is that owing to the interval of 6 months between the patient's birthday and the summer, his age at the time of the trauma must have been 0 years + 6 months, or 1 year + 6 months, or 2 years + 6 months, etc. The $0 + \frac{1}{2}$ is, however, already excluded in the footnote on p. 36.]

[4] In white underclothes: the *white* wolves.

[5] Why three times? He suddenly one day produced the statement that I had discovered this detail by interpretation. This was not the case. It was a spontaneous association, exempt from further criticism; in his usual way he passed it off on to me, and by this projection tried to make it seem more trustworthy.

[6] I mean that he understood it at the time of the dream when he was four years old, not at the time of the observation. He received the impressions when he was one and a half; his understanding of them was

he interrupted his parents' intercourse in a manner which will be discussed later [p. 80].

There is at bottom nothing extraordinary, nothing to give the impression of being the product of an extravagant imagination, in the fact that a young couple who had only been married a few years should have ended a *siesta* on a hot summer's afternoon with a love-scene, and should have disregarded the presence of their little boy of one and a half, asleep in his cot. On the contrary, such an event would, I think, be something entirely commonplace and *banal*; and even the position in which we have inferred that the coitus took place cannot in the least alter this judgement—especially as the evidence does not require that the intercourse should have been performed from behind each time. A single time would have been enough to give the spectator an opportunity for making observations which would have been rendered difficult or impossible by any other attitude of the lovers. The content of the scene cannot therefore in itself be an argument against its credibility. Doubts as to its probability will turn upon three other points: whether a child at the tender age of one and a half could be in a position to take in the perceptions of such a complicated process and to preserve them so accurately in his unconscious; secondly, whether it is possible at the age of four for a deferred revision of the impressions so received to penetrate the understanding; and finally, whether any procedure could succeed in bringing into consciousness coherently and convincingly the details of a scene of this kind which had been experienced and understood in such circumstances.[1]

Later on I shall carefully examine these and other doubts; but I can assure the reader that I am no less critically inclined

deferred, but became possible at the time of the dream owing to his development, his sexual excitations, and his sexual researches.

[1] The first of these difficulties cannot be reduced by assuming that the child at the time of his observation was after all probably a year older, that is to say *two* and a half, an age at which he may perhaps have been perfectly capable of talking. All the minor details of my patient's case almost excluded the possibility of shifting the date in this way. Moreover, the fact should be taken into account that these scenes of observing parental intercourse are by no means rarely brought to light in analysis. The condition of their occurrence, however, is precisely that it should be in the earliest period of childhood. The older the child is, the more carefully, with parents above a certain social level, will the child be deprived of the opportunity for this kind of observation.

than he towards an acceptance of this observation of the child's, and I will only ask him to join me in adopting a *provisional* belief in the reality of the scene. We will first proceed with the study of the relations between this 'primal scene'[1] and the patient's dream, his symptoms, and the history of his life; and we will trace separately the effects that followed from the essential content of the scene and from one of its visual impressions.

By the latter I mean the postures which he saw his parents adopt—the man upright, and the woman bent down like an animal. We have already heard [p. 30] that during his anxiety period his sister used to terrify him with a picture from the fairy-book, in which the wolf was shown standing upright, with one foot forward, with its claws stretched out and its ears pricked. He devoted himself with tireless perseverance during the treatment to the task of hunting in the second-hand bookshops till he had found the illustrated fairy-book of his childhood, and had recognized his bogy in an illustration to the story of 'The Wolf and the Seven Little Goats'. He thought that the posture of the wolf in this picture might have reminded him of that of his father during the constructed primal scene. At all events the picture became the point of departure for further manifestations of anxiety. Once when he was in his seventh or eighth year he was informed that next day a new tutor was coming for him. That night he dreamt of this tutor in the shape of a lion that came towards his bed roaring loudly and in the posture of the wolf in the picture; and once again he awoke in a state of anxiety. The wolf phobia had been overcome by that time, so he was free to choose himself a new anxiety-animal, and in this late dream he was recognizing the tutor as a father-surrogate. In the later years of his childhood each of his tutors and masters played the part of his father, and was endowed with his father's influence both for good and for evil.

While he was at his secondary school the Fates provided him with a remarkable opportunity of reviving his wolf phobia, and of using the relation which lay behind it as an occasion for severe inhibitions. The master who taught his form Latin was called Wolf. From the very first he felt cowed by him, and he was once taken severely to task by him for having made a stupid mistake

[1] ['*Urszene.*' This seems to be the earliest published use of the term. Freud had, however, used it in approximately the same sense in a letter to Fliess as early as May 2, 1897 (1950*a*, Letter 61).]

in a piece of Latin translation. From that time on he could not get free from a paralysing fear of this master, and it was soon extended to other masters besides. But the occasion on which he made his blunder in the translation was also to the purpose. He had to translate the Latin word '*filius*', and he did it with the French word '*fils*' instead of with the corresponding word from his own language. The wolf, in fact, was still his father.[1]

The first 'transitory symptom'[2] which the patient produced during the treatment went back once more to the wolf phobia and to the fairy tale of 'The Seven Little Goats'. In the room in which the first sessions were held there was a large grandfather clock opposite the patient, who lay on a sofa facing away from me. I was struck by the fact that from time to time he turned his face towards me, looked at me in a very friendly way as though to propitiate me, and then turned his look away from me to the clock. I thought at the time that he was in this way showing his eagerness for the end of the hour. A long time afterwards the patient reminded me of this piece of dumb show, and gave me an explanation of it; for he recalled that the youngest of the seven little goats hid himself in the case of the grandfather clock while his six brothers were eaten up by the wolf. So what he had meant was: 'Be kind to me! Must I be frightened of you? Are you going to eat me up? Shall I hide myself from you in the clock-case like the youngest little goat?'

The wolf that he was afraid of was undoubtedly his father; but his fear of the wolf was conditional upon the creature being in an upright posture. His recollection asserted most definitely that he had not been terrified by pictures of wolves going on all fours or, as in the story of 'Little Red Riding-Hood', lying in

[1] After this reprimand from the schoolmaster-wolf he learnt that it was the general opinion of his companions that, to be pacified, the master expected money from him. We shall return to this point later [p. 72 ff.].—I can see that it would greatly facilitate a rationalistic view of such a history of a child's development as this if it could be supposed that his whole fear of the wolf had really originated from the Latin master of that name, that it had been projected back into his childhood, and, supported by the illustration to the fairy tale, had caused the phantasy of the primal scene. But this is untenable; the chronological priority of the wolf phobia and its reference to the period of his childhood spent upon the first estate is far too securely attested. And his dream at the age of four?

[2] Ferenczi (1912).

bed. The posture which, according to our construction of the primal scene, he had seen the woman assume, was of no less significance; though in this case the significance was limited to the sexual sphere. The most striking phenomenon of his erotic life after maturity was his liability to compulsive attacks of falling physically in love which came on and disappeared again in the most puzzling succession. These attacks released a tremendous energy in him even at times when he was otherwise inhibited, and they were quite beyond his control. I must, for a specially important reason, postpone a full consideration of this compulsive love [see p. 91 ff.]; but I may mention here that it was subject to a definite condition, which was concealed from his consciousness and was discovered only during the treatment. It was necessary that the woman should have assumed the posture which we have ascribed to his mother in the primal scene. From his puberty he had felt large and conspicuous buttocks as the most powerful attraction in a woman; to copulate except from behind gave him scarcely any enjoyment. At this point a criticism may justly be raised: it may be objected that a sexual preference of this kind for the hind parts of the body is a general characteristic of people who are inclined to an obsessional neurosis, and that its presence does not justify us in referring it back to a special impression in childhood. It is part of the fabric of the anal-erotic disposition and is one of the archaic traits which distinguish that constitution. Indeed, copulation from behind—*more ferarum* [in the fashion of animals]—may, after all, be regarded as phylogenetically the older form. We shall return to this point too in a later discussion, when we have brought forward the supplementary material which showed the basis of the unconscious condition upon which his falling in love depended. [Cf. pp. 56 and 92.]

Let us now proceed with our discussion of the relations between his dream and the primal scene. We should so far have expected the dream to present the child (who was rejoicing at Christmas in the prospect of the fulfilment of his wishes) with this picture of sexual satisfaction afforded through his father's agency, just as he had seen it in the primal scene, as a model of the satisfaction that he himself was longing to obtain from his father. Instead of this picture, however, there appeared the material of the story which he had been told by his grandfather shortly before: the tree, the wolves, and the taillessness (in the over-compensated form of the bushy tails of the putative wolves). At this point some connection is missing, some associative bridge to lead from the content of the primal scene to that of the wolf story. This connection is provided once again by the postures and only by them. In his grandfather's story the tailless wolf asked the others *to climb upon him*. It was this detail that called up the recollection of the picture of the primal scene; and it was in this way that it became possible for the material of the primal scene to be represented by that of the wolf story, and at the same time for the *two* parents to be replaced, as was desirable, by *several* wolves. The content of the dream met with a further transformation, and the material of the wolf story was made to fit in with the content of the fairy tale of 'The Seven Little Goats', by borrowing from it the number seven.[1]

The steps in the transformation of the material, 'primal scene —wolf story—fairy tale of "The Seven Little Goats" ', are a reflection of the progress of the dreamer's thoughts during the construction of the dream: 'longing for sexual satisfaction from his father—realization that castration is a necessary condition of it—fear of his father'. It is only at this point, I think, that we can regard the anxiety-dream of this four-year-old boy as being exhaustively explained.[2]

[1] It says 'six or seven' in the dream. Six is the number of the children that were eaten; the seventh escaped into the clock-case. It is always a strict law of dream-interpretation that an explanation must be found for every detail.

[2] Now that we have succeeded in making a synthesis of the dream, I will try to give a comprehensive account of the relations between the manifest content of the dream and the latent dream-thoughts. [Cf. the synthesis of 'Dora's' first dream (1905*e*), *Standard Ed.*, **7**, 88 ff.]

It was night, I was lying in my bed. The latter part of this is the beginning of the reproduction of the primal scene. 'It was night' is a distortion of 'I had been asleep'. The remark, 'I know it was winter when I had the dream, and night-time', refers to the patient's recollection of the dream and is not part of its content. It is correct, for it was one of the nights before his birthday, that is, Christmas Day.

Suddenly the window opened of its own accord. That is to be translated: 'Suddenly I woke up of my own accord', a recollection of the primal scene. The influence of the wolf story, in which the wolf leapt in through the window, is making itself felt as a modifying factor, and transforms a direct expression into a plastic one. At the same time the introduction of the window serves the purpose of providing a contemporary reference for the subsequent content of the dream. On Christmas Eve the door opens suddenly and one sees before one the tree with the

After what has already been said I need only deal shortly with the pathogenic effect of the primal scene and the alteration which its revival produced in his sexual development. We will only trace that one of its effects to which the dream gave expression. Later on we shall have to make it clear that it was not only a single sexual current that started from the primal scene but a whole set of them, that his sexual life was positively

presents. Here therefore the influence of the actual expectation of Christmas (which comprises the wish for sexual satisfaction) is making itself felt.

The big walnut-tree. The representative of the Christmas tree, and therefore belonging to the current situation. But also the tree out of the wolf story, on which the tailor took refuge from pursuit, and under which the wolves were on the watch. Moreover, as I have often been able to satisfy myself, a high tree is a symbol of observing, of scopophilia. A person sitting on a tree can see everything that is going on below him and cannot himself be seen. Compare Boccaccio's well-known story, and similar *facetiae*.

The wolves. Their number: *six or seven*. In the wolf story there was a pack, and no number was given. The fixing of the number shows the influence of the fairy tale of 'The Seven Little Goats', six of whom were eaten up. The fact that the number two in the primal scene is replaced by a larger number, which would be absurd in the primal scene, is welcomed by the resistance as a means of distortion. In the illustration to the dream the dreamer brings forward the number five, which is probably meant to correct the statement 'It was night'.

They were sitting on the tree. In the first place they replace the Christmas presents hanging on the tree. But they are also transposed on to the tree because that can mean that they are looking. In his grandfather's story they were posted underneath the tree. Their relation to the tree has therefore been reversed in the dream; and from this it may be concluded that there are further reversals of the latent material to be found in the content of the dream.

They were looking at him with strained attention. This feature comes entirely from the primal scene, and has got into the dream at the price of being turned completely round.

They were quite white. This feature is unessential in itself, but is strongly emphasized in the dreamer's narrative. It owes its intensity to a copious fusion of elements from all the strata of the material, and it combines unimportant details from the other sources of the dream with a fragment of the primal scene which is more significant. This last part of its determination goes back to the white of his parents' bedclothes and underclothes, and to this is added the white of the flocks of sheep, and of the sheep-dogs, as an allusion to his sexual researches among animals, and the white in the fairy tale of 'The Seven Little Goats', in which the mother is recognized by the white of her hand. Later on we shall see that the white clothes are also an allusion to death. [There does not splintered up by it. We shall further bear in mind that the activation of this scene (I purposely avoid the word 'recollection') had the same effect as though it were a recent experience. The effects of the scene were deferred, but meanwhile it had lost none of its freshness in the interval between the ages of one and a half and four years. We shall perhaps find in what follows reason to suppose that it produced certain effects even

seem in fact to be any further clear reference to this point. The connection is perhaps with the episode of the winding-sheet (p. 98).

They sat there motionless. This contradicts the most striking feature of the observed scene, namely, its agitated movement, which, in virtue of the postures to which it led, constitutes the connection between the primal scene and the wolf story.

They had tails like foxes. This must be the contradiction of a conclusion which was derived from the action of the primal scene on the wolf story, and which must be recognized as the most important result of the dreamer's sexual researches: 'So there really is such a thing as castration.' The terror with which this conclusion was received finally broke out in the dream and brought it to an end.

The fear of being eaten up by the wolves. It seemed to the dreamer as though the motive force of this fear was not derived from the content of the dream. He said he need not have been afraid, for the wolves looked more like foxes or dogs, and they did not rush at him as though to bite him, but were very still and not at all terrible. We observe that the dream-work tries for some time to make the distressing content harmless by transforming it into its opposite. ('They aren't moving, and, only look, they have the loveliest tails!') Until at last this expedient fails, and the fear breaks out. It expresses itself by the help of the fairy tale, in which the goat-children are eaten up by the wolf-father. This part of the fairy tale may perhaps have acted as a reminder of threats made by the child's father in fun when he was playing with him; so that the fear of being eaten up by the wolf may be a reminiscence as well as a substitute by displacement.

The wishes which act as motive forces in this dream are obvious. First there are the superficial wishes of the day, that Christmas with its presents may already be here (a dream of impatience) and accompanying these is the deeper wish, now permanently present, for sexual satisfaction from the dreamer's father. This is immediately replaced by the wish to see once more what was then so fascinating. The mental process then proceeds on its way. Starting from the fulfilment of this last wish with the conjuring up of the primal scene, it passes on to what has now become inevitable—the repudiation of that wish and its repression.

The diffuseness and elaboration of this commentary have been forced on me by the effort to present the reader with some sort of equivalent for the convincing power of an analysis carried through by oneself; perhaps they may also serve to discourage him from asking for the publication of analyses which have stretched over several years.

at the time of its perception, that is, from the age of one and a half onwards.

When the patient entered more deeply into the situation of the primal scene, he brought to light the following pieces of self-observation. He assumed to begin with, he said, that the event of which he was a witness was an act of violence, but the expression of enjoyment which he saw on his mother's face did not fit in with this; he was obliged to recognize that the experience was one of gratification.[1] What was essentially new for him in his observation of his parents' intercourse was the conviction of the reality of castration—a possibility with which his thoughts had already been occupied previously. (The sight of the two girls micturating, his Nanya's threat, the governess's interpretation

[1] We might perhaps best do justice to this statement of the patient's by supposing that the object of his observation was in the first instance a coitus in the normal position, which cannot fail to produce the impression of being a sadistic act, and that only after this was the position altered, so that he had an opportunity for making other observations and judgements. This hypothesis, however, was not confirmed with certainty, and moreover does not seem to me indispensable. We must not forget the actual situation which lies behind the abbreviated description given in the text: the patient under analysis, at an age of over twenty-five years, was putting the impressions and impulses of his fourth year into words which he would never have found at that time. If we fail to notice this, it may easily seem comic and incredible that a child of four should be capable of such technical judgements and learned notions. This is simply another instance of *deferred action*. At the age of one and a half the child receives an impression to which he is unable to react adequately; he is only able to understand it and to be moved by it when the impression is revived in him at the age of four; and only twenty years later, during the analysis, is he able to grasp with his conscious mental processes what was then going on in him. The patient justifiably disregards the three periods of time, and puts his present ego into the situation which is so long past. And in this we follow him, since with correct self-observation and interpretation the effect must be the same as though the distance between the second and third periods of time could be neglected. Moreover, we have no other means of describing the events of the second period. [This theory of deferred action had already been put forward by Freud in the *Studies on Hysteria* (1895*d*) in discussing what he then called 'retention hysteria' (*Standard Ed.*, **2**, 161 ff.). He also gave a very elaborate account of its workings in hysteria in Part II of his posthumously-published 'Project' (1950*a*), also written in 1895. But in these earlier statements of the theory the effects of the primal scenes were deferred at least until the age of puberty, and the primal scenes themselves were never imagined as happening at so early an age as in the present case.]

of the sugar-sticks, the recollection of his father having beaten a snake to pieces.) For now he saw with his own eyes the wound of which his Nanya had spoken, and understood that its presence was a necessary condition of intercourse with his father. He could no longer confuse it with the bottom, as he had in his observation of the little girls.[1]

The dream ended in a state of anxiety, from which he did not recover until he had his Nanya with him. He fled, therefore, from his father to her. His anxiety was a repudiation of the wish for sexual satisfaction from his father—the trend which had put the dream into his head. The form taken by the anxiety, the fear of 'being eaten by the wolf', was only the (as we shall hear, regressive) transposition of the wish to be copulated with by his father, that is, to be given sexual satisfaction in the same way as his mother. His last sexual aim, the passive attitude towards his father, succumbed to repression, and fear of his father appeared in its place in the shape of the wolf phobia.

And the driving force of this repression? The circumstances of the case show that it can only have been his narcissistic genital libido, which, in the form of concern for his male organ, was fighting against a satisfaction whose attainment seemed to involve the renunciation of that organ. And it was from his threatened narcissism that he derived the masculinity with which he defended himself against his passive attitude towards his father.

We now observe that at this point in our narrative we must make an alteration in our terminology. During the dream he had reached a new phase in his sexual organization. Up to then the sexual opposites had been for him *active* and *passive*. Since his seduction his sexual aim had been a passive one, of being touched on the genitals; it was then transformed, by regression to the earlier stage of the sadistic-anal organization, into the masochistic aim of being beaten or punished. It was a matter of indifference to him whether he reached this aim with a man or with a woman. He had travelled, without considering the difference of sex, from his Nanya to his father; he had longed to have his penis touched by his Nanya, and had tried to provoke a beating from his father. Here his genitals were left out of account; though the connection with them which had been

[1] We shall learn later on [p. 77 ff.], when we come to trace out his anal erotism, how he further dealt with this portion of the problem.

concealed by the regression was still expressed in his phantasy of being beaten *on the penis*. The activation of the primal scene in the dream now brought him back to the genital organization. He discovered the vagina and the biological significance of masculine and feminine. He understood now that active was the same as masculine, while passive was the same as feminine. His passive sexual aim should now have been transformed into a feminine one, and have expressed itself as 'being copulated with by his father' instead of 'being beaten by him on the genitals or on the bottom'. This feminine aim, however, underwent repression and was obliged to let itself be replaced by fear of the wolf.

We must here break off the discussion of his sexual development until new light is thrown from the later stages of his history upon these earlier ones. For the proper appreciation of the wolf phobia we will only add that both his father and mother became wolves. His mother took the part of the castrated wolf, which let the others climb upon it; his father took the part of the wolf that climbed. But his fear, as we have heard him assure us, related only to the standing wolf, that is, to his father. It must further strike us that the fear with which the dream ended had a model in his grandfather's story. For in this the castrated wolf, which had let the others climb upon it, was seized with fear as soon as it was reminded of the fact of its taillessness. It seems, therefore, as though he had identified himself with his castrated mother during the dream, and was now fighting against that fact. 'If you want to be sexually satisfied by Father', we may perhaps represent him as saying to himself, 'you must allow yourself to be castrated like Mother; but I won't have that.' In short, a clear protest on the part of his masculinity! Let us, however, plainly understand that the sexual development of the case that we are now examining has a great disadvantage from the point of view of research, for it was by no means undisturbed. It was first decisively influenced by the seduction, and was then diverted by the scene of observation of the coitus, which in its deferred action operated like a second seduction.[1]

[1] [An attempt was later made by Rank (1926) to make use of the wolf dream to support his own views on the analysis of the transference. His arguments were criticized by Ferenczi (1927), who quoted the text of a letter from the 'Wolf Man' himself which had been put at his disposal by Freud.]

V

A FEW DISCUSSIONS

THE whale and the polar bear, it has been said, cannot wage war on each other, for since each is confined to his own element they cannot meet. It is just as impossible for me to argue with workers in the field of psychology or of the neuroses who do not recognize the postulates of psycho-analysis and who look on its results as artefacts. But during the last few years there has grown up another kind of opposition as well, among people who, in their own opinion at all events, take their stand upon the ground of analysis, who do not dispute its technique or results, but who merely think themselves justified in drawing other conclusions from the same material and in submitting it to other interpretations.

As a rule, however, theoretical controversy is unfruitful. No sooner has one begun to depart from the material on which one ought to be relying, than one runs the risk of becoming intoxicated with one's own assertions and, in the end, of supporting opinions which any observation would have contradicted. For this reason it seems to me to be incomparably more useful to combat dissentient interpretations by testing them upon particular cases and problems.

I have remarked above (see p. 38) that it will certainly be considered improbable, firstly, that 'a child at the tender age of one and a half could be in a position to take in the perceptions of such a complicated process and to preserve them so accurately in his unconscious; secondly, that it is possible at the age of four for a deferred revision of this material to penetrate the understanding; and finally, that any procedure could succeed in bringing into consciousness coherently and convincingly the details of a scene of this kind which had been experienced and understood in such circumstances'.

The last question is purely one of fact. Anyone who will take the trouble of pursuing an analysis into these depths by means of the prescribed technique will convince himself that it is decidedly possible. Anyone who neglects this, and breaks off the analysis in some higher stratum, has waived his right of forming a judgement on the matter. But the interpretation of what is arrived at in depth-analysis is not decided by this.

The two other doubts are based on a low estimate of the importance of early infantile impressions and an unwillingness to ascribe such enduring effects to them. The supporters of this view look for the causes of neuroses almost exclusively in the grave conflicts of later life; they assume that the importance of childhood is only held up before our eyes in analysis on account of the inclination of neurotics for expressing their present interests in reminiscences and symbols from the remote past. Such an estimate of the importance of the infantile factor would involve the disappearance of much that has formed part of the most intimate characteristics of analysis, though also, no doubt, of much that raises resistance to it and alienates the confidence of the outsider.

The view, then, that we are putting up for discussion is as follows. It maintains that scenes from early infancy, such as are brought up by an exhaustive analysis of neuroses (as, for instance, in the present case), are not reproductions of real occurrences, to which it is possible to ascribe an influence over the course of the patient's later life and over the formation of his symptoms. It considers them rather as products of the imagination, which find their instigation in mature life, which are intended to serve as some kind of symbolic representation of real wishes and interests, and which owe their origin to a regressive tendency, to a turning-away from the tasks of the present. If that is so, we can of course spare ourselves the necessity of attributing such a surprising amount to the mental life and intellectual capacity of children of the tenderest age.

Besides the desire which we all share for the rationalization and simplification of our difficult problem, there are all sorts of facts that speak in favour of this view. It is also possible to eliminate beforehand one objection to it which may arise, particularly in the mind of a practising analyst. It must be admitted that, if this view of these scenes from infancy were the right one, the carrying-out of analysis would not in the first instance be altered in any respect. If neurotics are endowed with the evil characteristic of diverting their interest from the present and of attaching it to these regressive substitutes, the products of their imagination, then there is absolutely nothing for it but to follow upon their tracks and bring these unconscious productions into consciousness; for, leaving on one side their lack of value from the point of view of reality, they are of the utmost value from our point of view, since they are for the moment the bearers and possessors of the interest which we want to set free so as to be able to direct it on to the tasks of the present. The analysis would have to run precisely the same course as one which had a *naïf* faith in the truth of the phantasies. The difference would only come at the end of the analysis, after the phantasies had been laid bare. We should then say to the patient: 'Very well, then; your neurosis proceeded *as though* you had received these impressions and spun them out in your childhood. You will see, of course, that that is out of the question. They were products of your imagination which were intended to divert you from the real tasks that lay before you. Let us now enquire what these tasks were, and what lines of communication ran between them and your phantasies.' After the infantile phantasies had been disposed of in this way, it would be possible to begin a second portion of the treatment, which would be concerned with the patient's real life.

Any shortening of this course, any alteration, that is, in psycho-analytic treatment, as it has hitherto been practised, would be technically inadmissible. Unless these phantasies are made conscious to the patient to their fullest extent, he cannot obtain command of the interest which is attached to them. If his attention is diverted from them as soon as their existence and their general outlines are divined, support is simply being given to the work of repression, thanks to which they have been put beyond the patient's reach in spite of all his pains. If he is given a premature sense of their unimportance, by being informed, for instance, that it will only be a question of phantasies, which, of course, have no real significance, his co-operation will never be secured for the task of bringing them into consciousness. A correct procedure, therefore, would make no alteration in the technique of analysis, whatever estimate might be formed of these scenes from infancy.

I have already mentioned that there are a number of facts which can be brought up in support of the view of these scenes being regressive phantasies. And above all there is this one: so far as my experience hitherto goes, these scenes from infancy are not reproduced during the treatment as recollections, they are the products of construction. Many people will certainly think that this single admission decides the whole dispute.

I am anxious not to be misunderstood. Every analyst knows —and he has met with the experience on countless occasions— that in the course of a successful treatment the patient brings up a large number of spontaneous recollections from his childhood, for the appearance of which (a first appearance, perhaps) the physician feels himself entirely blameless, since he has not made any attempt at a construction which could have put any material of the sort into the patient's head. It does not necessarily follow that these previously unconscious recollections are always true. They may be; but they are often distorted from the truth, and interspersed with imaginary elements, just like the so-called screen memories which are preserved spontaneously. All that I mean to say is this: scenes, like this one in my present patient's case, which date from such an early period and exhibit a similar content, and which further lay claim to such an extraordinary significance for the history of the case, are as a rule not reproduced as recollections, but have to be divined—constructed—gradually and laboriously from an aggregate of indications.[1] Moreover, it would be sufficient for the purposes of the argument if my admission that scenes of this kind do not become conscious in the shape of recollections applied only to cases of obsessional neurosis, or even if I were to limit my assertion to the case which we are studying here.

I am not of opinion, however, that such scenes must necessarily be phantasies because they do not reappear in the shape of recollections. It seems to me absolutely equivalent to a recollection, if the memories are replaced (as in the present case) by dreams the analysis of which invariably leads back to the same scene and which reproduce every portion of its content in an inexhaustible variety of new shapes. Indeed, dreaming is another kind of remembering, though one that is subject to the conditions that rule at night and to the laws of dream-formation. It is this recurrence in dreams that I regard as the explanation of the fact that the patients themselves gradually acquire a profound conviction of the reality of these primal scenes, a conviction which is in no respect inferior to one based on recollection.[2]

[1] [Cf. Freud's paper on 'Constructions in Analysis' (1937*d*).]

[2] A passage in the first edition of my *Interpretation of Dreams* (1900*a*) will show at what an early stage I was occupied with this problem. On

There is naturally no need for those who take the opposite view to abandon as hopeless their fight against such arguments. It is well known that dreams can be guided.[1] And the sense of conviction felt by the person analysed may be the result of suggestion, which is always having new parts assigned to it in the play of forces involved in analytic treatment. The old-fashioned psychotherapist, it might be maintained, used to suggest to his patient that he was cured, that he had overcome his inhibitions, and so on; while the psycho-analyst, on this view, suggests to him that when he was a child he had some experience or other, which he must now recollect in order to be cured. This would be the difference between the two.

Let it be clearly understood that this last attempt at an explanation on the part of those who take the view opposed to mine results in the scenes from infancy being disposed of far more fundamentally than was announced to begin with. What was argued at first was that they were not realities but phantasies. But what is argued now is evidently that they are phantasies not of the patient but of the analyst himself, who forces them upon the person under analysis on account of some complexes of his own. An analyst, indeed, who hears this reproach, will comfort himself by recalling how gradually the construction of this phantasy which he is supposed to have originated came about, and, when all is said and done, how independently of the physician's incentive many points in its development proceeded; how, after a certain phase of the treatment, everything seemed to converge upon it, and how later, in the synthesis, the most various and remarkable results radiated out from it; how not only the large problems but the smallest peculiarities in the history of the case were cleared up by this single assumption. And he will disclaim the possession of the amount of ingenuity necessary for the concoction of an occurrence which can fulfil all these demands. But even this plea will be without an effect

p. 126 [*Standard Ed.*, **4**, 184] of that work there is an analysis of a remark occurring in a dream: '*That's not obtainable any longer.*' It is explained that the phrase originated from myself. 'A few days earlier I had explained to the patient that the earliest experiences of childhood were "*not obtainable any longer* as such" but were replaced in analysis by "transferences" and dreams.'

[1] The *mechanism* of dreaming cannot be influenced; but dream *material* is to some extent subject to orders. [See Section VII of 'Remarks on the Theory and Practice of Dream-Interpretation' (1923*c*).]

on an adversary who has not experienced the analysis himself. On the one side there will be a charge of subtle self-deception, and on the other of obtuseness of judgement; it will be impossible to arrive at a decision.

Let us turn to another factor which supports this opposing view of these constructed scenes from infancy. It is as follows: There can be no doubt of the real existence of all the processes which have been brought forward in order to explain these doubtful structures as phantasies, and their importance must be recognized. The diversion of interest from the tasks of real life,[1] the existence of phantasies in the capacity of substitutes for unperformed actions, the regressive tendency which is expressed in these productions—regressive in more than one sense, in so far as there is involved simultaneously a shrinking-back from life and a harking-back to the past—all these things hold good, and are regularly confirmed by analysis. One might think that they would also suffice to explain the supposed reminiscences from early infancy which are under discussion; and in accordance with the principle of economy in science[2] such an explanation would have the advantage over one which is inadequate without the support of new and surprising assumptions.

I may here venture to point out that the antagonistic views which are to be found in the psycho-analytic literature of to-day are usually arrived at on the principle of *pars pro toto*. From a highly composite combination one part of the operative factors is singled out and proclaimed as the truth; and in its favour the other part, together with the whole combination, is then contradicted. If we look a little closer, to see which group of factors it is that has been given the preference, we shall find that it is the one that contains material already known from other sources or what can be most easily related to that material. Thus, Jung picks out actuality and regression, and Adler, egoistic motives. What is left over, however, and rejected as false, is precisely what is new in psycho-analysis and peculiar to it. This is the easiest method of repelling the revolutionary and inconvenient advances of psycho-analysis.

[1] I have good reasons for preferring to say 'the diversion of *libido* from current *conflicts*'. [For Freud's view of the relation between libido and interest, see the end of Section I of his paper on narcissism (1914*c*).]

[2] [Commonly known as 'Occam's razor'.]

It is worth while remarking that none of the factors which are adduced by the opposing view in order to explain these scenes from infancy had to wait for recognition until Jung brought them forward as novelties. The notion of a current conflict, of a turning away from reality, of a substitutive satisfaction obtained in phantasy, of a regression to material from the past—all of this (employed, moreover, in the same context, though perhaps with a slightly different terminology) had for years formed an integral part of my own theory. It was not the whole of it, however. It was only one part of the causes leading to the formation of neuroses—that part which, starting from reality, operates in a regressive direction. Side by side with this I left room for another influence which, starting from the impressions of childhood, operates in a forward direction, which points a path for the libido that is shrinking away from life, and which makes it possible to understand the otherwise inexplicable regression to childhood. Thus on my view the two factors co-operate in the formation of symptoms. But an earlier co-operation seems to me to be of equal importance. I am of opinion that *the influence of childhood makes itself felt already in the situation at the beginning of the formation of a neurosis, since it plays a decisive part in determining whether and at what point the individual shall fail to master the real problems of life.*

What is in dispute, therefore, is the significance of the infantile factor. The problem is to find a case which can establish that significance beyond any doubt. Such, however, is the case which is being dealt with so exhaustively in these pages and which is distinguished by the characteristic that the neurosis in later life was preceded by a neurosis in early childhood. It is for that very reason, indeed, that I have chosen it to report upon. Should any one feel inclined to reject it because the animal phobia strikes him as not sufficiently serious to be recognized as an independent neurosis, I may mention that the phobia was succeeded without any interval by an obsessional ceremonial, and by obsessional acts and thoughts, which will be discussed in the following sections of this paper.

The occurrence of a neurotic disorder in the fourth and fifth years of childhood proves, first and foremost, that infantile experiences are by themselves in a position to produce a neurosis, without there being any need for the addition of a flight from some task which has to be faced in real life. It may be objected that even a child is constantly being confronted with tasks which it would perhaps be glad to evade. That is so; but the life of a child under school age is easily observable, and we can examine it to see whether any 'tasks' are to be found in it capable of determining the causation of a neurosis. But we discover nothing but instinctual impulses which the child cannot satisfy and which it is not old enough to master, and the sources from which these impulses arise.

As was to be expected, the enormous shortening of the interval between the outbreak of the neurosis and the date of the childhood experiences which are under discussion reduces to the narrowest limits the regressive part of the causation, while it brings into full view the portion of it which operates in a forward direction, the influence of earlier impressions. The present case history will, I hope, give a clear picture of this position of things. But there are other reasons why neuroses of childhood give a decisive answer to the question of the nature of primal scenes—the earliest experiences of childhood that are brought to light in analysis.

Let us assume as an uncontradicted premise that a primal scene of this kind has been correctly educed technically, that it is indispensable to a comprehensive solution of all the conundrums that are set us by the symptoms of the infantile disorder, that all the consequences radiate out from it, just as all the threads of the analysis have led up to it. Then, in view of its content, it is impossible that it can be anything else than the reproduction of a reality experienced by the child. For a child, like an adult, can produce phantasies only from material which has been acquired from some source or other; and with children, some of the means of acquiring it (by reading, for instance) are cut off, while the space of time at their disposal for acquiring it is short and can easily be searched with a view to the discovery of any such sources.

In the present case the content of the primal scene is a picture of sexual intercourse between the boy's parents in a posture especially favourable for certain observations. Now it would be no evidence whatever of the reality of such a scene if we were to find it in a patient whose symptoms (the effects of the scene, that is) had appeared at some time or other in the later part of his life. A person such as this might have acquired the impressions, the ideas, and the knowledge on a great number of different occasions in the course of the long interval; he might then have transformed them into an imaginary picture, have projected them back into his childhood, and have attached them to his parents. If, however, the effects of a scene of this sort appear in the child's fourth or fifth year, then he must have witnessed the scene at an age even earlier than that. But in that case we are still faced with all the disconcerting consequences which have arisen from the analysis of this infantile neurosis. The only way out would be to assume that the patient not only unconsciously imagined the primal scene, but also concocted the alteration in his character, his fear of the wolf, and his religious obsession; but such an expedient would be contradicted by his otherwise sober nature and by the direct tradition in his family. It must therefore be left at this (I can see no other possibility): either the analysis based on the neurosis in his childhood is all a piece of nonsense from start to finish, or everything took place just as I have described it above.

At an earlier stage in the discussion [p. 41] we were brought up against an ambiguity in regard to the patient's predilection for female nates and for sexual intercourse in the posture in which they are especially prominent. It seemed necessary to trace this predilection back to the intercourse which he had observed between his parents, while at the same time a preference of this kind is a general characteristic of archaic constitutions which are predisposed to an obsessional neurosis. But the contradiction is easily resolved if we regard it as a case of overdetermination. The person who was the subject of his observation of this posture during intercourse was, after all, his father in the flesh, and it may also have been from him that he had inherited this constitutional predilection. Neither his father's subsequent illness nor his family history contradicts this; as has been mentioned already [p. 21 f.], a brother of his father's died in a condition which must be regarded as the outcome of a severe obsessional disorder.

In this connection we may recall that, at the time of his seduction as a boy of three and a quarter,[1] his sister had uttered a remarkable calumny against his good old nurse, to the effect that she stood all kinds of people on their heads and then took hold of them by their genitals (p. 20). We cannot fail to be struck by the idea that perhaps the sister, at a similar tender

[1] [In the editions before 1924 this read 'three and a half'.]

age, also witnessed the same scene as was observed by her brother later on, and that it was this that had suggested to her her notion about 'standing people on their heads' during the sexual act. This hypothesis would also give us a hint of the reason for her own sexual precocity.

[Originally [1] I had no intention of pursuing the discussion of the reality of 'primal scenes' any further in this place. Since, however, I have meanwhile had occasion in my *Introductory Lectures on Psycho-Analysis* [1916–17, Lecture XXIII] to treat the subject on more general lines and with no controversial aim in view, it would be misleading if I omitted to apply the considertaions which determined my other discussion of the matter to the case that is now before us. I therefore proceed as follows by way of supplement and rectification.—There remains the possibility of taking yet another view of the primal scene underlying the dream—a view, moreover, which obviates to a large extent the conclusion that has been arrived at above and relieves us of many of our difficulties. But the theory which seeks to reduce scenes from infancy to the level of regressive symbols will gain nothing even by this modification; and indeed that theory seems to me to be finally disposed of by this (as it would be by any other) analysis of an infantile neurosis.

This other view which I have in mind is that the state of affairs can be explained in the following manner. It is true that we cannot dispense with the assumption that the child observed a copulation, the sight of which gave him a conviction that castration might be more than an empty threat. Moreover, the significance which he subsequently came to attach to the postures of men and women, in connection with the development of anxiety on the one hand, and as a condition upon which his falling in love depended on the other hand, leaves us no choice but to conclude that it must have been a *coitus a tergo, more ferarum*. But there is another factor which is not so irreplaceable and which may be dropped. Perhaps what the child observed was not copulation between his parents but copulation between animals, which he then displaced on to his parents, as though he had inferred that his parents did things in the same way.

Colour is lent to this view above all by the fact that the wolves

[1] [Author's square bracket. See end of footnote, p. 7.]

in the dream were actually sheep-dogs and, moreover, appear as such in the drawing. Shortly before the dream the boy was repeatedly taken to visit the flocks of sheep [p. 30], and there he might see just such large white dogs and probably also observe them copulating. I should also like to bring into this connection the number three, which the dreamer introduced without adducing any further motive [p. 37, *n.* 5], and I would suggest that he had kept in his memory the fact that he had made three such observations with the sheep-dogs. What supervened during the expectant excitement of the night of his dream was the transference on to his parents of his recently acquired memory-picture, with *all* its details, and it was only thus that the powerful emotional effects which followed were made possible. He now arrived at a deferred understanding of the impressions which he may have received a few weeks or months earlier—a process such as all of us perhaps have been through in our own experiences. The transference from the copulating dogs on to his parents was accomplished not by means of his making an inference accompanied by words but by his searching out in his memory a real scene in which his parents had been together and which could be coalesced with the situation of the copulation. All the details of the scene which were established in the analysis of the dream may have been accurately reproduced. It was really on a summer's afternoon while the child was suffering from malaria, the parents were both present, dressed in white, when the child woke up from his sleep, but—the scene was innocent. The rest had been added by the inquisitive child's subsequent wish, based on his experiences with the dogs, to witness his parents too in their love-making; and the scene which was thus imagined now produced all the effects that we have catalogued, just as though it had been entirely real and not fused together out of two components, the one earlier and indifferent, the other later and profoundly impressive.

It is at once obvious how greatly the demands on our credulity are reduced. We need no longer suppose that the parents copulated in the presence of their child (a very young one, it is true)—which was a disagreeable idea for many of us. The period of time during which the effects were deferred is very greatly diminished; it now covers only a few months of the child's fourth year and does not stretch back at all into the first dark years of childhood. There remains scarcely anything strange in the child's conduct in making the transference from the dogs on to his parents and in being afraid of the wolf instead of his father. He was in that phase of the development of his attitude towards the world which I have described in *Totem and Taboo* [1912–13, Essay IV] as the return of totemism. The theory which endeavours to explain the primal scenes found in neuroses as retrospective phantasies of a later date seems to obtain powerful support from the present observation, in spite of our patient being of the tender age of four years. Young though he was, he was yet able to succeed in replacing an impression of his fourth year by an imaginary trauma at the age of one and a half. This regression, however, seems neither mysterious nor tendentious. The scene which was to be made up had to fulfil certain conditions which, in consequence of the circumstances of the dreamer's life, could only be found in precisely this early period; such, for instance, was the condition that he should be in bed in his parents' bedroom.

But something that I am able to adduce from the analytic findings in other cases will seem to most readers to be the decisive factor in favour of the correctness of the view here proposed. Scenes of observing sexual intercourse between parents at a very early age (whether they be real memories or phantasies) are as a matter of fact by no means rarities in the analyses of neurotic mortals. Possibly they are no less frequent among those who are not neurotics. Possibly they are part of the regular store in the—conscious or unconscious—treasury of their memories. But as often as I have been able by means of analysis to bring out a scene of this sort, it has shown the same peculiarity which startled us with our present patient too: it has related to *coitus a tergo*, which alone offers the spectator a possibility of inspecting the genitals. There is surely no need any longer to doubt that what we are dealing with is only a phantasy, which is invariably aroused, perhaps, by an observation of the sexual intercourse of animals. And yet more: I have hinted [p. 38] that my description of the 'primal scene' has remained incomplete because I have reserved for a later moment my account of the way in which the child interrupted his parents' intercourse. I must now add that this method of interruption is also the same in every case.

I can well believe that I have now laid myself open to grave aspersions on the part of the readers of this case history. If these arguments in favour of such a view of the 'primal scene' were at my disposal, how could I possibly have taken it on myself to begin by advocating one which seemed so absurd? Or have I made these new observations, which have obliged me to alter my original view, in the interval between the first draft of the case history and this addition, and am I for some reason or other unwilling to admit the fact? I will admit something else instead: I intend on this occasion to close the discussion of the reality of the primal scene with a *non liquet*.[1] This case history is not yet at an end; in its further course a factor will emerge which will shake the certainty which we seem at present to enjoy. Nothing, I think, will then be left but to refer my readers to the passages in my *Introductory Lectures* in which I have treated the problem of primal phantasies or primal scenes.]

[1] ['It is not clear'—a verdict where the evidence in a trial is inconclusive.]

- primal scene) ①
- seduction (3¼ YO)
- alteration of character) ②
- anxiety dream (4 YO)
- animal phobia) ③
- initiation into religion (4½ YO)) ④ no wolf phobia
- obsessional neurosis

10 YO

VI

THE OBSESSIONAL NEUROSIS

Now for the third time the patient came under a new influence that gave a decisive turn to his development. When he was four and a half years old, and as his state of irritability and apprehensiveness had still not improved, his mother determined to make him acquainted with the Bible story in the hope of distracting and elevating him. Moreover, she succeeded; his initiation into religion brought the previous phase to an end, but at the same time it led to the anxiety symptoms being replaced by obsessional symptoms. Up to then he had not been able to get to sleep easily because he had been afraid of having bad dreams like the one he had had that night before Christmas; now he was obliged before he went to bed to kiss all the holy pictures in the room, to recite prayers, and to make innumerable signs of the cross upon himself and upon his bed.

His childhood now falls clearly into the following epochs: first, the earliest period up to the seduction when he was three and a quarter years old, during which the primal scene took place; secondly, the period of the alteration in his character up to the anxiety dream (four years old); thirdly, the period of the animal phobia up to his initiation into religion (four and a half years old); and from then onwards the period of the obsessional neurosis up to a time later than his tenth year. That there should be an instantaneous and clear-cut displacement of one phase by the next was not in the nature of things or of our patient; on the contrary, the preservation of all that had gone before and the co-existence of the most different sorts of currents were characteristic of him. His naughtiness did not disappear when the anxiety set in, and persisted with slowly diminishing force during the period of piety. But there was no longer any question of a wolf phobia during this last phase. The obsessional neurosis ran its course discontinuously; the first attack was the longest and most intense, and others came on when he was eight and ten, following each time upon exciting causes which stood in a clear relationship to the content of the neurosis.

His mother told him the sacred story herself, and also

made his Nanya read aloud to him about it out of a book adorned with illustrations. The chief emphasis in the narrative was naturally laid upon the story of the passion. His Nanya, who was very pious and superstitious, added her own commentary on it, but was also obliged to listen to all the little critic's objections and doubts. If the battles which now began to convulse his mind finally ended in a victory for faith, his Nanya's influence was not without its share in this result.

What he related to me as his recollection of his reactions to this initiation was met by me at first with complete disbelief. It was impossible, I thought, that these could have been the thoughts of a child of four and a half or five; he had probably referred back to this remote past the thoughts which had arisen from the reflections of a grown man of thirty.[1] But the patient would not hear of this correction; I could not succeed, as in so many other differences of opinion between us, in convincing him; and in the end the correspondence between the thoughts which he had recollected and the symptoms of which he gave particulars, as well as the way in which the thoughts fitted into his sexual development, compelled me on the contrary to come to believe him. And I then reflected that this very criticism of the doctrines of religion, which I was unwilling to ascribe to the child, was only achieved by an infinitesimal minority of adults.

I shall now bring forward the material of his recollections, and not until afterwards try to find some path that may lead to an explanation of them.

The impression which he received from the sacred story was, to begin with, as he reported, by no means an agreeable one. He set his face, in the first place, against the feature of suffering in the figure of Christ, and then against his story as a whole. He turned his critical dissatisfaction against God the Father. If he

[1] I also repeatedly attempted to throw the patient's whole story forward by one year at all events, and in that way to refer the seduction to an age of four and a quarter, the dream to his fifth birthday, etc. As regards the intervals between the events there was no possibility of gaining any time. But the patient remained obdurate on the point, though he did not succeed entirely in removing my doubts. A postponement like this for one year would obviously be of no importance as regards the impression made by his story and as regards the discussions and implications attached to it.

were almighty, then it was his fault that men were wicked and tormented others and were sent to Hell for it. He ought to have made them good; he was responsible himself for all wickedness and all torments. The patient took objection to the command that we should turn the other cheek if our right cheek is smitten, and to the fact that Christ had wished on the Cross[1] that the cup might be taken away from him, as well as to the fact that no miracle had taken place to prove that he was the Son of God. Thus his acuteness was on the alert, and was able to search out with remorseless severity the weak points of the sacred narrative.

But to this rationalistic criticism there were very soon added ruminations and doubts, which betray to us that hidden impulses were also at work. One of the first questions which he addressed to his Nanya was whether Christ had had a behind too. His Nanya informed him that he had been a god and also a man. As a man he had had and done all the same things as other men. This did not satisfy him at all, but he succeeded in finding consolation of his own by saying to himself that the behind is really only a continuation of the legs. But hardly had he pacified his dread of having to humiliate the sacred figure, when it flared up again as the further question arose whether Christ used to shit too. He did not venture to put this question to his pious Nanya, but he himself found a way out, and she could not have shown him a better. Since Christ had made wine *out of* nothing, he could also have made food *into* nothing and in this way have avoided defaecating.

We shall be in a better position to understand these ruminations if we return to a piece of his sexual development which we have already mentioned. We know that, after the rebuff from his Nanya [p. 24 f.] and the consequent suppression of the beginnings of genital activity, his sexual life developed in the direction of sadism and masochism. He tormented and ill-treated small animals, imagined himself beating horses, and on the other hand imagined the heir to the throne being beaten.[2] In his sadism he maintained his ancient identification with his father; but in his masochism he chose him as a sexual object. He was deep in a phase of the pregenital organization which I

[1] [This should, of course, be the Mount of Olives. Freud informed the translators that the mistake originated from the patient himself.]

[2] Especially on the penis (see pp. 26 [and 47]).

regard as the predisposition to obsessional neurosis.[1] The operation of the dream, which brought him under the influence of the primal scene, could have led him to make the advance to the genital organization, and to transform his masochism towards his father into a feminine attitude towards him—into homosexuality. But the dream did not bring about this advance; it ended in a state of anxiety. His relation to his father might have been expected to proceed from the sexual aim of being beaten by him to the next aim, namely, that of being copulated with by him like a woman; but in fact, owing to the opposition of his narcissistic masculinity, this relation was thrown back to an even more primitive stage. It was displaced on to a father-surrogate, and at the same time split off in the shape of a fear of being eaten by the wolf. But this by no means disposed of it. On the contrary, we can only do justice to the apparent complexity of the state of affairs by bearing firmly in mind the co-existence of the three sexual trends which were directed by the boy towards his father. From the time of the dream onwards, in his unconscious he was homosexual, and in his neurosis he was at the level of cannibalism; while the earlier masochistic attitude remained the dominant one. All three currents had passive sexual aims; there was the same object, and the same sexual impulse, but that impulse had become split up along three different levels.

His knowledge of the sacred story now gave him a chance of sublimating his predominant masochistic attitude towards his father. He became Christ—which was made specially easy for him on account of their having the same birthday. Thus he became something great and also (a fact upon which enough stress was not laid for the moment) a man. We catch a glimpse of his repressed homosexual attitude in his doubting whether Christ could have a behind, for these ruminations can have had no other meaning but the question whether he himself could be used by his father like a woman—like his mother in the primal scene. When we come to the solution of the other obsessional ideas, we shall find this interpretation confirmed. His reflection that it was insulting to bring the sacred figure into relation with such insinuations corresponded to the repression of his passive homosexuality. It will be noticed that he was

[1] [See the paper Freud had written on the subject not long before the present one (1913*i*).]

endeavouring to keep his new sublimation free from the admixture which it derived from sources in the repressed. But he was unsuccessful.

We do not as yet understand why he also rebelled against the passive character of Christ and against his ill-treatment by his Father, and in this way began also to renounce his previous masochistic ideal, even in its sublimation. We may assume that this second conflict was especially favourable to the emergence of the humiliating obsessional thoughts from the first conflict (between the dominant masochistic and the repressed homosexual currents), for it is only natural that in a mental conflict all the currents upon one side or the other should combine with one another, even though they have the most diverse origins. Some fresh information teaches us the motive of this rebelling and at the same time of the criticisms which he levelled at religion.

His sexual researches, too, gained something from what he was told about the sacred story. So far he had had no reason for supposing that children only came from women. On the contrary, his Nanya had given him to believe that he was his father's child, while his sister was his mother's [p. 17]; and this closer connection with his father had been very precious to him. He now heard that Mary was called the Mother of God. So all children came from women, and what his Nanya had said to him was no longer tenable. Moreover, as a result of what he was told, he was bewildered as to who Christ's father really was. He was inclined to think it was Joseph, as he heard that he and Mary had always lived together, but his Nanya said that Joseph was only 'like' his father and that his real father was God. He could make nothing of that. He only understood this much: if the question was one that could be argued about at all, then the relation between father and son could not be such an intimate one as he had always imagined it to be.

The boy had some kind of inkling of the ambivalent feelings towards the father which are an underlying factor in all religions, and attacked his religion on account of the slackening which it implied in this relation between son and father. Naturally his opposition soon ceased to take the form of doubting the truth of the doctrine, and turned instead directly against the figure of God. God had treated his son harshly and cruelly, but he was no better towards men; he had sacrificed his own son and had ordered Abraham to do the same. He began to fear God.

If he was Christ, then his father was God. But the God which religion forced upon him was not a true substitute for the father whom he had loved and whom he did not want to have stolen from him. His love for this father of his gave him his critical acuteness. He resisted God in order to be able to cling to his father; and in doing this he was really upholding the old father against the new. He was faced by a trying part of the process of detaching himself from his father.

His old love for his father, which had been manifest in his earliest period, was therefore the source of his energy in struggling against God and of his acuteness in criticizing religion. But on the other hand this hostility to the new God was not an original reaction either; it had its prototype in a hostile impulse against his father, which had come into existence under the influence of the anxiety-dream, and it was at bottom only a revival of that impulse. The two opposing currents of feeling, which were to rule the whole of his later life, met here in the ambivalent struggle over the question of religion. It followed, moreover, that what this struggle produced in the shape of symptoms (the blasphemous ideas, the compulsion which came over him of thinking 'God—shit', 'God—swine') were genuine compromise-products, as we shall see from the analysis of these ideas in connection with his anal erotism.

Some other obsessional symptoms of a less typical sort pointed with equal certainty to his father, while at the same time showing the connection between the obsessional neurosis and the earlier occurrences.

A part of the pious ritual by means of which he eventually atoned for his blasphemies was the command to breathe in a ceremonious manner under certain conditions. Each time he made the sign of the cross he was obliged to breathe in deeply or to exhale forcibly. In his native tongue 'breath' is the same word as 'spirit', so that here the Holy Ghost came in. He was obliged to breathe in the Holy Spirit, or to breathe out the evil spirits which he had heard and read about.[1] He ascribed too to these evil spirits the blasphemous thoughts for which he had to inflict such heavy penance upon himself. He was, however, also

[1] This symptom, as we shall hear, had developed after his sixth year and when he could already read.

obliged to exhale when he saw beggars, or cripples, or ugly, old, or wretched-looking people; but he could think of no way of connecting this obsession with the spirits. The only account he could give to himself was that he did it so as not to become like such people.

Eventually, in connection with a dream, the analysis elicited the information that the breathing out at the sight of pitiable-looking people had begun only after his sixth year and was related to his father. He had not seen his father for many months, when one day his mother said she was going to take the children with her to the town and show them something that would very much please them. She then took them to a sanatorium, where they saw their father again; he looked ill, and the boy felt very sorry for him. His father was thus the prototype of all the cripples, beggars, and poor people in whose presence he was obliged to breathe out; just as a father is the prototype of the bogies that people see in anxiety-states, and of the caricatures that are drawn to bring derision upon some one. We shall learn elsewhere [p. 88] that this attitude of compassion was derived from a particular detail of the primal scene, a detail which only became operative in the obsessional neurosis at this late moment.

Thus his determination not to become like cripples (which was the motive of his breathing out in their presence) was his old identification with his father transformed into the negative. But in so doing he was also copying his father in the positive sense, for the heavy breathing was an imitation of the noise which he had heard coming from his father during the intercourse.[1] He had derived the Holy Ghost from this manifestation of male sensual excitement. Repression had turned this breathing into an evil spirit, which had another genealogy as well: namely, the malaria [p. 37] from which he had been suffering at the time of the primal scene.

His repudiation of these evil spirits corresponded to an unmistakable strain of asceticism in him which also found expression in other reactions. When he heard that Christ had once cast out some evil spirits into a herd of swine which then rushed down a precipice, he thought of how his sister in the earliest years of her childhood, before he could remember, had rolled down on to the beach from the cliff-path above the harbour. She too was an evil spirit and a swine. It was a short

[1] Assuming the reality of the primal scene.

road from here to 'God—swine'. His father himself had shown that he was no less of a slave to sensuality. When he was told the story of the first of mankind he was struck by the similarity of his lot to Adam's. In conversation with his Nanya he professed hypocritical surprise that Adam should have allowed himself to be dragged into misfortune by a woman, and promised her that he would never marry. A hostility towards women, due to his seduction by his sister, found strong expression at this time. And it was destined to disturb him often enough in his later erotic life. His sister came to be the permanent embodiment for him of temptation and sin. After he had been to confession he seemed to himself pure and free from sin. But then it appeared to him as though his sister were lying in wait to drag him again into sin, and in a moment he had provoked a quarrel with her which made him sinful once more. Thus he was obliged to keep on reproducing the event of his seduction over and over again. Moreover, he had never given away his blasphemous thoughts at confession, in spite of their being such a weight on his mind.

We have been led unawares into a consideration of the symptoms of the later years of the obsessional neurosis; and we shall therefore pass over the occurrences of the intervening period and shall proceed to describe its termination. We already know that, apart from its permanent strength, it underwent occasional intensifications: once—though the episode must for the present remain obscure to us—at the time of the death of a boy living in the same street, with whom he was able to identify himself. When he was ten years old he had a German tutor, who very soon obtained a great influence over him. It is most instructive to observe that the whole of his strict piety dwindled away, never to be revived, after he had noticed and had learnt from enlightening conversations with his tutor that this father-surrogate attached no importance to piety and set no store by the truth of religion. His piety sank away along with his dependence upon his father, who was now replaced by a new and more sociable father. This did not take place, however, without one last flicker of the obsessional neurosis; and from this he particularly remembered the obsession of having to think of the Holy Trinity whenever he saw three heaps of dung lying together in the road. In fact he never gave way to fresh ideas without making one last attempt at clinging to what had lost its values for him. When his tutor discouraged him from his cruelties to small animals he did indeed put an end to those misdeeds, but not until he had again cut up caterpillars for a last time to his thorough satisfaction. He still behaved in just the same way during the analytic treatment, for he showed a habit of producing transitory 'negative reactions'; every time something had been conclusively cleared up, he attempted to contradict the effect for a short while by an aggravation of the symptom which had been cleared up. It is quite the rule, as we know, for children to treat prohibitions in the same kind of way. When they have been rebuked for something (for instance, because they are making an unbearable din), they repeat it once more after the prohibition before stopping it. In this way they gain the point of apparently stopping of their own accord and of disobeying the prohibition.

Under the German tutor's influence there arose a new and better sublimation of the patient's sadism, which, with the approach of puberty, had then gained the upper hand over his masochism. He developed an enthusiasm for military affairs, for uniforms, weapons and horses, and used them as food for continual day-dreams. Thus, under a man's influence, he had got free from his passive attitudes, and found himself for the time being on fairly normal lines. It was as an after-effect of his affection for the tutor, who left him soon afterwards, that in his later life he preferred German things (as, for instance, physicians, sanatoria, women) to those belonging to his native country (representing his father)—a fact which was incidentally of great advantage to the transference during the treatment.

There was another dream, which belongs to the period before his emancipation by the tutor, and which I mention because it was forgotten until its appearance during the treatment. He saw himself riding on a horse and pursued by a gigantic caterpillar. He recognized in this dream an allusion to an earlier one from the period before the tutor, which we had interpreted long before. In this earlier dream he saw the Devil dressed in black and in the upright posture with which the wolf and the lion had terrified him so much in their day. He was pointing with his out-stretched finger at a gigantic snail. The patient had soon guessed that this Devil was the Demon out of a well-known poem,[1] and that the dream itself was a version of a very popular picture representing the Demon in a love-scene

[1] [Lermontov's 'The Demon'.]

with a girl. The snail was in the woman's place, as being a perfect female sexual symbol. Guided by the Demon's pointing gesture, we were soon able to give as the dream's meaning that the patient was longing for some one who should give him the last pieces of information that were still missing upon the riddle of sexual intercourse, just as his father had given him the first in the primal scene long before.

In connection with the later dream, in which the female symbol was replaced by the male one, he remembered a particular event which had occurred a short time before the dream. Riding on the estate one day, he passed a peasant who was lying asleep with his little boy beside him. The latter woke his father and said something to him, whereupon the father began to abuse the rider and to pursue him till he rode off hastily. There was also a second recollection, that on the same estate there were trees that were quite white, spun all over by caterpillars. We can see that he took flight from the realization of the phantasy of the son lying with his father, and that he brought in the white trees in order to make an allusion to the anxiety-dream of the white wolves on the walnut tree. It was thus a direct outbreak of dread of the feminine attitude towards men against which he had at first protected himself by his religious sublimation and was soon to protect himself still more effectively by the military one [p. 69].

It would, however, be a great mistake to suppose that after the removal of the obsessional symptoms no permanent effects of the obsessional neurosis remained behind. The process had led to a victory for the faith of piety over the rebelliousness of critical research, and had had the repression of the homosexual attitude as its necessary condition. Lasting disadvantages resulted from both these factors. His intellectual activity remained seriously impaired after this first great defeat. He developed no zeal for learning, he showed no more of the acuteness with which at the tender age of five he had criticized and dissected the doctrines of religion. The repression of his overpowerful homosexuality, which was accomplished during the anxiety-dream, reserved that important impulse for the unconscious, kept it directed towards its original aim, and withdrew it from all the sublimations to which it is susceptible in other circumstances. For this reason the patient was without all those social interests which give a content to life. It was only when, during the analytic treatment, it became possible to liberate his shackled homosexuality that this state of affairs showed any improvement; and it was a most remarkable experience to see how (without any direct advice from the physician) each piece of homosexual libido which was set free sought out some application in life and some attachment to the great common concerns of mankind.

VII

ANAL EROTISM AND THE CASTRATION COMPLEX

I MUST beg the reader to bear in mind that I obtained this history of an infantile neurosis as a by-product, so to speak, during the analysis of an illness in mature years. I have therefore been obliged to put it together from even smaller fragments than are usually at one's disposal for purposes of synthesis. This task, which is not difficult in other respects, finds a natural limit when it is a question of forcing a structure which is itself in many dimensions on to the two-dimensional descriptive plane. I must therefore content myself with bringing forward fragmentary portions, which the reader can then put together into a living whole. The obsessional neurosis that has been described grew up, as has been repeatedly emphasized, on the basis of a sadistic-anal constitution. But we have hitherto discussed only one of the two chief factors—the patient's sadism and its transformations. Everything that concerns his anal erotism has intentionally been left on one side so that it might be brought together and discussed at this later stage.

Analysts have long been agreed that the multifarious instinctual impulses which are comprised under the name of anal erotism play an extraordinarily important part, which it would be quite impossible to over-estimate, in building up sexual life and mental activity in general. It is equally agreed that one of the most important manifestations of the transformed erotism derived from this source is to be found in the treatment of money,[1] for in the course of life this precious material attracts on to itself the psychical interest which was originally proper to faeces, the product of the anal zone. We are accustomed to trace back interest in money, in so far as it is of a libidinal and not of a rational character, to excretory pleasure, and we expect normal people to keep their relations to money entirely free from libidinal influences and regulate them according to the demands of reality.

In our patient, at the time of his later illness, these relations

[1] [See Freud's paper on 'Character and Anal Erotism' (1908*b*).]

were disturbed to a particularly severe degree, and this fact was not the least considerable element in his lack of independence and his incapacity for dealing with life. He had become very rich through legacies from his father and uncle; it was obvious that he attached great importance to being taken for rich, and he was liable to feel very much hurt if he was undervalued in this respect. But he had no idea how much he possessed, what his expenditure was, or what balance was left over. It was hard to say whether he ought to be called a miser or a spendthrift. He behaved now in this way and now in that, but never in a way that seemed to show any consistent intention. Some striking traits, which I shall further discuss below, might have led one to regard him as a hardened plutocrat, who considered his wealth as his greatest personal advantage, and who would never for a moment allow emotional interests to weigh against pecuniary ones. Yet he did not value other people by their wealth, and, on the contrary, showed himself on many occasions unassuming, helpful, and charitable. Money, in fact, had been withdrawn from his conscious control, and meant for him something quite different.

I have already mentioned (p. 23) that I viewed with grave suspicion the way in which he consoled himself for the loss of his sister, who had become his closest companion during her latter years, with the reflection that now he would not have to share his parents' inheritance with her. But what was perhaps even more striking was the calmness with which he was able to relate this, as though he had no comprehension of the coarseness of feeling to which he was thus confessing. It is true that analysis rehabilitated him by showing that his grief for his sister had merely undergone a displacement; but it then became quite inexplicable why he should have tried to find a substitute for his sister in an increase of wealth.

He himself was puzzled by his behaviour in another connection. After his father's death the property that was left was divided between him and his mother. His mother administered it, and, as he himself admitted, met his pecuniary claims irreproachably and liberally. Yet every discussion of money matters that took place between them used to end with the most violent reproaches on his side, to the effect that she did not love him, that she was trying to economize at his expense, and that she would probably rather see him dead so as to have sole control over the money. His mother used then to protest her disinterestedness with tears, and he would thereupon grow ashamed of himself and declare with justice that he thought nothing of the sort of her. But he was sure to repeat the same scene at the first opportunity.

Many incidents, of which I will relate two, show that, for a long time before the analysis, faeces had had this significance of money for him. At a time when his bowel as yet played no part in his complaint, he once paid a visit to a poor cousin of his in a large town. As he left him he reproached himself for not giving this relative financial support, and immediately afterwards had what was 'perhaps the most urgent need for relieving his bowels that he had experienced in his life'. Two years later he did in fact settle an annuity upon this cousin. Here is the other case. At the age of eighteen, while he was preparing for his leaving-examination at school, he visited a friend and came to an agreement with him on a plan which seemed advisable on account of the dread which they shared of failing in the examination.[1] It had been decided to bribe the school servant, and the patient's share of the sum to be provided was naturally the larger. On the way home he thought to himself that he should be glad to give even more if only he could succeed in getting through, if only he could be sure that nothing would happen to him in the examination—and an accident of another sort really did happen to him[2] before he reached his own front door.

We shall be prepared to hear that during his later illness he suffered from disturbances of his intestinal function which were very obstinate, though various circumstances caused them to fluctuate in intensity. When he came under my treatment he had become accustomed to enemas, which were given him by an attendant; spontaneous evacuations did not occur for months at a time, unless a sudden excitement from some particular direction intervened, as a result of which normal activity of the bowels might set in for a few days. His principal subject of

[1] [The German word '*Durchfall*' means literally 'falling through'; it is used in the sense of 'failing', as in an examination, and also of 'diarrhoea'.] The patient informed me that his native tongue has no parallel to the familiar German use of '*Durchfall*' as a description for disturbances of the bowels.

[2] This expression has the same meaning in the patient's native tongue as in German. [The German idiom refers euphemistically to the excretory processes.]

complaint was that for him the world was hidden in a veil, or that he was cut off from the world by a veil. This veil was torn only at one moment—when, after an enema, the contents of the bowel left the intestinal canal; and he then felt well and normal again.[1]

The colleague to whom I referred the patient for a report upon his intestinal condition was perspicacious enough to explain it as being a functional one, or even psychically determined, and to abstain from any active medicinal treatment. Moreover, neither this nor dieting were of any use. During the years of analytic treatment there was no spontaneous motion—apart from the sudden influences that I have mentioned. The patient allowed himself to be convinced that if the intractable organ received more intensive treatment things would only be made worse, and contented himself with bringing on an evacuation once or twice a week by means of an enema or a purgative.

In discussing these intestinal troubles I have given more space to the patient's later illness than has been my plan elsewhere in this work, which is concerned with his infantile neurosis. I have done so for two reasons: first, because the intestinal symptoms were in point of fact carried forward from the infantile neurosis into the later one with little alteration, and secondly, because they played a principal part in the conclusion of the treatment.

We know how important doubt is to the physician who is analysing an obsessional neurosis.[2] It is the patient's strongest weapon, the favourite expedient of his resistance. This same doubt enabled our patient to lie entrenched behind a respectful indifference and to allow the efforts of the treatment to slip past him for years together. Nothing changed, and there was no way of convincing him. At last I recognized the importance of the intestinal trouble for my purposes; it represented the small trait of hysteria which is regularly to be found at the root of an obsessional neurosis.[3] I promised the patient a

[1] The effect was the same whether he had the enema given him by some one else or whether he managed it himself.

[2] [Cf. the case history of the 'Rat Man' (1909*d*), *Standard Ed.*, **10**, 241–3.]

[3] [Freud had already remarked on this at the beginning of Section II of his second paper on 'The Neuro-Psychoses of Defence' (1896*b*). He alluded to the point again in Chapter V of *Inhibitions, Symptoms and Anxiety* (1926*d*).]

complete recovery of his intestinal activity, and by means of this promise made his incredulity manifest. I then had the satisfaction of seeing his doubt dwindle away, as in the course of the work his bowel began, like a hysterically affected organ, to 'join in the conversation',[1] and in a few weeks' time recovered its normal functions after their long impairment.

I now turn back to the patient's childhood—to a time at which it was impossible that faeces could have had the significance of money for him.

Intestinal disorders set in very early with him, and especially in the form which is the most frequent and, among children, the most normal—namely, incontinence. We shall certainly be right, however, in rejecting a pathological explanation of these earliest occurrences, and in regarding them only as evidence of the patient's intention not to let himself be disturbed or checked in the pleasure attached to the function of evacuation. He found a great deal of enjoyment (such as would tally with the natural coarseness of many classes of society, though not of his) in anal jokes and exhibitions, and this enjoyment had been retained by him until after the beginning of his later illness.

During the time of the English governess it repeatedly happened that he and his Nanya had to share that obnoxious lady's bedroom. His Nanya noticed with comprehension the fact that precisely on those nights he made a mess in his bed, though otherwise this had ceased to happen a long time before. He was not in the least ashamed of it; it was an expression of defiance against the governess.

A year later (when he was four and a half), during the anxiety period, he happened to make a mess in his knickerbockers in the day-time. He was terribly ashamed of himself, and as he was being cleaned he moaned that he could not go on living like that. So that in the meantime something had changed; and by following up his lament we came upon the traces of this something. It turned out that the words 'he could not go on living like that' were repeated from some one else. His mother had once[2] taken him with her when she was walking

[1] [This phrase ('*mitsprechen*') goes back to the *Studies on Hysteria* (1895*d*), *Standard Ed.*, 2, 296 f.]

[2] When this happened was not exactly fixed; but in any case before the anxiety-dream when he was four, and probably before his parents' absence from home.

down to the station with the doctor who had come to visit her. During this walk she had lamented over her pains and haemorrhages and had broken out in the same words, 'I cannot go on living like this', without imagining that the child whose hand she was holding would keep them in his memory. Thus his lament (which, moreover, he was to repeat on innumerable occasions during his later illness) had the significance of an identification with his mother.

There soon appeared in his recollection what was evidently, in respect both of its date and of its content, a missing intermediate link between these two events. It once happened at the beginning of his anxiety period that his apprehensive mother gave orders that precautions were to be taken to protect the children from dysentery, which had made its appearance in the neighbourhood of the estate. He made enquiries as to what that might be; and after hearing that when you have dysentery you find blood in your stool he became very nervous and declared that there was blood in his own stool; he was afraid he would die of dysentery, but allowed himself to be convinced by an examination that he had made a mistake and had no need to be frightened. We can see that in this dread he was trying to put into effect an identification with his mother, whose haemorrhages he had heard about in the conversation with her doctor. In his later attempt at identification (when he was four and a half) he had dropped any mention of the blood; he no longer understood himself, for he imagined that he was ashamed of himself and was not aware that he was being shaken by a dread of death, though this was unmistakably revealed in his lament.

At that time his mother, suffering as she was from an abdominal affection, was in general nervous, both about herself and the children; it is most probable that his own nervousness, besides its other motives, was based on an identification with his mother.

Now what can have been the meaning of this identification with his mother?

Between the impudent use he made of his incontinence when he was three and a half, and the horror with which he viewed it when he was four and a half, there lies the dream with which his anxiety period began—the dream which gave him a deferred comprehension of the scene he had experienced when he was one and a half (p. 45), and an explanation of the part played by women in the sexual act. It is only another step to connect the change in his attitude towards defaecation with this same great revulsion. Dysentery was evidently his name for the illness which he had heard his mother lamenting about, and which it was impossible to go on living with; he did not regard his mother's disease as being abdominal but as being intestinal. Under the influence of the primal scene he came to the conclusion that his mother had been made ill by what his father had done to her;[1] and his dread of having blood in his stool, of being as ill as his mother, was his repudiation of being identified with her in this sexual scene—the same repudiation with which he awoke from the dream. But the dread was also a proof that in his later elaboration of the primal scene he had put himself in his mother's place and had envied her this relation with his father. The organ by which his identification with women, his passive homosexual attitude to men, was able to express itself was the anal zone. The disorders in the function of this zone had acquired the significance of feminine impulses of tenderness, and they retained it during the later illness as well.

At this point we must consider an objection, the discussion of which may contribute much to the elucidation of the apparent confusion of the circumstances. We have been driven to assume that during the process of the dream he understood that women are castrated, that instead of a male organ they have a wound which serves for sexual intercourse, and that castration is the necessary condition of femininity; we have been driven to assume that the threat of this loss induced him to repress his feminine attitude towards men, and that he awoke from his homosexual enthusiasm in anxiety. Now how can this comprehension of sexual intercourse, this recognition of the vagina, be brought into harmony with the selection of the bowel for the purpose of identification with women? Are not the intestinal symptoms based on what is probably an older notion, and one which in any case completely contradicts the dread of castration—the notion, namely, that sexual intercourse takes place at the anus?

To be sure, this contradiction is present; and the two views are entirely inconsistent with each other. The only question is whether they need be consistent. Our bewilderment arises

[1] A conclusion which was probably not far from the truth.

only because we are always inclined to treat unconscious mental processes like conscious ones and to forget the profound differences between the two psychical systems.

When his Christmas dream, with its excitement and expectancy, conjured up before him the picture of the sexual intercourse of his parents as it had once been observed (or construed) by him, there can be no doubt that the first view of it to come up was the old one, according to which the part of the female body which received the male organ was the anus. And, indeed, what else could he have supposed when at the age of one and a half he was a spectator of the scene?[1] But now came the new event that occurred when he was four years old. What he had learnt in the meantime, the allusions which he had heard to castration, awoke and cast a doubt on the 'cloacal theory'; they brought to his notice the difference between the sexes and the sexual part played by women. In this contingency he behaved as children in general behave when they are given an unwished-for piece of information—whether sexual or of any other kind. He rejected what was new (in our case from motives connected with his fear of castration) and clung fast to what was old. He decided in favour of the intestine and against the vagina, just as, for similar motives, he later on took his father's side against God. He rejected the new information and clung to the old theory. The latter must have provided the material for his identification with women, which made its appearance later as a dread of death in connection with the bowels, and for his first religious scruples, about whether Christ had had a behind, and so on. It is not that his new insight remained without any effect; quite the reverse. It developed an extraordinarily powerful effect, for it became a motive for keeping the whole process of the dream under repression and for excluding it from being worked over later in consciousness. But with that its effect was exhausted; it had no influence in deciding the sexual problem. That it should have been possible from that time onwards for a fear of castration to exist side by side with an identification with women by means of the bowel admittedly involved a contradiction. But it was only a logical contradiction—which is not saying much. On the contrary, the whole process is characteristic of the way in which the unconscious works. A

[1] Or so long as he did not grasp the sense of the copulation between the dogs.

repression is something very different from a condemning judgement.

When we were studying the genesis of the wolf phobia, we followed the effect of his new insight into the sexual act; but now that we are investigating the disturbances of the intestinal function, we find ourselves working on the basis of the old cloacal theory. The two points of view remained separated from each other by a stage of repression. His feminine attitude towards men, which had been repudiated by the act of repression, drew back, as it were, into the intestinal symptoms, and expressed itself in the attacks of diarrhoea, constipation, and intestinal pain, which were so frequent during the patient's childhood. His later sexual phantasies, which were based on a correct sexual knowledge, were thus able to express themselves regressively as intestinal troubles. But we cannot understand them until we have explained the modifications which take place in the significance of faeces from the first years of childhood onward.[1]

I have already hinted at an earlier point in my story [p. 38] that one portion of the content of the primal scene has been kept back. I am now in a position to produce this missing portion. The child finally interrupted his parents' intercourse by passing a stool, which gave him an excuse for screaming. All the considerations which I have raised above in discussing the rest of the content of the same scene apply equally to the criticism of this additional piece. The patient accepted this concluding act when I had constructed it, and appeared to confirm it by producing 'transitory symptoms'. A further additional piece which I had proposed, to the effect that his father was annoyed at the interruption and gave vent to his ill-humour by scolding him, had to be dropped. The material of the analysis did not react to it.

The additional detail which I have now brought forward cannot of course be put on a level with the rest of the content of the scene. Here it is not a question of an impression from outside, which must be expected to re-emerge in a number of later indications, but of a reaction on the part of the child himself. It would make no difference to the story as a whole if this

[1] Cf. 'On Transformations of Instinct as Exemplified in Anal Erotism' (1917*c*). [See below, p. 125. Though that paper was published before he present case history, it was probably written later.]

demonstration had not occurred, or if it had been taken from a later period and inserted into the course of the scene. But there can be no question of how we are to regard it. It is a sign of a state of excitement of the anal zone (in the widest sense). In other similar cases an observation like this of sexual intercourse has ended with a discharge of urine; a grown-up man in the same circumstances would feel an erection. The fact that our little boy passed a stool as a sign of his sexual excitement is to be regarded as a characteristic of his congenital sexual constitution. He at once assumed a passive attitude, and showed more inclination towards a subsequent identification with women than with men.

At the same time, like every other child, he was making use of the content of the intestines in one of its earliest and most primitive meanings. Faeces are the child's first *gift*, the first sacrifice on behalf of his affection, a portion of his own body which he is ready to part with, but only for the sake of some one he loves.[1] To use faeces as an expression of defiance, as our patient did against the governess when he was three and a half, is merely to turn this earlier 'gift' meaning into the negative. The '*grumus merdae*' [heap of faeces] left behind by criminals upon the scene of their misdeeds seems to have both these meanings: contumely, and a regressive expression of making amends. It is always possible, when a higher stage has been reached, for use still to be made of the lower one in its negative and debased sense. The contrariety is a manifestation of repression.[2]

[1] I believe there can be no difficulty in substantiating the statement that infants only soil with their excrement people whom they know and are fond of; they do not consider strangers worthy of this distinction. In my *Three Essays on the Theory of Sexuality* (1905*d*) [*Standard Ed.*, 7, 185–7] I mentioned the very first purpose to which faeces are put—namely, the auto-erotic stimulation of the intestinal mucous membrane. We now reach a further stage, at which a decisive part in the process of defaecation is played by the child's attitude to some object to whom he thus shows himself obedient or agreeable. This relation is one that persists; for even older children will only allow themselves to be assisted in defaecating and urinating by particular privileged persons, though in this connection the prospect of other forms of satisfaction is also involved.

[2] In the unconscious, as we are aware, 'No' does not exist, and there is no distinction between contraries. Negation is only introduced by the process of repression. [See 'The Unconscious' (1915*e*), Section V, and the later paper on 'Negation' (1925*h*).]

At a later stage of sexual development faeces take on the meaning of a *baby*. For babies, like faeces, are born through the anus. The 'gift' meaning of faeces readily admits of this transformation. It is a common usage to speak of a baby as a 'gift'. The more frequent expression is that the woman has 'given' the man a baby; but in the usage of the unconscious equal attention is justly paid to the other aspect of the relation, namely, to the woman having 'received'[1] the baby as a gift from the man.

The meaning of faeces as *money* branches off from the 'gift' meaning in another direction.

The deeper significance of our patient's early screen memory, to the effect that he had his first fit of rage because he was not given enough presents one Christmas, is now revealed to us. What he was feeling the want of was sexual satisfaction, which he had taken as being anal. His sexual researches came during the course of the dream to understand what they had been prepared for finding before the dream, namely, that the sexual act solved the problem of the origin of babies. Even before the dream he had disliked babies. Once, when he had come upon a small unfledged bird that had fallen out of its nest, he had taken it for a human baby and been horrified at it. The analysis showed that all small animals, such as caterpillars and insects, that he had been so enraged with, had had the meaning of babies to him.[2] His position in regard to his elder sister had given him every opportunity for reflecting upon the relation between elder and younger children. His Nanya had once told him that his mother was so fond of him because he was the youngest, and this gave him good grounds for wishing that no younger child might come after him. His dread of this youngest child was revived under the influence of the dream which brought up before him his parents' intercourse.

To the sexual currents that are already known to us we must therefore add a further one, which, like the rest, started from the primal scene reproduced in the dream. In his identification with women (that is, with his mother) he was ready to give his father a baby, and was jealous of his mother, who had already done so and would perhaps do so again.

[1] [The word '*empfangen*' in the German means both 'received' and 'conceived'.]

[2] Just as vermin often stand for babies in dreams and phobias.

In a roundabout way, since both 'money' and 'baby' have the sense of 'gift', money can take over the meaning of baby and can thus become the means of expressing feminine (homosexual) satisfaction. This was what occurred with our patient when—he and his sister were staying at a German sanatorium at the time—he saw his father give his sister two large bank notes. In imagination he had always had suspicions of his father's relations with his sister; and at this his jealousy awoke. He rushed at his sister as soon as they were alone, and demanded a share of the money with so much vehemence and such reproaches that his sister, in tears, threw him the whole of it. What had excited him was not merely the actual money, but rather the 'baby'—anal sexual satisfaction from his father. And he was able to console himself with this when, in his father's lifetime, his sister died. The revolting thought which occurred to him when he heard the news of her death [p. 73] in fact meant no more than this: 'Now I am the only child. Now Father will have to love me only.' But though his reflection was in itself perfectly capable of becoming conscious, yet its homosexual background was so intolerable that it was possible for its disguise in the shape of the most sordid avarice to come as a great relief.

Similarly, too, when after his father's death he reproached his mother so unjustifiably with wanting to cheat him out of the money and with being fonder of the money than of him [p. 73 f.]. His old jealousy of her for having loved another child besides him, the possibility of her having wanted another child after him, drove him into making charges which he himself knew were unwarranted.

This analysis of the meaning of faeces makes it clear that the obsessive thoughts which obliged him to connect God with faeces had a further significance beyond the disparagement which he saw in them himself. They were in fact true compromise-products, in which a part was played no less by an affectionate current of devotion than by a hostile current of abuse. 'God—shit' was probably an abbreviation for an offering that one occasionally hears mentioned in its unabbreviated form. 'Shitting on God' ['*auf Gott scheissen*'] or 'shitting something for God' ['*Gott etwas scheissen*'] also means giving him a baby or getting him to give one a baby. The old 'gift' meaning in its negative and debased form and the 'baby' meaning that was later developed from it are combined with each other in the obsessional phrase. In the latter of these meanings a feminine tenderness finds expression: a readiness to give up one's masculinity if in exchange for it one can be loved like a woman. Here, then, we have precisely the same impulse towards God which was expressed in unambiguous words in the delusional system of the paranoic Senatspräsident Schreber [Freud, 1911*c*, end of Section I].

When later on I come to describing the final clearing up of my patient's symptoms, the way in which the intestinal disorder had put itself at the service of the homosexual current and had given expression to his feminine attitude towards his father will once again become evident. Meanwhile we shall mention a further meaning of faeces, which will lead us on to a discussion of the castration complex.

Since the column of faeces stimulates the erotogenic mucous membrane of the bowel, it plays the part of an active organ in regard to it; it behaves just as the penis does to the vaginal mucous membrane, and acts as it were as its forerunner during the cloacal epoch. The handing over of faeces for the sake of (out of love for) some one else becomes a prototype of castration; it is the first occasion upon which an individual parts with a piece of his own body[1] in order to gain the favour of some other person whom he loves. So that a person's love of his own penis, which is in other respects narcissistic, is not without an element of anal erotism. 'Faeces', 'baby' and 'penis' thus form a unity, an unconscious concept (*sit venia verbo*)—the concept, namely, of 'a little one' that can become separated from one's body. Along these paths of association the libidinal cathexis may become displaced or intensified in ways which are pathologically important and which are revealed by analysis.

We are already acquainted with the attitude which our patient first adopted to the problem of castration. He rejected castration, and held to his theory of intercourse by the anus. When I speak of his having rejected it, the first meaning of the phrase is that he would have nothing to do with it, in the sense of having repressed it. This really involved no judgement upon the question of its existence, but it was the same as if it did not exist. Such an attitude, however, could not have been his final one, even at the time of his infantile neurosis. We find good

[1] It is as such that faeces are invariably treated by children.

subsequent evidence of his having recognized castration as a fact. In this connection, once again, he behaved in the manner which was so characteristic of him, but which makes it so difficult to give a clear account of his mental processes or to feel one's way into them. First he resisted and then he yielded; but the second reaction did not *do away with* the first. In the end there were to be found in him two contrary currents side by side, of which one abominated the idea of castration, while the other was prepared to accept it and console itself with feminity as a compensation. But beyond any doubt a third current, the oldest and deepest, which did not as yet even raise the question of the reality of castration, was still capable of coming into activity. I have elsewhere[1] reported a hallucination which this same patient had at the age of five and upon which I need only add a brief commentary here.

' "When I was five years old, I was playing in the garden near my nurse, and was carving with my pocket-knife in the bark of one of the walnut-trees that come into my dream as well.[2] Suddenly, to my unspeakable terror, I noticed that I had cut through the little finger of my (right or left?) hand, so that it was only hanging on by its skin. I felt no pain, but great fear. I did not venture to say anything to my nurse, who was only a few paces distant, but I sank down on the nearest seat and sat there incapable of casting another glance at my finger. At last I calmed down, took a look at the finger, and saw that it was entirely uninjured." '

After he had received his instruction in the Bible story at the age of four and a half he began, as we know, to make the intense effort of thought which ended in his obsessional piety. We may therefore assume that this hallucination belongs to the period in which he brought himself to recognize the reality of castration and it is perhaps to be regarded as actually marking this step. Even the small correction [see footnote] made by the patient is not without interest. If he had a hallucination of the same

[1] '*Fausse Reconnaissance* ("*Déjà Raconté*") in Psycho-Analytic Treatment' (1914*a*), [*Standard Ed.*, **13**, 204 f.].

[2] 'Cf. "The Occurrence in Dreams of Material from Fairy Tales" [1913*d*]. In telling the story again on a later occasion he made the following correction: "I don't believe I was cutting the tree. That was a confusion with another recollection, which must also have been hallucinatorily falsified, of having made a cut in a tree with my knife and of *blood* having come out of the tree." '

dreadful experience which Tasso, in his *Gerusalemme Liberata*, tells of his hero Tancred,[1] we shall perhaps be justified in reaching the interpretation that the tree meant a woman to my little patient as well. Here, then, he was playing the part of his father, and was connecting his mother's familiar haemorrhages with the castration of women, which he now recognized,—with the 'wound'.

His hallucination of the severed finger was instigated, as he reported later on, by the story that a female relation of his had been born with six toes and that the extra one had immediately afterwards been chopped off with an axe. Women, then, had no penis because it was taken away from them at birth. In this manner he came, at the period of the obsessional neurosis, to accept what he had already learned during the dream but had at the time rejected by repression. He must also have become acquainted, during the readings and discussions of the sacred story, with the ritual circumcision of Christ and of the Jews in general.

There is no doubt whatever that at this time his father was turning into the terrifying figure that threatened him with castration. The cruel God with whom he was then struggling—who made men sinful, only to punish them afterwards, who sacrificed his own son and the sons of men—this God threw back his character on to the patient's father, though, on the other hand, the boy was at the same time trying to defend his father against the God. At this point the boy had to fit into a phylogenetic pattern, and he did so, although his personal experiences may not have agreed with it. Although the threats or hints of castration which had come his way had emanated from women,[2] this could not hold up the final result for long. In spite of everything it was his father from whom in the end he came to fear castration. In this respect heredity triumphed over accidental experience; in man's prehistory it was unquestionably the father who practised castration as a punishment and who later softened it down into circumcision. The further

[1] [The soul of Tancred's beloved Clorinda was imprisoned in a tree; and when, in ignorance of this, he slashed at it with his sword, blood flowed from the cut. This story is told by Freud at greater length in connection with the 'compulsion to repeat' in Chapter III of *Beyond the Pleasure Principle* (1920*g*), *Standard Ed.*, **18**, 22.]

[2] We already know this as regards his Nanya, and we shall hear of it again in connection with another woman.

the patient went in repressing sensuality during the course of the development of the obsessional neurosis,[1] the more natural it must have become to him to attribute these evil intentions to his father, who was the true representative of sensual activity.

His identification of his father with the castrator[2] became important as being the source of an intense unconscious hostility towards him (which reached the pitch of a death-wish) and of a sense of guilt which reacted against it. Up to this point, however, he was behaving normally—that is to say, like every neurotic who is possessed by a positive Oedipus complex. But the astonishing thing was that even against this there was a counter-current working in him, which, on the contrary, regarded his father as the one who had been castrated and as calling, therefore, for his sympathy.

When I analysed his ceremonial of breathing out whenever he saw cripples, beggars, and such people, I was able to show that that symptom could also be traced back to his father, whom he had felt sorry for when he visited him as a patient in the sanatorium [p. 67]. The analysis made it possible to follow this thread even further back. At a very early period, probably before his seduction (at the age of three and a quarter), there had been on the estate an old day-labourer whose business it was to carry the water into the house. He could not speak, ostensibly because his tongue had been cut out. (He was probably a deaf mute.) The little boy was very fond of him and pitied him deeply. When he died, he looked for him in the sky.[3] Here, then, was the first of the cripples for whom he had felt sympathy, and, as was shown by the context and the point at which

[1] For evidence of this see pp. 67–8.

[2] Among the most tormenting, though at the same time the most grotesque, symptoms of his later illness was his relation to every tailor from whom he ordered a suit of clothes: his deference and timidity in the presence of this high functionary, his attempts to get into his good books by giving him extravagant tips, and his despair over the results of the work however it might in fact have turned out. [The German word for 'tailor' is '*Schneider*', from the verb '*schneiden*' ('to cut'), a compound of which, '*beschneiden*', means 'to circumcise'. It will be remembered, too, that it was a tailor who pulled off the wolf's tail (pp. 30–1).]

[3] In this connection I may mention some dreams which he had, later than the anxiety-dream, but while he was still on the first estate. These dreams represented the scene of coition as an event taking place between heavenly bodies.

identification → (1) Group psych

the episode came out in the analysis, an undoubted father-surrogate.

In the analysis this man was associated with the recollection of other servants whom the patient had liked and about whom he emphasized the fact that they had been either sickly or Jews (which implied circumcision). The footman, too, who had helped to clean him after his accident at four and a half [p. 76], had been a Jew and a consumptive and had been an object of his compassion. All of these figures belong to the period before his visit to his father at the sanatorium, that is, before the formation of the symptom; the latter must therefore rather have been intended to ward off (by means of the breathing out) any identification with the object of the patient's pity. Then suddenly, in connection with a dream, the analysis plunged back into the prehistoric period, and led him to assert that during the copulation in the primal scene he had observed the penis disappear, that he had felt compassion for his father on that account, and had rejoiced at the reappearance of what he thought had been lost. So here was a fresh emotional impulse, starting once again from the primal scene. Moreover, the narcissistic origin of compassion (which is confirmed by the word itself)[1] is here quite unmistakably revealed.

[1] [German '*Mitleid*', literally 'suffering with'.]

VIII

FRESH MATERIAL FROM THE PRIMAL PERIOD—SOLUTION

It happens in many analyses that as one approaches their end new recollections emerge which have hitherto been kept carefully concealed. Or it may be that on one occasion some unpretentious remark is thrown out in an indifferent tone of voice as though it were superfluous; that then, on another occasion, something further is added, which begins to make the physician prick his ears; and that at last he comes to recognize this despised fragment of a memory as the key to the weightiest secrets that the patient's neurosis has veiled.

Early in the analysis my patient had told me of a memory of the period in which his naughtiness had been in the habit of suddenly turning into anxiety. He was chasing a beautiful big butterfly with yellow stripes and large wings which ended in pointed projections—a swallow-tail, in fact [see p. 16]. Suddenly, when the butterfly had settled on a flower, he was seized with a dreadful fear of the creature, and ran away screaming.

This memory recurred occasionally during the analysis, and called for an explanation; but for a long time none was to be found. Nevertheless it was to be assumed as a matter of course that a detail like this had not kept its place in his recollection on its own account, but that it was a screen-memory, representing something of more importance with which it was in some way connected. One day he told me that in his language a butterfly was called '*babushka*', 'granny'. He added that in general butterflies had seemed to him like women and girls, and beetles and caterpillars like boys. So there could be little doubt that in this anxiety scene a recollection of some female person had been aroused. I will not hide the fact that at that time I put forward the possibility that the yellow stripes on the butterfly had reminded him of similar stripes on a piece of clothing worn by some woman. I only mention this as an illustration to show how inadequate the physician's constructive efforts usually are for clearing up questions that arise, and how unjust it is to attribute the results of analysis to the physician's imagination and suggestion.

Many months later, in quite another connection, the patient remarked that the opening and shutting of the butterfly's wings while it was settled on the flower had given him an uncanny feeling. It had looked, so he said, like a woman opening her legs, and the legs then made the shape of a Roman V, which, as we know, was the hour at which, in his boyhood, and even up to the time of the treatment, he used to fall into a depressed state of mind [p. 37].

This was an association which I could never have arrived at myself, and which gained importance from a consideration of the thoroughly infantile nature of the train of association which it revealed. The attention of children, as I have often noticed, is attracted far more readily by movements than by forms at rest; and they frequently base associations upon a similarity of movement which is overlooked or neglected by adults.

After this the little problem was once more left untouched for a long time; but I may mention the facile suspicion that the points or stick-like projections of the butterfly's wings might have had the meaning of genital symbols.

One day there emerged, timidly and indistinctly, a kind of recollection that at a very early age, even before the time of the nurse, he must have had a nursery-maid who was very fond of him. Her name had been the same as his mother's. He had no doubt returned her affection. It was, in fact, a first love that had faded into oblivion. But we agreed that something must have occurred at that time that became of importance later on.

Then on another occasion he emended this recollection. She could not have had the same name as his mother; that had been a mistake on his part, and it showed, of course, that in his memory she had become fused with his mother. Her real name, he went on, had occurred to him in a roundabout way. He had suddenly thought of a store-room, on the first estate, in which fruit was kept after it had been picked, and of a particular sort of pear with a most delicious taste—a big pear with yellow stripes on its skin. The word for 'pear' in his language was '*grusha*', and that had also been the name of the nursery-maid.

It thus became clear that behind the screen memory of the hunted butterfly the memory of the nursery-maid lay concealed.

But the yellow stripes were not on her dress, but on the pear whose name was the same as hers. What, however, was the origin of the anxiety which had arisen when the memory of her had been activated? The obvious answer to this might have been the crude hypothesis that it had been this girl whom, when he was a small child, he had first seen making the movements with her legs which he had fixed in his mind with the Roman V—movements which allow access to the genitals. We spared ourselves such theorizing as this and waited for more material.

Very soon after this there came the recollection of a scene, incomplete, but, so far as it was preserved, definite. Grusha was kneeling on the floor, and beside her a pail and a short broom made of a bundle of twigs; he was also there, and she was teasing him or scolding him.

The missing elements could easily be supplied from other directions. During the first months of the treatment he had told me of how he had suddenly fallen in love in a compulsive manner with a peasant girl from whom, in his eighteenth year, he had contracted the precipitating cause of his later illness.[1] When he told me this he had displayed a most extraordinary unwillingness to give me the girl's name. It was an entirely isolated instance of resistance, for apart from it he obeyed the fundamental rule of analysis unreservedly. He asserted, however, that the reason for his being so much ashamed of mentioning the name was that it was a purely peasant name and that no girl of gentle birth could possibly be called by it. When eventually the name was produced, it turned out to be Matrona, which has a motherly ring about it. The shame was evidently displaced. He was not ashamed of the fact that these love-affairs were invariably concerned with girls of the humblest origin; he was ashamed only of the name. If it should turn out that the affair with Matrona had something in common with the Grusha scene, then the shame would have to be transferred back to that early episode.

He had told me another time that when he heard the story of John Huss he had been greatly moved, and that his attention had been held by the bundles of firewood that were dragged up when he was burnt at the stake. Now his sympathy for Huss created a perfectly definite suspicion in my mind, for I have

[1] [A gonorrhoeal infection. Cf. p. 7.]

often come upon this sympathy in youthful patients and I have always been able to explain it in the same way. One such patient even went so far as to produce a dramatized version of Huss's career; he began to write his play on the day on which he lost the object with whom he was secretly in love. Huss perished by fire, and (like others who possess the same qualification) he becomes the hero of people who have at one time suffered from enuresis. My patient himself connected the bundles of firewood used for the execution of Huss with the nursery-maid's broom or bundle of twigs.

This material fitted together spontaneously and served to fill in the gaps in the patient's memory of the scene with Grusha. When he saw the girl scrubbing the floor he had micturated in the room and she had rejoined, no doubt jokingly, with a threat of castration.[1]

I do not know if my readers will have already guessed why it is that I have given such a detailed account of this episode from the patient's early childhood.[2] It provides an important link between the primal scene and the later compulsive love [p. 41] which came to be of such decisive significance in his subsequent career, and it further shows us a condition upon which his falling in love depended and which elucidates that compulsion.

When he saw the girl on the floor engaged in scrubbing it, and kneeling down, with her buttocks projecting and her back horizontal, he was faced once again with the posture which his mother had assumed in the copulation scene. She became

[1] It is very remarkable that the reaction of shame should be so intimately connected with involuntary emptying of the bladder (whether in the day-time or at night) and not equally so, as one would have expected, with incontinence of the bowels. Experience leaves no room for doubt upon the point. The regular relation that is found to exist between incontinence of the bladder and fire also provides matter for reflection. It is possible that these reactions and relations represent precipitates from the history of human civilization derived from a lower stratum than anything that is preserved for us in the traces surviving in myths or folklore. [Freud had discussed the connection between enuresis and dreaming of fire in his case history of 'Dora' (1905*e*), *Standard Ed.*, 7, 71–2. He returned to the subject in a footnote in Chapter III of *Civilization and its Discontents* (1930*a*) and later devoted a paper to it (1932*a*).]

[2] It may be assigned to a time at which he was about two and a half: between his supposed observation of intercourse and his seduction.

his mother to him; he was seized with sexual excitement owing to the activation of this picture;[1] and, like his father (whose action he can only have regarded at the time as micturition), he behaved in a masculine way towards her. His micturition on the floor was in reality an attempt at a seduction, and the girl replied to it with a threat of castration, just as though she had understood what he meant.

The compulsion which proceeded from the primal scene was transferred on to this scene with Grusha and was carried forward by it. But the condition upon which his falling in love depended underwent a change which showed the influence of the second scene: it was transferred from the woman's posture to the occupation on which she was engaged while in that posture. This was clear, for instance, in the episode of Matrona. He was walking through the village which formed part of their (later) estate [cf. p. 15], when he saw a peasant girl kneeling by the pond and employed in washing clothes in it. He fell in love with the girl instantly and with irresistible violence, although he had not yet been able to get even a glimpse of her face. By her posture and occupation she had taken the place of Grusha for him. We can now see how it was that the shame which properly related to the content of the scene with Grusha could become attached to the name of Matrona.

Another attack of falling in love, dating from a few years earlier, shows even more clearly the compelling influence of the Grusha scene. A young peasant girl, who was a servant in the house, had long attracted him, but he succeeded in keeping himself from approaching her. One day, when he came upon her in a room by herself, he was overwhelmed by his love. He found her kneeling on the floor and engaged in scrubbing it, with a pail and a broom beside her—in fact, exactly as he had seen the girl in his childhood.

Even his final choice of object, which played such an important part in his life, is shown by its details (though they cannot be adduced here) to have been dependent upon the same condition and to have been an offshoot of the compulsion which, starting from the primal scene and going on to the scene with Grusha, had dominated his love-choice. I have remarked on an earlier page that I recognize in the patient an endeavour to debase his love-object. This is to be explained as

[1] This was *before* the dream.

a reaction against pressure from the sister who was so much his superior. But I promised at the same time (see pp. 22–3) to show that this self-assertive motive was not the only determinant, but that it concealed another and deeper one based on purely erotic motives. These were brought to light by the patient's memory of the nursery-maid scrubbing the floor—*physically* debased too, by the by. All his later love-objects were surrogates for this one person, who through the accident of her attitude had herself become his first mother-surrogate. The patient's first association in connection with the problem of his fear of the butterfly can now easily be explained retrospectively as a distant allusion to the primal scene (the hour of five). He confirmed the connection between the Grusha scene and the threat of castration by a particularly ingenious dream, which he himself succeeded in deciphering. 'I had a dream,' he said, 'of a man tearing off the wings of an *Espe*.' '*Espe*?' I asked; 'what do you mean by that?' 'You know; that insect with yellow stripes on its body, that stings.' I could now put him right: 'So what you mean is a *Wespe* [wasp].' 'Is it called a *Wespe*? I really thought it was called an *Espe*.' (Like so many other people, he used his difficulties with a foreign language as a screen for symptomatic acts.) 'But *Espe*, why, that's myself: S. P.' (which were his initials).[1] The *Espe* was of course a mutilated *Wespe*. The dream said clearly that he was avenging himself on Grusha for her threat of castration.

The action of the two-and-a-half-year-old boy in the scene with Grusha is the earliest effect of the primal scene which has come to our knowledge. It represents him as copying his father, and shows us a tendency towards development in a direction which would later deserve the name of masculine. His seduction drove him into passivity—for which, in any case, the way was prepared by his behaviour when he was a witness of his parents' intercourse.

I must here turn for a moment to the history of the treatment. When once the Grusha scene had been assimilated—the first experience that he could really remember, and one which he had remembered without any conjectures or intervention on my part—the problem of the treatment had every appearance of having been solved. From that time forward there were no more resistances; all that remained to be done was to collect

[1] [In Austria '*Espe*' and '*S.P.*' would be pronounced exactly alike.]

and to co-ordinate. The old trauma theory of the neuroses,[1] which was after all built up upon impressions gained from psycho-analytic practice, had suddenly come to the front once more. Out of critical interest I made one more attempt to force upon the patient another view of his story, which might commend itself more to sober common sense. It was true that there could be no doubt about the scene with Grusha, but, I suggested, in itself that scene meant nothing; it had been emphasized *ex post facto* by a regression from the circumstances of his object-choice, which, as a result of his intention to debase, had been diverted from his sister on to servant girls. On the other hand, his observation of intercourse, I argued, was a phantasy of his later years; its historical nucleus may perhaps have been an observation or an experience by the patient of the administration of an innocent enema. Some of my readers will possibly be inclined to think that with such hypotheses as these I was for the first time beginning to approach an understanding of the case; but the patient looked at me uncomprehendingly and a little contemptuously when I put this view before him, and he never reacted to it again. I have already stated my own arguments against any such rationalization at their proper point in the discussion. [Section V above.]

[Thus[2] the Grusha scene, by explaining the conditions governing the patient's object-choice—conditions which were of decisive importance in his life—prevents our over-estimating the significance of his intention to debase women. But it does more than this. It affords me a justification for having refused on an earlier page (see p. 60) to adopt unhesitatingly, as the only tenable explanation, the view that the primal scene was derived from an observation made upon animals shortly before the dream. The Grusha scene emerged in the patient's memory spontaneously and through no effort of mine. His fear of the yellow-striped butterfly, which went back to that scene, proved that the scene had had a significant content, or that he had been able to attach this significance to its content subsequently. By means of the accompanying associations and the inferences

[1] [See the discussion of this in Freud's paper on the part played by sexuality in the aetiology of the neuroses (1906*a*), *Standard Ed.*, 7, 273 ff.]

[2] [Author's square bracket. See end of footnote, p. 7.]

that followed from them, it was possible with certainty to supply this significant element which was lacking in the patient's memory. It then appeared that his fear of the butterfly was in every respect analogous to his fear of the wolf; in both cases it was a fear of castration, which was, to begin with, referred to the person who had first uttered the threat of castration, but was then transposed on to another person to whom it was bound to become attached in accordance with phylogenetic precedent. The scene with Grusha had occurred when the patient was two and a half, but the anxiety-episode with the yellow butterfly was certainly subsequent to the anxiety-dream. It was easy to understand how the patient's later comprehension of the possibility of castration had retrospectively brought out the anxiety in the scene with Grusha. But that scene in itself contained nothing objectionable or improbable; on the contrary, it consisted entirely of commonplace details which gave no grounds for scepticism. There was nothing in it which could lead one to attribute its origin to the child's imagination; such a supposition, indeed, seemed scarcely possible.

The question now arises whether we are justified in regarding the fact that the boy micturated, while he stood looking at the girl on her knees scrubbing the floor, as a proof of sexual excitement on his part. If so, the excitement would be evidence of the influence of an earlier impression, which might equally have been the actual occurrence of the primal scene or an observation made upon animals before the age of two and a half. Or are we to conclude that the situation as regards Grusha was entirely innocent, that the child's emptying his bladder was purely accidental, and that it was not until later that the whole scene became sexualized in his memory, after he had come to recognize the importance of similar situations?

On these issues I can venture upon no decision. I must confess, however, that I regard it as greatly to the credit of psychoanalysis that it should even have reached the stage of *raising* such questions as these. Nevertheless, I cannot deny that the scene with Grusha, the part it played in the analysis, and the effects that followed from it in the patient's life can be most naturally and completely explained if we consider that the primal scene, which may in other cases be a phantasy, was a reality in the present one. After all, there is nothing impossible about it; and the hypothesis of its reality is entirely compatible with the inciting action of the observations upon animals which are indicated by the sheep-dogs in the dream-picture.

I will now turn from this unsatisfactory conclusion to a consideration of the problem which I have attempted in my *Introductory Lectures on Psycho-Analysis* [Lecture XXIII]. I should myself be glad to know whether the primal scene in my present patient's case was a phantasy or a real experience; but, taking other similar cases into account, I must admit that the answer to this question is not in fact a matter of very great importance. These scenes of observing parental intercourse, of being seduced in childhood, and of being threatened with castration are unquestionably an inherited endowment, a phylogenetic heritage, but they may just as easily be acquired by personal experience. With my patient, his seduction by his elder sister was an indisputable reality; why should not the same have been true of his observation of his parents' intercourse?

All that we find in the prehistory of neuroses is that a child catches hold of this phylogenetic experience where his own experience fails him. He fills in the gaps in individual truth with prehistoric truth; he replaces occurrences in his own life by occurrences in the life of his ancestors. I fully agree with Jung[1] in recognizing the existence of this phylogenetic heritage; but I regard it as a methodological error to seize on a phylogenetic explanation before the ontogenetic possibilities have been exhausted. I cannot see any reason for obstinately disputing the importance of infantile prehistory while at the same time freely acknowledging the importance of ancestral prehistory. Nor can I overlook the fact that phylogenetic motives and productions themselves stand in need of elucidation, and that in quite a number of instances this is afforded by factors in the childhood of the individual. And, finally, I cannot feel surprised that what was originally produced by certain circumstances in prehistoric times and was then transmitted in the shape of a predisposition to its re-acquirement should, since the same circumstances persist, emerge once more as a concrete event in the experience of the individual.]

Room must also be found in the interval between the primal

[1] *Die Psychologie der unbewussten Prozesse*, 1917. This was published too late for it to have influenced my *Introductory Lectures*.

preconception

scene and the seduction (from the age of one and a half to the age of three and a quarter) for the dumb water-carrier [p. 87]. He served the patient as a father-surrogate just as Grusha served him as a mother-surrogate. I do not think there is any justification for regarding this as an example of the intention to debase, even though it is true that both parents have come to be represented by servants. A child pays no regard to social distinctions, which have little meaning for him as yet; and he classes people of inferior rank with his parents if such people love him as his parents do. Nor is the intention to debase any more responsible for the substitution of animals for a child's parents, for children are very far indeed from taking a disparaging view of animals.[1] Uncles and aunts are used as parent-surrogates without any regard to the question of debasing, and this was in fact done by our present patient, as many of his recollections showed.

There also belongs in this period a phase, which was obscurely remembered, in which he would not eat anything except sweet things, until alarm was felt on the score of his health. He was told about one of his uncles who had refused to eat in the same way and had wasted away to death while he was still young. He was also informed that when he himself was three months old he had been so seriously ill (with pneumonia?) that his winding-sheet had been got ready for him. In this way they succeeded in alarming him, so that he began eating again; and in the later years of his childhood he used actually to overdo this duty, as though to guard himself against the threat of death. The fear of death, which was evoked at that time for his own protection, made its reappearance later when his mother warned him of the danger of dysentery [p. 77]. Later still, it brought on an attack of his obsessional neurosis (see p. 68). We shall try below [p. 107] to go into its origins and meanings.

I am inclined to the opinion that this disturbance of appetite should be regarded as the very first of the patient's neurotic illnesses. If so, the disturbance of appetite, the wolf phobia, and the obsessional piety would constitute the complete series of infantile disorders which laid down the predisposition for his neurotic break-down after he had passed the age of puberty. It will be objected that few children escape such disorders as a

[1] [This point was dealt with by Freud at greater length in his paper 'A Difficulty in the Path of Psycho-Analysis' (1917*a*), below p. 140.]

temporary loss of appetite or an animal phobia. But this argument is exactly what I should wish for. I am ready to assert that every neurosis in an adult is built upon a neurosis which has occurred in his childhood but has not invariably been severe enough to strike the eye and be recognized as such. This objection only serves to emphasize the theoretical importance of the part which infantile neuroses must play in our view of those later disorders which we treat as neuroses and endeavour to attribute entirely to the effects of adult life. If our present patient had not suffered from obsessional piety in addition to his disturbance of appetite and his animal phobia, his story would not have been noticeably different from that of other children, and we should have been the poorer by the loss of precious material which may guard us against certain plausible errors.

The analysis would be unsatisfactory if it failed to explain the phrase used by the patient for summing up the troubles of which he complained. The world, he said, was hidden from him by a veil [p. 75]; and our psycho-analytic training forbids our assuming that these words can have been without significance or have been chosen at haphazard. The veil was torn, strange to say, in one situation only; and that was at the moment when, as a result of an enema, he passed a motion through his anus. He then felt well again, and for a very short while he saw the world clearly. The interpretation of this 'veil' progressed with as much difficulty as we met with in clearing up his fear of the butterfly. Nor did he keep to the veil. It became still more elusive, as a feeling of twilight, '*ténèbres*', and of other impalpable things.

It was not until just before taking leave of the treatment that he remembered having been told that he was born with a caul. He had for that reason always looked on himself as a special child of fortune whom no ill could befall.[1] He did not lose that conviction until he was forced to realize that his gonorrhoeal infection constituted a serious injury to his body. The blow to his narcissism was too much for him and he went to pieces. It may be said that in so doing he was repeating a mechanism that he had already brought into play once before. For his wolf phobia had broken out when he found himself

[1] [The German word for 'caul' (*Glückshaube*'), like the corresponding Scots expression 'sely how', means literally 'lucky hood'.]

JENNA "no entry" anorexia

faced by the fact that such a thing as castration was possible; and he clearly classed his gonorrhoea as castration.

Thus the caul was the veil which hid him from the world and hid the world from him. The complaint that he made was in reality a fulfilled wishful phantasy: it exhibited him as back once more in the womb, and was, in fact, a wishful phantasy of flight from the world. It can be translated as follows: 'Life makes me so unhappy! I must get back into the womb!'

But what can have been the meaning of the fact that this veil, which was now symbolic but had once been real, was torn at the moment at which he evacuated his bowels after an enema, and that under this condition his illness left him? The context enables us to reply. If this birth-veil was torn, then he saw the world and was re-born. The stool was the child, as which he was born a second time, to a happier life. Here, then, we have the phantasy of re-birth, to which Jung has recently drawn attention and to which he has assigned such a dominating position in the imaginative life of neurotics.

This would be all very well, if it were the whole story. But certain details of the situation, and a due regard for the connection between it and this particular patient's life-history, compel us to pursue the interpretation further. The necessary condition of his re-birth was that he should have an enema administered to him by a man. (It was not until later on that he was driven by necessity to take this man's place himself.) This can only have meant that he had identified himself with his mother, that the man was acting as his father, and that the enema was repeating the act of copulation, as the fruit of which the excrement-baby (which was once again himself) would be born. The phantasy of re-birth was therefore bound up closely with the necessary condition of sexual satisfaction from a man. So that the translation now runs to this effect: only on condition that he took the woman's place and substituted himself for his mother, and thus let himself be sexually satisfied by his father and bore him a child—only on that condition would his illness leave him. Here, therefore, the phantasy of re-birth was simply a mutilated and censored version of the homosexual wishful phantasy.

If we look into the matter more closely we cannot help remarking that in this condition which he laid down for his recovery the patient was simply repeating the state of affairs at the time of the 'primal scene'. At that moment he had wanted to substitute himself for his mother; and, as we assumed long ago, it was he himself who, in the scene in question, had produced the excrement-baby. He still remained fixated, as though by a spell, to the scene which had such a decisive effect on his sexual life, and the return of which during the night of the dream brought the onset of his illness. The tearing of the veil was analogous to the opening of his eyes and to the opening of the window. The primal scene had become transformed into the necessary condition for his recovery.

It is easy to make a unified statement of what was expressed on the one hand by the complaint he made and on the other hand by the single exceptional condition under which the complaint no longer held good, and thus to make clear the whole meaning that underlay the two factors: he wished he could be back in the womb, not simply in order that he might then be re-born, but in order that he might be copulated with there by his father, might obtain sexual satisfaction from him, and might bear him a child.

The wish to be born of his father (as he had at first believed was the case), the wish to be sexually satisfied by him, the wish to present him with a child—and all of this at the price of his own masculinity, and expressed in the language of anal erotism—these wishes complete the circle of his fixation upon his father. In them homosexuality has found its furthest and most intimate expression.[1]

This instance, I think, throws light on the meaning and origin of the womb-phantasy as well as that of re-birth. The former, the womb-phantasy, is frequently derived (as it was in the present case) from an attachment to the father. There is a wish to be inside the mother's womb in order to replace her during intercourse—in order to take her place in regard to the father. The phantasy of re-birth, on the other hand, is in all probability regularly a softened substitute (a euphemism, one might say) for the phantasy of incestuous intercourse with the

[1] A possible subsidiary explanation, namely that the veil represented the hymen which is torn at the moment of intercourse with a man, does not harmonize completely with the necessary condition for his recovery. Moreover it has no bearing on the life of the patient, for whom virginity carried no significance.

mother; to make use of Silberer's expression, it is an *anagogic* [1] abbreviation of it. There is a wish to be back in a situation in which one was in the mother's genitals; and in this connection the man is identifying himself with his own penis and is using it to represent himself. Thus the two phantasies are revealed as each other's counterparts: they give expression, according as the subject's attitude is feminine or masculine, to his wish for sexual intercourse with his father or with his mother. We cannot dismiss the possibility that in the complaint made by our present patient and in the necessary condition laid down for his recovery the two phantasies, that is to say the two incestuous wishes, were united. [2]

I will make a final attempt at re-interpreting the last findings of this analysis in accordance with the scheme of my opponents. The patient lamented his flight from the world in a typical womb-phantasy and viewed his recovery as a typically conceived re-birth. In accordance with the predominant side of his disposition, he expressed the latter in anal symptoms. He next concocted, on the model of his anal phantasy of re-birth, a childhood scene which repeated his wishes in an archaic-symbolic medium of expression. His symptoms were then strung together as though they had been derived from a primal scene of that kind. He was driven to embark on this long backward course either because he had come up against some task in life which he was too lazy to perform, or because he had every reason to be aware of his own inferiority and thought he could best protect himself from being slighted by elaborating such contrivances as these.

All this would be very nice, if only the unlucky wretch had not had a dream when he was no more than four years old, which signalized the beginning of his neurosis, which was instigated by his grandfather's story of the tailor and the wolf, and the interpretation of which necessitates the assumption of this primal scene. All the alleviations which the theories of Jung and Adler seek to afford us come to grief, alas, upon such paltry but unimpeachable facts as these. As things stand, it

[1] [This term of Silberer's is explained and discussed in an addition made in 1919 to *The Interpretation of Dreams* (1900*a*), *Standard Ed.*, **5**, 524.]

[2] [See the discussion of the 'complete' Oedipus complex in Chapter III of *The Ego and the Id* (1923*b*).]

seems to me more probable that the phantasy of re-birth was a derivative of the primal scene than that, conversely, the primal scene was a reflection of the phantasy of re-birth. And we may perhaps suppose, too, that the patient, at a time only four years after his birth, may after all have been too young to be already wishing to be born again. But no, I must take this last argument back; for my own observations show that we have rated the powers of children too low and that there is no knowing what they cannot be given credit for.[1]

[1] I admit that this is the most delicate question in the whole domain of psycho-analysis. I did not require the contributions of Adler or Jung to induce me to consider the matter with a critical eye, and to bear in mind the possibility that what analysis puts forward as being forgotten experiences of childhood (and of an improbably early childhood) may on the contrary be based uponphantasies created on occasions occurring late in life. According to this view, wherever we seemed in analyses to see traces of the after-effects of an infantile impression of the kind in question, we should rather have to assume that we were faced by the manifestation of some constitutional factor or of some disposition that had been phylogenetically maintained. On the contrary, no doubt has troubled me more; no other uncertainty has been more decisive in holding me back from publishing my conclusions. I was the first—a point to which none of my opponents have referred—to recognize both the part played by phantasies in symptom-formation and also the 'retrospective phantasying' of late impressions into childhood and their sexualization after the event. (See my *Interpretation of Dreams* (1900*a*), First Edition, p. 49, and 'Notes upon a Case of Obsessional Neurosis', (1909*d*) [*Standard Ed.*, **10**, 206 ff., footnote].) If, in spite of this, I have held to the more difficult and more improbable view, it has been as a result of arguments such as are forced upon the investigator by the case described in these pages or by any other infantile neurosis—arguments which I once again lay before my readers for their decision.

[The reference to p. 49 of the first edition of *Die Traumdeutung* which is given in all editions of this paper would correspond to *Standard Ed.*, **4**, 70–1. No relevant passage, however, occurs there and evidently a wrong page number has been given. It seems likely that Freud had in mind a passage occurring in *Standard Ed.*, **4**, 288, which corresponds to p. 198 of the first edition of *Die Traumdeutung*. He there uses the same term 'retrospective phantasy' ('*zurückphantasieren*') as in the present footnote.]

IX

RECAPITULATIONS AND PROBLEMS

I do not know if the reader of this report of an analysis will have succeeded in forming a clear picture of the origin and development of the patient's illness. I fear that, on the contrary, this will not have been the case. But though on other occasions I have said very little on behalf of my powers in the art of exposition, I should like in the present instance to plead mitigating circumstances. The description of such early phases and of such deep strata of mental life has been a task which has never before been attacked; and it is better to perform that task badly than to take flight before it—a proceeding which would moreover (or so we are told) involve the coward in risks of a certain kind. I prefer, therefore, to put a bold face on it and show that I have not allowed myself to be held back by a sense of my own inferiority.

The case itself was not a particularly favourable one. The advantage of having a wealth of information about the patient's childhood (an advantage which was made possible by the fact that the child could be studied through the medium of the adult) had to be purchased at the expense of the analysis being most terribly disjointed and of the exposition showing corresponding gaps. Personal peculiarities in the patient and a national character that was foreign to ours made the task of feeling one's way into his mind a laborious one. The contrast between the patient's agreeable and affable personality, his acute intelligence and his nice-mindedness on the one hand, and his completely unbridled instinctual life on the other, necessitated an excessively long process of preparatory education, and this made a general perspective more difficult. But the patient himself has no responsibility for that feature of the case which put the severest obstacles in the way of any description of it. In the psychology of adults we have fortunately reached the point of being able to divide mental processes into conscious and unconscious and of being able to give a clearly-worded description of both. With children this distinction leaves us almost completely in the lurch. It is often embarrassing to decide what one would choose to call conscious and what unconscious. Processes which have become the dominant ones, and which from their subsequent behaviour must be equated with conscious ones, have nevertheless not been conscious in the child. It is easy to understand why. In children the conscious has not yet acquired all its characteristics; it is still in process of development, and it does not as yet fully possess the capacity for transposing itself into verbal images. We are constantly guilty of making a confusion between the phenomenon of emergence as a perception in consciousness and the fact of belonging to a hypothetical psychical system to which we ought to assign some conventional name, but which we in fact also call 'consciousness' (the system *Cs.*). This confusion does no harm when we are giving a psychological description of an adult, but it is misleading when we are dealing with that of a young child. Nor should we be much assisted here if we introduced the 'preconscious'; for a child's preconscious may, in just the same way, fail to coincide with an adult's. We must be content, therefore, with having clearly recognized the obscurity.

It is obvious that a case such as that which is described in these pages might be made an excuse for dragging into the discussion every one of the findings and problems of psycho-analysis. But this would be an endless and unjustifiable labour. It must be recognized that everything cannot be learnt from a single case and that everything cannot be decided by it; we must content ourselves with exploiting whatever it may happen to show most clearly. There are in any case narrow limits to what a psycho-analysis is called upon to explain. For, while it is its business to explain the striking symptoms by revealing their genesis, it is not its business to explain but merely to describe the psychical mechanisms and instinctual processes to which one is led by that means. In order to derive fresh generalizations from what has thus been established with regard to the mechanisms and instincts, it would be essential to have at one's disposal numerous cases as thoroughly and deeply analysed as the present one. But they are not easily to be had, and each one of them requires years of labour. So that advances in these spheres of knowledge must necessarily be slow. There is no doubt a great temptation to content oneself with 'scratching' the mental surface of a number of people and of replacing what is left undone by speculation—the latter being put under the patronage of some school or other of philosophy. Practical requirements may also be adduced in favour of this procedure; but no substitute can satisfy the requirements of science.

I shall now attempt to sketch out a synthetic survey of my patient's sexual development, beginning from its earliest indications. The first that we hear of it is in the disturbance of his appetite [p. 98]; for, taking other observations into account, I am inclined, though with due reservations, to regard that as a result of some process in the sphere of sexuality. I have been driven to regard as the earliest recognizable sexual organization the so-called 'cannibalistic' or 'oral' phase, during which the original attachment of sexual excitation to the nutritional instinct still dominates the scene.[1] It is not to be expected that we should come upon direct manifestations of this phase, but only upon indications of it where disturbances have been set up. Impairment of the nutritional instinct (though this can of course have other causes) draws our attention to a failure on the part of the organism to master its sexual excitation. In this phase the sexual aim could only be cannibalism—devouring; it makes its appearance with our present patient through regression from a higher stage, in the form of fear of 'being eaten by the wolf'. We were, indeed, obliged to translate this into a fear of being copulated with by his father. It is well known that there is a neurosis in girls which occurs at a much later age, at the time of puberty or soon afterwards, and which expresses aversion to sexuality by means of anorexia. This neurosis will have to be brought into relation with the oral phase of sexual life. The erotic aim of the oral organization further makes its appearance at the height of a lover's paroxysm (in such phrases as 'I could eat you up with love') and in affectionate relations with children, when the grown-up person is pretending to be a child himself. I have elsewhere given voice to a suspicion that the father of our present patient used himself to indulge in 'affectionate abuse', and may have played at wolf or dog with the little boy and have threatened as a joke to gobble him up (p. 32). The patient confirmed this suspicion by his curious behaviour in the transference. Whenever he shrank back on to the transference from the difficulties of the treatment, he used

[1] [See a section added in 1915 to Freud's *Three Essays* (1905*d*), *Standard Ed.*, **7**, 198, and 'Instincts and their Vicissitudes' (1915*c*).]

to threaten me with eating me up and later with all kinds of other ill-treatment—all of which was merely an expression of affection.

Permanent marks have been left by this oral phase of sexuality upon the usages of language. People commonly speak for instance, of an 'appetizing' love-object, and describe persons they are fond of as 'sweet'. It will be remembered, too, that our little patient would only eat sweet things. In dreams sweet things and sweetmeats stand regularly for caresses or sexual gratifications.

It appears, moreover, that there is an anxiety belonging to this phase (only, of course, where some disturbance has arisen) which manifests itself as a fear of death and may be attached to anything that is pointed out to the child as being suitable for the purpose. With our patient it was employed to induce him to overcome his loss of appetite and indeed to overcompensate for it. A possible origin of this disturbance of his appetite will be found, if we bear in mind (basing ourselves on the hypothesis that we have so often discussed) that his observation of copulation at the age of one and a half, which produced so many deferred effects, certainly occurred before the time of these difficulties in his eating. So we may perhaps suppose that it accelerated the processes of sexual maturing and consequently did in fact also produce *immediate* effects, though these were insignificant in appearance.

I am of course aware that it is possible to explain the symptoms of this period (the wolf anxiety and the disturbance of appetite) in another and simpler manner, without any reference to sexuality or to a pregenital stage of its organization. Those who like to neglect the indications of neurosis and the interconnections between events will prefer this other explanation, and I shall not be able to prevent their doing so. It is hard to discover any cogent evidence in regard to these beginnings of sexual life except by such roundabout paths as I have indicated.

In the scene with Grusha (at the age of two and a half) we see the little boy at the beginning of a development which, except perhaps for its prematureness, deserves to be considered normal; thus we find in it identification with his father, and urethral erotism representing masculinity. It was also completely under the sway of the primal scene. We have hitherto regarded his identification with his father as being narcissistic; but if we take the content of the primal scene into account we cannot deny that it had already reached the stage of genital organization. His male genital organ had begun to play its part and it continued to do so under the influence of his seduction by his sister.

But his seduction gives the impression not merely of having encouraged his sexual development but of having, to an even greater extent, disturbed and diverted it. It offered him a passive sexual aim, which was ultimately incompatible with the action of his male genital organ. At the first external obstacle, the threat of castration from his Nanya, his genital organization, half-hearted as it still was, broke down (at the age of three and a half[1]) and regressed to the stage which had preceded it, namely to that of the sadistic-anal organization, which he might otherwise have passed through, perhaps, with as slight indications as other children.

The sadistic-anal organization can easily be regarded as a continuation and development of the oral one. The violent muscular activity, directed upon the object, by which it is characterized, is to be explained as an action preparatory to eating. The eating then ceases to be a sexual aim, and the preparatory action becomes a sufficient aim in itself. The essential novelty, as compared with the previous stage, is that the receptive passive function becomes disengaged from the oral zone and attached to the anal zone. In this connection we can hardly fail to think of biological parallels or of the theory that the pregenital organizations in man should be regarded as vestiges of conditions which have been permanently retained in several classes of animals. The building up of the instinct for research out of its various components is another characteristic feature of this stage of development.

The boy's anal erotism was not particularly noticeable. Under the influence of his sadism the affectionate significance of faeces gave place to an aggressive one. A part was played in the transformation of his sadism into masochism by a sense of guilt, the presence of which points to developmental processes in spheres other than the sexual one.

His seduction continued to make its influence felt, by maintaining the passivity of his sexual aim. It transformed his sadism

[1] [In the editions before 1924 this read 'three and three quarters'.]

to a great extent into the masochism which was its passive counterpart. But it is questionable whether the seduction can be made entirely responsible for this characteristic of passivity, for the child's reaction to his observation of intercourse at the age of one and a half was already preponderantly a passive one. His sympathetic sexual excitement expressed itself by his passing a stool, though it is true that in this behaviour an active element is also to be distinguished. Side by side with the masochism which dominated his sexual impulsions and also found expression in phantasies, his sadism, too, persisted and was directed against small animals. His sexual researches had set in from the time of the seduction and had been concerned, in essence, with two problems: the origin of children and the possibility of losing the genitals. These researches wove themselves into the manifestations of his instinctual impulses, and directed his sadistic propensities on to small animals as being representatives of small children.

We have now carried our account down to about the time of the boy's fourth birthday, and it was at that point that the dream brought into deferred operation his observation of intercourse at the age of one and a half. It is not possible for us completely to grasp or adequately to describe what now ensued. The activation of the picture, which, thanks to the advance in his intellectual development, he was now able to understand, operated not only like a fresh event, but like a new trauma, like an interference from outside analogous to the seduction. The genital organization which had been broken off was re-established at a single blow; but the advance that was achieved in the dream could not be maintained. On the contrary, there came about, by means of a process that can only be equated with a repression, a repudiation of the new element and its replacement by a phobia.

Thus the sadistic-anal organization continued to exist during the phase of the animal phobia which now set in, only it suffered an admixture of anxiety-phenomena. The child persisted in his sadistic as well as in his masochistic activities, but he reacted with anxiety to a portion of them; the conversion of his sadism into its opposite probably made further progress.

The analysis of the anxiety-dream shows us that the repression was connected with his recognition of the existence of castration. The new element was rejected because its acceptance would have cost him his penis. Closer consideration leads us to some such conclusion as the following. What was repressed was the homosexual attitude understood in the genital sense, an attitude which had been formed under the influence of this recognition of castration. But that attitude was retained as regards the unconscious and set up as a dissociated and deeper stratum. The motive force of the repression seems to have been the narcissistic masculinity which attached to the boy's genitals, and which had come into a long-prepared conflict with the passivity of his homosexual sexual aim. The repression was thus a result of his masculinity.

One might be tempted at this point to introduce a slight alteration into psycho-analytic theory. It would seem palpably obvious that the repression and the formation of the neurosis must have originated out of the conflict between masculine and feminine tendencies, that is out of bisexuality. This view of the situation, however, is incomplete. Of the two conflicting sexual impulses one was ego-syntonic, while the other offended the boy's narcissistic interest; it was on *that* account that the latter underwent repression. So that in this case, too, it was the ego that put the repression into operation, for the benefit of one of the sexual tendencies. In other cases there is no such conflict between masculinity and femininity; there is only a single sexual tendency present, which seeks for acceptance, but offends against certain forces of the ego and is consequently repelled. Indeed, conflicts between sexuality and the *moral* ego trends are far more common than such as take place within the sphere of sexuality; but a moral conflict of this kind is lacking in our present case. To insist that bisexuality is the motive force leading to repression is to take too narrow a view; whereas if we assert the same of the conflict between the ego and the sexual tendencies (that is, the libido) we shall have covered all possible cases.

The theory of the 'masculine protest', as it has been developed by Adler, is faced by the difficulty that repression by no means always takes the side of masculinity against femininity; there are quite large classes of cases in which it is masculinity that has to submit to repression by the ego.

Moreover, a juster appreciation of the process of repression in our present case would lead us to deny that narcissistic masculinity was the sole motive force. The homosexual attitude which came into being during the dream was of such overwhelming intensity that the little boy's ego found itself unable to cope with it and so defended itself against it by the process of repression.[1] The narcissistic masculinity which attached to his genitals, being opposed to the homosexual attitude, was drawn in, in order to assist the ego in carrying out the task. Merely to avoid misunderstandings, I will add that all narcissistic impulses operate from the ego and have their permanent seat in the ego, and that repressions are directed against libidinal object-cathexes.[2]

Let us now leave the process of repression, though we have perhaps not succeeded in dealing with it exhaustively, and let us turn to the boy's state when he awoke from the dream. If it had really been his masculinity that had triumphed over his homosexuality (or femininity) during the dream-process, then we should necessarily find that the dominant trend was an active sexual trend of a character already explicitly masculine. But there is no question of this having happened. The essentials of the sexual organization had not been changed; the sadistic-anal phase persisted, and remained the dominant one. The triumph of his masculinity was shown only in this: that thenceforward he reacted with anxiety to the passive sexual aims of the dominant organization—aims which were masochistic but not feminine. We are not confronted by a triumphant masculine sexual trend, but only by a passive one and a struggle against it.

I can well imagine the difficulties that the reader must find in the sharp distinction (unfamiliar but essential) which I have drawn between 'active' and 'masculine' and between 'passive' and 'feminine'. I shall therefore not hesitate to repeat myself. The state of affairs, then, after the dream, may be described as follows. The sexual trends had been split up; in the unconscious the stage of the genital organization had been reached, and a

[1] [Freud had insisted from very early times, e.g. in Section 6 of Part I of his 'Project for a Scientific Psychology' (1950*a* [1895]), on the traumatic effects of excessive excitation. In Chapter II of *Inhibitions, Symptoms and Anxiety* (1926*d*), he writes: 'It is highly probable that the immediate precipitating causes of primal repressions are quantitative factors such as an excessive degree of excitation and the breaking through of the protective shield against stimuli.']

[2] [Adler's theory of repression is considered by Freud in greater detail in the last part of his paper on beating-phantasies (1919*e*), below p. 201 ff.]

very intense homosexuality set up; on the top of this (virtually in the conscious) there persisted the earlier sadistic and predominantly masochistic sexual current; the ego had on the whole changed its attitude towards sexuality, for it now repudiated sexuality and rejected the dominant masochistic aims with anxiety, just as it had reacted to the deeper homosexual aims with the formation of a phobia. Thus the result of the dream was not so much the triumph of a masculine current, as a reaction against a feminine and passive one. It would be very forced to ascribe the quality of masculinity to this reaction. The truth is that the ego has no sexual currents, but only an interest in its own self-protection and in the preservation of its narcissism.

Let us now consider the phobia. It came into existence on the level of the genital organization, and shows us the relatively simple mechanism of an anxiety-hysteria. The ego, by developing anxiety, was protecting itself against what it regarded as an overwhelming danger, namely, homosexual satisfaction. But the process of repression left behind it a trace which cannot be overlooked. The object to which the dangerous sexual aim had been attached had to have its place taken in consciousness by another one. What became conscious was fear not of the *father* but of the *wolf*. Nor did the process stop at the formation of a phobia with a single content. A considerable time afterwards the wolf was replaced by the lion [p. 39]. Simultaneously with sadistic impulses against small animals there was a phobia directed towards them, in their capacity of representatives of the boy's rivals, the possible small children. The origin of the butterfly phobia is of especial interest. It was like a repetition of the mechanism that produced the wolf phobia in the dream. Owing to a chance stimulus an old experience, the scene with Grusha, was activated; her threat of castration thus produced deferred effects, though at the time it was uttered it had made no impression.[1]

[1] The Grusha scene was, as I have said, a spontaneous product of the patient's memory, and no construction or stimulation by the physician played any part in evoking it. The gaps in it were filled up by the analysis in a fashion which must be regarded as unexceptionable, if any value at all is attached to the analytic method of work. The only possible rationalistic explanation of the phobia would be the following. There is nothing extraordinary, it might be said, in a child that was inclined to be nervous having had an anxiety attack in connection with

It may truly be said that the anxiety that was concerned in the formation of these phobias was a fear of castration. This statement involves no contradiction of the view that the anxiety originated from the repression of homosexual libido. Both modes of expression refer to the same process: namely, the withdrawal of libido by the ego from the homosexual wishful impulse, the libido having then become converted into free anxiety and subsequently bound in phobias.[1] The first method of statement merely mentions in addition the motive by which the ego was actuated.

If we look into the matter more closely we shall see that our patient's first illness (leaving the disturbance of appetite out of account) is not exhausted when we have extracted the phobia from it. It must be regarded as a true hysteria showing not merely anxiety-symptoms but also phenomena of conversion. A portion of the homosexual impulse was retained by the organ concerned in it; from that time forward, and equally during his adult life, his bowel behaved like a hysterically affected organ. The unconscious repressed homosexuality withdrew into his bowel. It was precisely this trait of hysteria which was of such great service in helping to clear up his later illness.

We must now summon up our courage to attack the still more complicated structure of the obsessional neurosis. Let us once more bear the situation in mind: a dominant masochistic

a yellow-striped butterfly, probably as a result of some inherited tendency to anxiety. (See Stanley Hall, 'A Synthetic Genetic Study of Fear', 1914.) In ignorance of the true causation of his fear, this explanation would proceed, the patient looked about for something in his childhood to which he could connect it; he made use of the chance similarity of names and the recurrence of the stripes as a ground for the construction of an imaginary adventure with the nursery-maid whom he still remembered. When, however, we observe that the trivial details of this event (which, according to this view, was in itself an innocent one)—the scrubbing, the pail and the broom—had enough power over the patient's later life to determine his object-choice permanently and compulsively, then the butterfly phobia seems to have acquired an inexplicable importance. The state of things on this hypothesis is thus seen to be at least as remarkable as on mine, and any advantage that might be claimed for a rationalistic reading of the scene has melted away. The Grusha scene is of particular value to us, since in relation to it we can prepare our judgement upon the less certain primal scene.

[1] [Freud's subsequent change of view on the relation between repression and anxiety is explained in his *Inhibitions, Symptoms and Anxiety* (1926*d*), especially in Chapter IV and Chapter XI, A (b).]

sexual current and a repressed homosexual one, and an ego deep in hysterical repudiation of them. What processes transformed this condition into one of obsessional neurosis?

The transformation did not occur spontaneously, through internal development, but through an outside influence. Its visible effect was that the patient's relation to his father, which stood in the foreground, and which had so far found expression in the wolf phobia, was now manifested in obsessional piety. I cannot refrain from pointing out that the course of events in this part of the patient's history affords an unmistakable confirmation of an assertion which I made in *Totem and Taboo* upon the relation of the totem animal to the deity.[1] I there decided in favour of the view that the idea of God was not a development from the totem, but replaced it after arising independently from a root common to both ideas. The totem, I maintained, was the first father-surrogate, and the god was a later one, in which the father had regained his human shape. And we find the same thing with our patient. In his wolf phobia he had gone through the stage of the totemic father-surrogate; but that stage was now broken off, and, as a result of new relations between him and his father, was replaced by a phase of religious piety.

The influence that provoked this transformation was the acquaintance which he obtained through his mother's agency with the doctrines of religion and with the Bible story. This educational measure had the desired effect. The sadistic-masochistic sexual organization came slowly to an end, the wolf phobia quickly vanished, and, instead of sexuality being repudiated with anxiety, a higher method of suppressing it made its appearance. Piety became the dominant force in the child's life. These victories, however, were not won without struggles, of which his blasphemous thoughts were an indication, and of which the establishment of an obsessive exaggeration of religious ceremonial was the result.

Apart from these pathological phenomena, it may be said that in the present case religion achieved all the aims for the sake of which it is included in the education of the individual. It put a restraint on his sexual impulsions by affording them a sublimation and a safe mooring; it lowered the importance of his family relationships, and thus protected him from the threat of isolation by giving him access to the great community of man-

[1] *Totem and Taboo* (1912–13), *Standard Ed.*, **13**, 148.

kind. The untamed and fear-ridden child became social, well-behaved, and amenable to education.

The chief motive force of the influence which religion had on him was his identification with the figure of Christ, which came particularly easily to him owing to the accident of the date of his birth. Along this path his extravagant love of his father, which had made the repression necessary, found its way at length to an ideal sublimation. As Christ, he could love his father, who was now called God, with a fervour which had sought in vain to discharge itself so long as his father had been a mortal. The means by which he could bear witness to this love were laid down by religion, and they were not haunted by that sense of guilt from which his individual feelings of love could not set themselves free. In this way it was still possible for him to drain off his deepest sexual current, which had already been precipitated in the form of unconscious homosexuality; and at the same time his more superficial masochistic impulsion found an incomparable sublimation, without much renunciation, in the story of the Passion of Christ, who, at the behest of his divine Father and in his honour, had let himself be ill-treated and sacrificed. So it was that religion did its work for the hard-pressed child—by the combination which it afforded the believer of satisfaction, of sublimation, of diversion from sensual processes to purely spiritual ones, and of access to social relationships.[1]

The opposition which he at first offered to religion had three different points of origin. To begin with, there was, in general, his characteristic (which we have seen exemplified already) of fending off all novelties. Any position of the libido which he had once taken up was obstinately defended by him from fear of what he would lose by giving it up and from distrust of the probability of a complete substitute being afforded by the new position that was in view. This is an important and fundamental psychological peculiarity, which I described in my *Three Essays on the Theory of Sexuality* (1905*d*) as a susceptibility to 'fixation'.[2] Under the name of psychical 'inertia' Jung has attempted to erect it into the principal cause of all the failures of neurotics. I think he is wrong in this; for this factor has a far more general

[1] [The value of religion to the individual is further discussed in *The Future of an Illusion* (1927*c*).]

[2] [*Standard Ed.*, 7, 242–3.]

application and plays an important part in the lives of the non-neurotic as well. Great mobility or sluggishness of libidinal cathexes (as well as of other kinds of energic cathexes) are special characteristics which attach to many normal people and by no means to all neurotics, and which have hitherto not been brought into relation with other qualities. They are, as it were, like prime numbers, not further divisible. We only know one thing about them, and that is that mobility of the mental cathexes is a quality which shows striking diminution with the advance of age. This has given us one of the indications of the limits within which psycho-analytic treatment is effective. There are some people, however, who retain this mental plasticity far beyond the usual age-limit, and others who lose it very prematurely. If the latter are neurotics, we make the unwelcome discovery that it is impossible to undo developments in them which, in apparently similar circumstances, have been easily dealt with in other people. So that in considering the conversion of psychical energy no less than of physical, we must make use of the concept of an *entropy*, which opposes the undoing of what has already occurred.[1]

A second point of attack was afforded by the circumstance that religious doctrine is itself based upon a by no means unambiguous relation to God the Father, and in fact bears the stamp of the ambivalent attitude which presided over its origin. The patient's own ambivalence, which he possessed in a high degree of development, helped him to detect the same feature in religion, and he brought to bear on that feature those acute powers of criticism whose presence could not fail to astonish us in a child of four and a half.

But there was a third factor at work, which was certainly the most important of all, and to the operation of which we must ascribe the pathological products of his struggle against religion. The truth was that the mental current which impelled him to turn to men as sexual objects and which should have been

[1] [Entropy is the force which, according to the Second Law of Thermodynamics, tends to make certain physical changes irreversible.—The topic of 'psychical inertia' was discussed by Freud at the end of his paper on 'A Case of Paranoia Running Counter to the Psycho-Analytic Theory of the Disease' (1915*f*). Though this was published earlier than the present case history, it was probably written later. An Editor's footnote at the end of that paper gives a number of references to other passages in which Freud considered the same topic.]

sublimated by religion was no longer free; a portion of it was cut off by repression and so withdrawn from the possibility of sublimation and tied to its original sexual aim. In virtue of this state of things, the repressed portion kept making efforts to forge its way through to the sublimated portion or to drag down the latter to itself. The first ruminations which he wove round the figure of Christ already involved the question whether that sublime son could also fulfil the sexual relationship to his father which the patient had retained in his unconscious. The only result of his repudiation of these efforts was the production of apparently blasphemous obsessive thoughts, in which his physical affection for God asserted itself in the form of a debasement. A violent defensive struggle against these compromises then inevitably led to an obsessive exaggeration of all the activities which are prescribed for giving expression to piety and a pure love of God. Religion won in the end, but its instinctual foundations proved themselves to be incomparably stronger than the durability of the products of their sublimation. As soon as the course of events presented him with a new father-surrogate, who threw his weight into the scale against religion, it was dropped and replaced by something else. Let us further bear in mind, as an interesting complication, that his piety originated under the influence of women (his mother and his nurse), while it was a masculine influence that set him free from it.

The origin of this obsessional neurosis on the basis of the sadistic-anal organization confirms on the whole what I have said elsewhere on the predisposition to obsessional neurosis (1913*i*). The previous existence, however, of a severe hysteria in the present case makes it more obscure in this respect.

I will conclude my survey of the patient's sexual development by giving some brief glimpses of its later vicissitudes. During the years of puberty a markedly sensual, masculine current, with a sexual aim suitable to the genital organization, made its appearance in him; it must be regarded as normal, and its history occupied the period up to the time of his later illness. It was connected directly with the Grusha scene, from which it borrowed its characteristic feature—a compulsive falling in love that came on and passed off by sudden fits. This current had to struggle against the inhibitions that were derived from his infantile neurosis. There had been a violent revulsion in the direction of women, and he had thus won his way to complete masculinity. From that time forward he retained women as his sexual object; but he did not enjoy this possession, for a powerful, and now entirely unconscious, inclination towards men, in which were united all the forces of the earlier phases of his development, was constantly drawing him away from his female objects and compelling him in the intervals to exaggerate his dependence upon women. He kept complaining during the treatment that he could not bear having to do with women, and all our labours were directed towards disclosing to him his unconscious relation to men. The whole situation might be summarized in the shape of a formula. His childhood had been marked by a wavering between activity and passivity, his puberty by a struggle for masculinity, and the period after he had fallen ill by a fight for the object of his masculine desires. The precipitating cause of his neurosis was not one of the types of onset which I have been able to put together as special cases of 'frustration,' [1] and it thus draws attention to a gap in that classification. He broke down after an organic affection of the genitals had revived his fear of castration, shattered his narcissism, and compelled him to abandon his hope of being personally favoured by destiny. He fell ill, therefore, as the result of a *narcissistic* 'frustration'. This excessive strength of his narcissism was in complete harmony with the other indications of an inhibited sexual development: with the fact that so few of his psychical trends were concentrated in his heterosexual object-choice, in spite of all its energy, and that his homosexual attitude, standing so much nearer to narcissism, persisted in him as an unconscious force with such very great tenacity. Naturally, where disturbances like these are present, psycho-analytic treatment cannot bring about any instantaneous revolution or put matters upon a level with a normal development: it can only get rid of the obstacles and clear the path, so that the influences of life may be able to further development along better lines.

I shall now bring together some peculiarities of the patient's mentality which were revealed by the psycho-analytic treatment but were not further elucidated and were accordingly not susceptible to direct influence. Such were his tenacity of fixation, which has already been discussed, his extraordinary propensity to ambivalence, and (as a third trait in a constitution which deserves the name of archaic) his power of maintaining

[1] 'Types of Onset of Neurosis' (1912*c*).

simultaneously the most various and contradictory libidinal cathexes, all of them capable of functioning side by side. His constant wavering between these (a characteristic which for a long time seemed to block the way to recovery and progress in the treatment) dominated the clinical picture during his adult illness, which I have scarcely been able to touch upon in these pages. This was undoubtedly a trait belonging to the general character of the unconscious, which in his case had persisted into processes that had become conscious. But it showed itself only in the products of affective impulses; in the region of pure logic he betrayed, on the contrary, a peculiar skill in unearthing contradictions and inconsistencies. So it was that his mental life impressed one in much the same way as the religion of Ancient Egypt, which is so unintelligible to us because it preserves the earlier stages of its development side by side with the end-products, retains the most ancient gods and their attributes along with the most modern ones, and thus, as it were, spreads out upon a two-dimensional surface what other instances of evolution show us in the solid.

I have now come to the end of what I had to say about this case. There remain two problems, of the many that it raises, which seem to me to deserve special emphasis. The first relates to the phylogenetically inherited schemata, which, like the categories of philosophy, are concerned with the business of 'placing' the impressions derived from actual experience. I am inclined to take the view that they are precipitates from the history of human civilization. The Oedipus complex, which comprises a child's relation to his parents, is one of them—is, in fact, the best known member of the class. Wherever experiences fail to fit in with the hereditary schema, they become remodelled in the imagination—a process which might very profitably be followed out in detail. It is precisely such cases that are calculated to convince us of the independent existence of the schema. We are often able to see the schema triumphing over the experience of the individual; as when in our present case the boy's father became the castrator and the menace of his infantile sexuality in spite of what was in other respects an inverted Oedipus complex. A similar process is at work where a nurse comes to play the mother's part or where the two become fused together. The contradictions between experience and the schema seem to supply the conflicts of childhood with an abundance of material.

The second problem is not far removed from the first, but it is incomparably more important. If one considers the behaviour of the four-year-old child towards the re-activated primal scene,[1] or even if one thinks of the far simpler reactions of the one-and-a-half-year-old child when the scene was actually experienced, it is hard to dismiss the view that some sort of hardly definable knowledge, something, as it were, preparatory to an understanding, was at work in the child at the time.[2] We can form no conception of what this may have consisted in; we have nothing at our disposal but the single analogy—and it is an excellent one—of the far-reaching *instinctive* [3] knowledge of animals.

If human beings too possessed an instinctive endowment such as this, it would not be surprising that it should be very particularly concerned with the processes of sexual life, even though it could not be by any means confined to them. This instinctive factor would then be the nucleus of the unconscious, a primitive kind of mental activity, which would later be dethroned and overlaid by human reason, when that faculty came to be acquired, but which in some people, perhaps in every one, would retain the power of drawing down to it the higher mental processes. Repression would be the return to this instinctive stage, and man would thus be paying for his great new acquisition with his liability to neurosis, and would be bearing witness by the possibility of the neuroses to the existence of those earlier, instinct-like, preliminary stages. The significance of the traumas of early childhood would lie in their contributing material to this unconscious which would save it from being worn away by the subsequent course of development.

[1] I may disregard the fact that it was not possible to put this behaviour into words until twenty years afterwards; for all the effects that we traced back to the scene had already been manifested in the form of symptoms, obsessions, etc., in the patient's childhood and long before the analysis. It is also a matter of indifference in this connection whether we choose to regard it as a primal *scene* or as a primal *phantasy*.

[2] I must once more emphasize the fact that these reflections would be vain if the dream and the neurosis had not themselves occurred in infancy.

[3] [The German word used here and in what follows is '*instinktiv*' not '*triebhaft*', which is regularly translated 'instinctual'.]

I am aware that expression has been given in many quarters to thoughts like these, which emphasize the hereditary, phylogenetically acquired factor in mental life. In fact, I am of opinion that people have been far too ready to find room for them and ascribe importance to them in psycho-analysis. I consider that they are only admissible when psycho-analysis strictly observes the correct order of precedence, and, after forcing its way through the strata of what has been acquired by the individual, comes at last upon traces of what has been inherited.[1]

[1] (*Footnote added* 1923:) I will once more set out here the chronology of the events mentioned in this case history.

Born on Christmas Day.

1½ *years old*: Malaria. Observation of his parents copulating; or observation of them when they were together, into which he later introduced a phantasy of them copulating.

Just before 2½: Scene with Grusha.

2½: Screen memory of his parents' departure with his sister. This showed him alone with his Nanya and so disowned Grusha and his sister.

Before 3¼: His mother's laments to the doctor.

3¼: Beginning of his seduction by his sister. Soon afterwards the threat of castration from his Nanya.

3½: The English governess. Beginning of the change in his character.

4: The wolf dream. Origin of the phobia.

4½: Influence of the Bible story. Appearance of the obsessional symptoms.

Just before 5: Hallucination of the loss of his finger.

5: Departure from the first estate.

After 6: Visit to his sick father [compulsion to breathe out].

8:
10: } Final outbreaks of the obsessional neurosis.

[17: Breakdown, precipitated by gonorrhoea.]

[23: Beginning of treatment.]

[The dates of the following events are not exactly established

Between primal scene (1½) *and seduction* (3¼): Disturbance of appetite.

Same period: Dumb water-carrier.

Before 4: Possible observation of dogs copulating.

After 4: Anxiety at swallow-tail butterfly.]

It will have been easy to guess from my account that the patient was a Russian. I parted from him, regarding him as cured, a few weeks before the unexpected outbreak of the Great War [1914]; and I did not see him again until the shifting chances of the war had given the Central European Powers access to South Russia. He then came to Vienna and reported that immediately after the end of the treatment he had been seized with a longing to tear himself free from my influence. After a few months' work, a piece of the transference which had not hitherto been overcome was successfully dealt with. Since then the patient has felt normal and has behaved unexceptionably, in spite of the war having robbed him of his home, his possessions, and all his family relationships. It may be that his very misery, by gratifying his sense of guilt, contributed to the consolidation of his recovery.

[Some further notes on the later history of the case may be of interest. The original course of treatment lasted from February, 1910, to July, 1914. The patient returned to Vienna in the spring of 1919, and Freud treated him again from November, 1919, till February, 1920. In some further remarks on the case, at the beginning of his 'Analysis Terminable and Interminable' (1937*c*), Freud reports that after this second treatment the patient continued living in Vienna and on the whole maintained his health, though with occasional interruptions. These later episodes were dealt with, on Freud's advice, by one of his pupils, Dr. Ruth Mack Brunswick. She herself reported in detail on this later phase of the treatment, which extended from October, 1926, to February, 1927 (Brunswick, 1928). Her report was reprinted in *The Psycho-Analytic Reader*, edited by R. Fliess (1950), with an added note by Dr. Mack Brunswick (dated September, 1945) giving a short account of the patient's further history up to 1940. A still later report, on his great external difficulties during the Second World War, and his reaction to them, has since been published by Muriel Gardiner (1952). A full account of the case will be found in the second volume of Ernest Jones's biography (1955), pp. 306-12.]

APPENDIX

List of Freud's Longer Case Histories

The date at the beginning of each entry is approximately that of the year during which the work in question was written. The date at the end is that of publication; and under that date fuller particulars of the work will be found in the Bibliography at the end of this volume.

1894 Frau Emmy von N.
Miss Lucy R.
Katharina
Fräulein Elisabeth von R.
in *Studies on Hysteria* (1895*d*)

1901 'Fragment of an Analysis of a Case of Hysteria' ('Dora') (1905*e*)

1909 'Analysis of a Phobia in a Five-Year-Old Boy' ('Little Hans') (1909*b* and 1922*c*)
'Notes upon a Case of Obsessional Neurosis' (The 'Rat Man') (1909*d* and 1955*a*)

1910 'Psycho-Analytic Notes on an Autobiographical Account of a Case of Paranoia' (Schreber) (1911*c* and 1912*a*)

1914 'From the History of an Infantile Neurosis' (The 'Wolf Man') (1918*b*)

1915 'A Case of Paranoia Running Counter to the Psycho-Analytic Theory of the Disease' (1915*f*)

1919 'The Psychogenesis of a Case of Homosexuality in a Woman' (1920*a*)

ON TRANSFORMATIONS OF INSTINCT AS EXEMPLIFIED IN ANAL EROTISM (1917)

ÜBER TRIEBUMSETZUNGEN, INSBESONDERE DER ANALEROTIK

(*a*) German Editions:

1917 *Int. Z. Psychoanal.*, **4** (3), 125–30.
1918 *S.K.S.N.*, **4**, 139–48 (1922, 2nd. ed.).
1924 *G.S.*, **5**, 268–76.
1926 *Psychoanalyse der Neurosen*, 40–9.
1931 *Sexualtheorie und Traumlehre*, 116–24.
1946 *G.W.*, **10**, 402–10.

(*b*) English Translation:

'On the Transformation of Instincts with Special Reference to Anal Erotism'

1924 *C.P.*, **2**, 164–71. (Tr. E. Glover.)

The present translation, with a modified title, is based on that published in 1924.

Though this paper was not published until 1917, it was probably written considerably earlier—perhaps even in 1915. Long delays in publication were inevitable at this period, owing to the difficulties of war conditions. The gist of it had already been given in a paragraph added to the 1915 edition of Freud's *Three Essays* (1905*d*), *Standard Ed.*, **7**, 186. Moreover, many conclusions reached here seem to be derived from the analysis of the 'Wolf Man' (1918*b*), whose case history was mostly written during the autumn of 1914. The later part of Section VII (p. 80 ff.) of that case history exemplifies in some detail the thesis of the present paper.

ON TRANSFORMATIONS OF INSTINCT AS EXEMPLIFIED IN ANAL EROTISM

SOME years ago, observations made during psycho-analysis led me to suspect that the constant co-existence in any one of the three character-traits of *orderliness*, *parsimony* and *obstinacy* indicated an intensification of the anal-erotic components in his sexual constitution, and that these modes of reaction, which were favoured by his ego, had been established during the course of his development through the assimilation of his anal erotism.[1]

In that publication my main object was to make known the fact of this established relation; I was little concerned about its theoretical significance. Since then there has been a general consensus of opinion that each one of the three qualities, avarice, pedantry and obstinacy, springs from anal-erotic sources—or, to express it more cautiously and more completely—draws powerful contributions from those sources. The cases in which these defects of character were combined and which in consequence bore a special stamp (the 'anal character') were merely extreme instances, which were bound to betray the particular connection that interests us here even to an unobservant eye.

As a result of numerous impressions, and in particular of one specially cogent analytical observation, I came to the conclusion a few years later that in the development of the libido in man the phase of genital primacy must be preceded by a 'pregenital organization' in which sadism and anal erotism play the leading parts.[2]

From that moment we had to face the problem of the later history of the anal-erotic instinctual impulses. What becomes of them when, owing to the establishment of a definitive genital organization, they have lost their importance in sexual life? Do they preserve their original nature, but in a state of repression? Are they sublimated or assimilated by

[1] 'Character and Anal Erotism' (1908*b*).

[2] 'The Predisposition to Obsessional Neurosis' (1913*i*).

transformation into character-traits? Or do they find a place within the new organization of sexuality characterized by genital primacy? Or, since none of these vicissitudes of anal erotism is likely to be the only one, to what extent and in what way does each of them share in deciding its fate? For the organic sources of anal erotism cannot of course be buried as a result of the emergence of the genital organization.

One would think that there could be no lack of material from which to provide an answer, since the processes of development and transformation in question must have taken place in everyone undergoing analysis. Yet the material is so obscure, the abundance of ever-recurring impressions so confusing, that even now I am unable to solve the problem fully and can do no more than make some contributions to its solution. In making them I need not refrain from mentioning, where the context allows it, other instinctual transformations besides anal-erotic ones. Finally, it scarcely requires to be emphasized that the developmental events here described—just as the others found in psycho-analysis—have been inferred from the regressions into which they had been forced by neurotic processes.

As a starting-point for this discussion we may take the fact that it appears as if in the products of the unconscious—spontaneous ideas, phantasies and symptoms—the concepts *faeces* (money, gift),[1] *baby* and *penis* are ill-distinguished from one another and are easily interchangeable. We realize, of course, that to express oneself in this way is incorrectly to apply to the sphere of the unconscious terms which belong properly to other regions of mental life, and that we have been led astray by the advantages offered by an analogy. To put the matter in a form less open to objection, these elements in the unconscious are often treated as if they were equivalent and could replace one another freely.

This is most easily seen in the relation between 'baby' and 'penis'. It cannot be without significance that in the symbolic language of dreams, as well as of everyday life, both may be replaced by the same symbol; both baby and penis are called a 'little one', ['*das Kleine*'].[2] It is a well-known fact that symbolic

[1] [The relations between aeces and money, or gold, are discussed at some length in the paper already referred to (Freud, 1908*b*).]

[2] [A dream illustrating this will be found in *The Interpretation of Dreams* (1900*a*), *Standard Ed.*, 5, 362f.]

speech often ignores difference of sex. The 'little one', which originally meant the male genital organ, may thus have acquired a secondary application to the female genitals.

If we penetrate deeply enough into the neurosis of a woman, we not infrequently meet with the repressed wish to possess a penis like a man. We call this wish 'envy for a penis' and include it in the castration complex. Chance mishaps in the life of such a woman, mishaps which are themselves frequently the result of a very masculine disposition, have re-activated this infantile wish and, through the backward flow of libido, made it the chief vehicle of her neurotic symptoms. In other women we find no evidence of this wish for a penis; it is replaced by the wish for a baby, the frustration of which in real life can lead to the outbreak of a neurosis. It looks as if such women had understood (although this could not possibly have acted as a motive) that nature has given babies to women as a substitute for the penis that has been denied them. With other women, again, we learn that both wishes were present in their childhood and that one replaced the other. At first they had wanted a penis like a man; then at a later, though still childish, stage there appeared instead the wish for a baby. The impression is forced upon us that this variety in our findings is caused by accidental factors during childhood (e.g. the presence or absence of brothers or the birth of a new baby at some favourable time of life), so that the wish for a penis and the wish for a baby would be fundamentally identical.

We can say what the ultimate outcome of the infantile wish for a penis is in women in whom the determinants of a neurosis in later life are absent: it changes into the wish for a *man*, and thus puts up with the man as an appendage to the penis. This transformation, therefore, turns an impulse which is hostile to the female sexual function into one which is favourable to it. Such women are in this way made capable of an erotic life based on the masculine type of object-love, which can exist alongside the feminine one proper, derived from narcissism. We already know [1] that in other cases it is only a baby that makes the transition from narcissistic self-love to object-love possible. So that in this respect too a baby can be represented by the penis.

[1] [See the later part of Section II of Freud's paper on narcissism (1914*c*).]

I have had occasional opportunities of being told women's dreams that had occurred after their first experience of intercourse. They revealed an unmistakable wish in the woman to keep for herself the penis which she had felt. Apart from their libidinal origin, then, these dreams indicated a temporary regression from man to penis as the object of her wish. One would certainly be inclined to trace back the wish for a man in a purely rationalistic way to the wish for a baby, since a woman is bound to understand sooner or later that there can be no baby without the co-operation of a man. It is, however, more likely that the wish for a man arises independently of the wish for a baby, and that when it arises—from understandable motives belonging entirely to ego-psychology—the original wish for a penis becomes attached to it as an unconscious libidinal reinforcement. The importance of the process described lies in the fact that a part of the young woman's narcissistic masculinity is thus changed into femininity, and so can no longer operate in a way harmful to the female sexual function.

Along another path, a part of the erotism of the pregenital phase, too, becomes available for use in the phase of genital primacy. The baby is regarded as 'lumf'[1] (cf. the analysis of 'Little Hans'), as something which becomes detached from the body by passing through the bowel. A certain amount of libidinal cathexis which originally attached to the contents of the bowel can thus be extended to the baby born through it. Linguistic evidence of this identity of baby and faeces is contained in the expression 'to give someone a baby'. For its faeces are the infant's first gift, a part of his body which he will give up only on persuasion by someone he loves, to whom indeed, he will make a spontaneous gift of it as a token of affection; for, as a rule, infants do not dirty strangers. (There are similar if less intense reactions with urine.) Defaecation affords the first occasion on which the child must decide between a narcissistic and an object-loving attitude. He either parts obediently with his faeces, 'sacrifices' them to his love, or else retains them for purposes of auto-erotic satisfaction and later as a means of asserting his own will. If he makes the latter choice we are in the presence of defiance (obstinacy) which, accordingly, springs from a narcissistic clinging to anal erotism.

It is probable that the first meaning which a child's interest

[1] ['Little Hans's' word for faeces. Cf. *Standard Ed.*, **10**, 54 and 68*n.*]

in faeces develops is that of 'gift' rather than 'gold' or 'money'. The child knows no money apart from what is given him—no money acquired and none inherited of his own. Since his faeces are his first gift, the child easily transfers his interest from that substance to the new one which he comes across as the most valuable gift in life. Those who question this derivation of gifts should consider their experience of psycho-analytic treatment, study the gifts they receive as doctors from their patients, and watch the storms of transference which a gift from them can rouse in their patients.

Thus the interest in faeces is continued partly as interest in money, partly as a wish for a baby, in which latter an anal-erotic and a genital impulse ('envy for a penis') converge. But the penis has another anal-erotic significance apart from its relation to the interest in a baby. The relationship between the penis and the passage lined with mucous membrane which it fills and excites already has its prototype in the pregenital, anal-sadistic phase. The faecal mass, or as one patient called it, the faecal 'stick', represents as it were the first penis, and the stimulated mucous membrane of the rectum represents that of the vagina. There are people whose anal erotism remains vigorous and unmodified up to the age preceding puberty (ten to twelve years); we learn from them that during the pregenital phase they had already developed in phantasy and in perverse play an organization analogous to the genital one, in which penis and vagina were represented by the faecal stick and the rectum. In other people—obsessional neurotics—we can observe the result of a regressive debasement of the genital organization. This is expressed in the fact that every phantasy originally conceived on the genital level is transposed to the anal level—the penis being replaced by the faecal mass and the vagina by the rectum.

As the interest in faeces recedes in a normal way, the organic analogy we have described here has the effect of transferring the interest on to the penis. When, later, in the course of the child's researches [1] he discovers that babies are born from the bowel, they inherit the greater part of his anal erotism; they have, however, been preceded by the penis in this as well as in another sense.

I feel sure that by this time the manifold interrelations of

[1] [See Freud's paper 'On the Sexual Theories of Children' (1908*c*).]

the series—faeces, penis, baby—have become totally unintelligible; so I will try to remedy the defect by presenting them diagramatically, and in considering the diagram [Fig. 2] we can review the same material in a different order. Unfortunately, this technical device is not sufficiently pliable for our purpose, or possibly we have not yet learned to use it with effect. In any case I hope the reader will not expect too much from it.

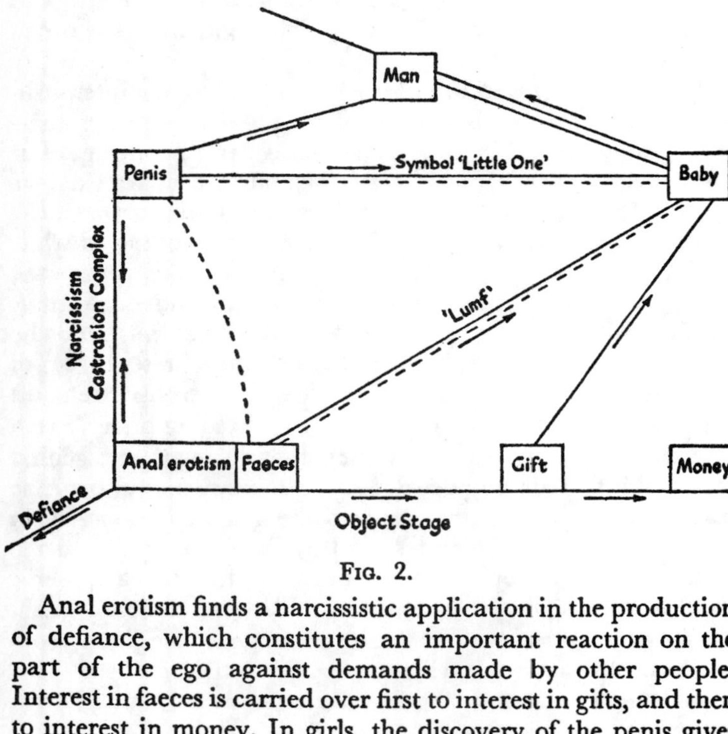

Fig. 2.

Anal erotism finds a narcissistic application in the production of defiance, which constitutes an important reaction on the part of the ego against demands made by other people. Interest in faeces is carried over first to interest in gifts, and then to interest in money. In girls, the discovery of the penis gives rise to envy for it, which later changes into the wish for a man as the possessor of a penis. Even before this the wish for a penis has changed into the wish for a baby, or the latter wish has taken the place of the former one. An organic analogy between penis and baby (dotted line) is expressed by the existence of a symbol ('little one') common to both. A rational wish (double line) then leads from the wish for a baby to the wish for a man: we have already appreciated the importance of this instinctual transformation.

Another part of the nexus of relations can be observed much more clearly in the male. It arises when the boy's sexual researches lead him to the discovery of the absence of a penis in women. He concludes that the penis must be a detachable part of the body, something analogous to faeces, the first piece of bodily substance the child had to part with. Thus the old anal defiance enters into the composition of the castration complex. The organic analogy which enabled the intestinal contents to be the forerunner of the penis during the pregenital phase cannot come into account as a motive; but the boy's sexual researches lead him to a psychical substitute for it. When a baby appears on the scene he regards it as 'lumf', in accordance with those researches, and he cathects it with powerful anal-erotic interest. When social experiences teach that a baby is to be regarded as a love-token, a gift, the wish for a baby receives a second contribution from the same source. Faeces, penis and baby are all three solid bodies; they all three, by forcible entry or expulsion, stimulate a membranous passage, i.e. the rectum and the vagina, the latter being as it were 'taken on lease' from the rectum, as Lou Andreas-Salomé aptly remarks.[1] Infantile sexual researches can only lead to the conclusion that the baby follows the same route as the faecal mass. The function of the penis is not usually discovered by those researches. But it is interesting to note that after so many détours an organic correspondence reappears in the psychical sphere as an unconscious identity.

[1] In her paper ' "Anal" und "Sexual" ' (1916). [Freud added a footnote in 1920 to the second of his *Three Essays on Sexuality* (1905*d*, *Standard Ed.*, 7, 187*n*.), in which he summarized the contents of that paper.]

A DIFFICULTY IN THE PATH OF PSYCHO-ANALYSIS (1917)

EINE SCHWIERIGKEIT DER PSYCHOANALYSE

(*a*) German Editions:

(1917 *Nyugat* (Budapest), **10** (1), 47–52. In a Hungarian translation.)

1917 *Imago*, **5** (1), 1–7.

1918 *S.K.S.N.*, **4**, 553–63 (1922, 2nd. ed.).

1924 *G.S.*, **10**, 347–56.

1947 *G.W.*, **12**, 3–12.

(*b*) English Translation:

'One of the Difficulties of Psycho-Analysis'

1920 *Int. J. Psycho-Anal.*, **1**, 17–23. (Tr. Joan Riviere.)

1925 *C.P.*, **4**, 347–56. (Same translator.)

The present translation, with a new title 'A Difficulty in the Path of Psycho-Analysis', is based on the one published in 1925.

A leading Hungarian man of letters of the day, H. Ignotus, invited Freud to contribute an article to the periodical *Nyugat*, of which he was editor, and this paper, evidently designed for an educated but uninstructed audience, was the result. The article was written at the end of 1916 and was first published in a Hungarian translation (under the title 'A pszihoanalizis egy nehézségéröl') in the early days of 1917. The original German appeared in *Imago* two or three months afterwards. A more general discussion of the resistances to the theories of psycho-analysis will be found in a paper of Freud's written some years later (1925*e*). The earlier part of the present work is, of course, a brief summary of the paper on narcissism (1914*c*). The three 'blows to human narcissism' are also described at the end of Lecture XVIII of Freud's *Introductory Lectures* (1916–17), the composition of which was completed at about the time at which the present paper was written.

A DIFFICULTY IN THE PATH OF PSYCHO-ANALYSIS

I WILL say at once that it is not an intellectual difficulty I am thinking of, not anything that makes psycho-analysis hard for the hearer or reader to understand, but an affective one—something that alienates the feelings of those who come into contact with it, so that they become less inclined to believe in it or take an interest in it. As will be observed, the two kinds of difficulty amount to the same thing in the end. Where sympathy is lacking, understanding will not come very easily.

My present readers, I take it, have not so far had anything to do with the subject and I shall be obliged, therefore, to go back some distance. Out of a great number of individual observations and impressions something in the nature of a theory has at last shaped itself in psycho-analysis, and this is known by the name of the 'libido theory'. As is well known, psycho-analysis is concerned with the elucidation and removal of what are called nervous disorders. A starting-point had to be found from which to approach this problem, and it was decided to look for it in the instinctual life of the mind. Hypotheses about the instincts in man came to form the basis, therefore, of our conception of nervous disease.

Psychology as it is taught academically gives us but very inadequate replies to questions concerning our mental life, but in no direction is its information so meagre as in this matter of the instincts.

It is open to us to make our first soundings as we please. The popular view distinguishes between hunger and love, as being the representatives of the instincts which aim respectively at the preservation of the individual and at the reproduction of the species. We accept this very evident distinction, so that in psycho-analysis too we make a distinction between the self-preservative or ego-instincts on the one hand and the sexual instincts on the other. The force by which the sexual instinct is represented in the mind we call 'libido'—sexual desire—and we regard it as something analogous to hunger, the will to power, and so on, where the ego-instincts are concerned.

With this as a starting-point we go on to make our first important discovery. We learn that, when we try to understand neurotic disorders, by far the greater significance attaches to the sexual instincts; that in fact neuroses are the specific disorders, so to speak, of the sexual function; that in general whether or not a person develops a neurosis depends on the quantity of his libido, and on the possibility of satisfying it and of discharging it through satisfaction; that the form taken by the disease is determined by the way in which the individual passes through the course of development of his sexual function, or, as we put it, by the fixations his libido has undergone in the course of its development; and, further, that by a special, not very simple technique for influencing the mind we are able to throw light on the nature of some groups of neuroses and at the same time to do away with them. Our therapeutic efforts have their greatest success with a certain class of neuroses which proceed from a conflict between the ego-instincts and the sexual instincts. For in human beings it may happen that the demands of the sexual instincts, whose reach of course extends far beyond the individual, seem to the ego to constitute a danger which threatens its self-preservation or its self-esteem. The ego then assumes the defensive, denies the sexual instincts the satisfaction they desire and forces them into those by-paths of substitutive satisfaction which become manifest as nervous symptoms.

The psycho-analytic method of treatment is then able to subject this process of repression to revision and to bring about a better solution of the conflict—one that is compatible with health. Unintelligent opposition accuses us of one-sidedness in our estimate of the sexual instincts. 'Human beings have other interests besides sexual ones,' they say. We have not forgotten or denied this for a moment. Our one-sidedness is like that of the chemist, who traces all compounds back to the force of chemical attraction. He is not on that account denying the force of gravity; he leaves that to the physicist to deal with.

During the work of treatment we have to consider the distribution of the patient's libido; we look for the object-presentations to which it is bound and free it from them, so as to place it at the disposal of the ego. In the course of this, we have come to form a very curious picture of the original, primal distribution of libido in human beings. We have been driven to assume that at the beginning of the development of the individual all his libido (all his erotic tendencies, all his capacity for love) is tied to himself—that as we say, it cathects his own ego. It is only later that, being attached to the satisfaction of the major vital needs, the libido flows over from the ego on to external objects. Not till then are we able to recognize the libidinal instincts as such and distinguish them from the ego-instincts. It is possible for the libido to become detached from these objects and withdrawn again into the ego.

The condition in which the ego retains the libido is called by us 'narcissism', in reference to the Greek legend of the youth Narcissus who was in love with his own reflection.

Thus in our view the individual advances from narcissism to object-love. But we do not believe that the *whole* of the libido ever passes over from the ego to objects. A certain quantity of libido is always retained in the ego; even when object-love is highly developed, a certain amount of narcissism persists. The ego is a great reservoir from which the libido that is destined for objects flows out and into which it flows back from those objects. Object-libido was at first ego-libido and can be transformed back into ego-libido. For complete health it is essential that the libido should not lose this full mobility. As an illustration of this state of things we may think of an amoeba, whose viscous substance puts out pseudopodia, elongations into which the substance of the body extends but which can be retracted at any time so that the form of the protoplasmic mass is restored.

What I have been trying to describe in this outline is the *libido theory* of the neuroses, upon which are founded all our conceptions of the nature of these morbid states, together with our therapeutic measures for relieving them. We naturally regard the premises of the libido theory as valid for normal behaviour as well. We speak of the narcissism of small children, and it is to the excessive narcissism of primitive man that we ascribe his belief in the omnipotence of his thoughts and his consequent attempts to influence the course of events in the external world by the technique of magic.

After this introduction I propose to describe how the universal narcissism of men, their self-love, has up to the present suffered three severe blows from the researches of science.

(*a*) In the early stages of his researches, man believed at first that his dwelling-place, the earth, was the stationary centre of the universe, with the sun, moon and planets circling round it.

In this he was naïvely following the dictates of his sense-perceptions, for he felt no movement of the earth, and wherever he had an unimpeded view he found himself in the centre of a circle that enclosed the external world. The central position of the earth, moreover, was a token to him of the dominating part played by it in the universe and appeared to fit in very well with his inclination to regard himself as lord of the world.

The destruction of this narcissistic illusion is associated in our minds with the name and work of Copernicus in the sixteenth century. But long before his day the Pythagoreans had already cast doubts on the privileged position of the earth, and in the third century B.C. Aristarchus of Samos had declared that the earth was much smaller than the sun and moved round that celestial body. Even the great discovery of Copernicus, therefore, had already been made before him. When this discovery achieved general recognition, the self-love of mankind suffered its first blow, the *cosmological* one.

(*b*) In the course of the development of civilization man acquired a dominating position over his fellow-creatures in the animal kingdom. Not content with this supremacy, however, he began to place a gulf between his nature and theirs. He denied the possession of reason to them, and to himself he attributed an immortal soul, and made claims to a divine descent which permitted him to break the bond of community between him and the animal kingdom. Curiously enough, this piece of arrogance is still foreign to children, just as it is to primitive and primaeval man. It is the result of a later, more pretentious stage of development. At the level of totemism primitive man had no repugnance to tracing his descent from an animal ancestor. In myths, which contain the precipitate of this ancient attitude of mind, the gods take animal shapes, and in the art of earliest times they are portrayed with animals' heads. A child can see no difference between his own nature and that of animals. He is not astonished at animals thinking and talking in fairy-tales; he will transfer an emotion of fear which he feels for his human father onto a dog or a horse, without intending any derogation of his father by it. Not until he is grown up does he become so far estranged from animals as to use their names in vilification of human beings.

We all know that little more than half a century ago the researches of Charles Darwin and his collaborators and forerunners put an end to this presumption on the part of man. Man is not a being different from animals or superior to them; he himself is of animal descent, being more closely related to some species and more distantly to others. The acquisitions he has subsequently made have not succeeded in effacing the evidences, both in his physical structure and in his mental dispositions, of his parity with them. This was the second, the *biological* blow to human narcissism.

(*c*) The third blow, which is psychological in nature, is probably the most wounding.

Although thus humbled in his external relations, man feels himself to be supreme within his own mind. Somewhere in the core of his ego he has developed an organ of observation to keep a watch on his impulses and actions and see whether they harmonize with its demands. If they do not, they are ruthlessly inhibited and withdrawn. His internal perception, consciousness, gives the ego news of all the important occurrences in the mind's working, and the will, directed by these reports, carries out what the ego orders and modifies anything that seeks to accomplish itself spontaneously. For this mind is not a simple thing; on the contrary, it is a hierarchy of superordinated and subordinated agencies, a labyrinth of impulses striving independently of one another towards action, corresponding with the multiplicity of instincts and of relations with the external world, many of which are antagonistic to one another and incompatible. For proper functioning it is necessary that the highest of these agencies should have knowledge of all that is going forward and that its will should penetrate everywhere, so as to exert its influence. And in fact the ego feels secure both as to the completeness and trustworthiness of the reports it receives and as to the openness of the channels through which it enforces its commands.

In certain diseases—including the very neuroses of which we have made special study—things are different. The ego feels uneasy; it comes up against limits to its power in its own house, the mind. Thoughts emerge suddenly without one's knowing where they come from, nor can one do anything to drive them away. These alien guests even seem to be more powerful than those which are at the ego's command. They resist all the well-proved measures of enforcement used by the will, remain unmoved by logical refutation, and are unaffected by the contradictory assertions of reality. Or else impulses appear which seem like those of a stranger, so that the ego disowns them; yet it has to fear them and take precautions against them. The ego says to itself: 'This is an illness, a foreign invasion.' It increases its vigilance, but cannot understand why it feels so strangely paralysed.

Psychiatry, it is true, denies that such things mean the intrusion into the mind of evil spirits from without; beyond this, however, it can only say with a shrug: 'Degeneracy, hereditary disposition, constitutional inferiority!' Psycho-analysis sets out to explain these uncanny disorders; it engages in careful and laborious investigations, devises hypotheses and scientific constructions, until at length it can speak thus to the ego:—

'Nothing has entered into you from without; a part of the activity of your own mind has been withdrawn from your knowledge and from the command of your will. That, too, is why you are so weak in your defence; you are using one part of your force to fight the other part and you cannot concentrate the whole of your force as you would against an external enemy. And it is not even the worst or least important part of your mental forces that has thus become antagonistic to you and independent of you. The blame, I am bound to say, lies with yourself. You over-estimated your strength when you thought you could treat your sexual instincts as you liked and could utterly ignore their intentions. The result is that they have rebelled and have taken their own obscure paths to escape this suppression; they have established their rights in a manner you cannot approve. How they have achieved this, and the paths which they have taken, have not come to your knowledge. All you have learned is the *outcome* of their work—the symptom which you experience as suffering. Thus you do not recognize it as a derivative of your own rejected instincts and do not know that it is a substitutive satisfaction of them.

'The whole process, however, only becomes possible through the single circumstance that you are mistaken in another important point as well. You feel sure that you are informed of all that goes on in your mind if it is of any importance at all, because in that case, you believe, your consciousness gives you news of it. And if you have had no information of something in your mind you confidently assume that it does not exist there. Indeed, you go so far as to regard what is "mental" as identical with what is "conscious"—that is, with what is known to you—in spite of the most obvious evidence that a great deal more must constantly be going on in your mind than can be known to your consciousness. Come, let yourself be taught something on this one point! What is in your mind does not coincide with what you are conscious of; whether something is going on in your mind and whether you hear of it, are two different things. In the ordinary way, I will admit, the intelligence which reaches your consciousness is enough for your needs; and you may cherish the illusion that you learn of all the more important things. But in some cases, as in that of an instinctual conflict such as I have described, your intelligence service breaks down and your will then extends no further than your knowledge. In every case, however, the news that reaches your consciousness is incomplete and often not to be relied on. Often enough, too, it happens that you get news of events only when they are over and when you can no longer do anything to change them. Even if you are not ill, who can tell all that is stirring in your mind of which you know nothing or are falsely informed? You behave like an absolute ruler who is content with the information supplied him by his highest officials and never goes among the people to hear their voice. Turn your eyes inward, look into your own depths, learn first to know yourself! Then you will understand why you were bound to fall ill; and perhaps, you will avoid falling ill in future.'

It is thus that psycho-analysis has sought to educate the ego. But these two discoveries—that the life of our sexual instincts cannot be wholly tamed, and that mental processes are in themselves unconscious and only reach the ego and come under its control through incomplete and untrustworthy perceptions—these two discoveries amount to a statement that *the ego is not master in its own house*. Together they represent the third blow to man's self-love, what I may call the *psychological* one. No wonder, then, that the ego does not look favourably upon psycho-analysis and obstinately refuses to believe in it.

Probably very few people can have realized the momentous significance for science and life of the recognition of unconscious mental processes. It was not psycho-analysis, however, let us hasten to add, which first took this step. There are famous philosophers who may be cited as forerunners—above all the great thinker Schopenhauer, whose unconscious 'Will' is equivalent to the mental instincts of psycho-analysis. It was this same thinker, moreover, who in words of unforgettable impressiveness admonished mankind of the importance, still so greatly under-estimated by it, of its sexual craving. Psycho-analysis has this advantage only, that it has not affirmed these two propositions which are so distressing to narcissism—the psychical importance of sexuality and the unconsciousness of mental life—on an *abstract* basis, but has demonstrated them in matters that touch every individual personally and force him to take up some attitude towards these problems. It is just for this reason, however, that it brings on itself the aversion and resistances which still hold back in awe before the great name of the philosopher.

A CHILDHOOD RECOLLECTION FROM *DICHTUNG UND WAHRHEIT* (1917)

EINE KINDHEITSERINNERUNG AUS *DICHTUNG UND WAHRHEIT*

(*a*) German Editions:

1917 *Imago*, **5** (2), 49–57.
1918 *S.K.S.N.*, **4**, 564–77 (1922, 2nd. ed.).
1924 *G.S.*, **10**, 357–68.
1924 *Dichtung und Kunst*, 87–98.
1947 *G.W.*, **12**, 15–26.

(*b*) English Translation:

'A Childhood Recollection from *Dichtung und Wahrheit*'
1925 *C.P.*, **4**, 357–67. (Tr. C. J. M. Hubback.)

The present translation is a considerably modified version of that published in 1925.

Freud gave the first part of this paper before the Vienna Psycho-Analytical Society on December 13, 1916 and the second part before the same society on April 18, 1917. The paper was not actually *written* by him until September, 1917, in the train on his way back from a summer holiday in the Tatra Mountains in Hungary. The date of publication is uncertain, since *Imago* appeared very irregularly at that time, owing to war conditions. A summary of his conclusions will be found in a long footnote which he added in 1919 to Chapter II of his study of a childhood memory of Leonardo da Vinci's (1910*c*).

A CHILDHOOD RECOLLECTION FROM *DICHTUNG UND WAHRHEIT*

'If we try to recollect what happened to us in the earliest years of childhood, we often find that we confuse what we have heard from others with what is really a possession of our own derived from what we ourselves have witnessed.' This remark is found on one of the first pages of Goethe's account of his life [*Dichtung und Wahrheit*], which he began to write at the age of sixty. It is preceded only by some information about his birth, which 'took place on August 28, 1749, at midday on the stroke of twelve'. The stars were in a favourable conjunction and may well have been the cause of his survival, for at his entry into the world he was 'as though dead', and it was only after great efforts that he was brought to life. There follows on this a short description of the house and of the place in it where the children—he and his younger sister—best liked to play. After this, however, Goethe relates in fact only one single event which can be assigned to the 'earliest years of childhood' (the years up to four?) and of which he seems to have preserved a recollection of his own.

The account of it runs as follows: 'And three brothers (von Ochsenstein by name) who lived over the way became very fond of me; they were orphan sons of the late magistrate, and they took an interest in me and used to tease me in all sorts of ways.

'My people used to like to tell of all kinds of pranks in which these men, otherwise of a serious and retiring disposition, used to encourage me. I will quote only one of these exploits. The crockery-fair was just over, and not only had the kitchen been fitted up from it with what would be needed for some time to come, but miniature utensils of the same sort had been bought for us children to play with. One fine afternoon, when all was quiet in the house, I was playing with my dishes and pots in the hall' (a place which had already been described, opening on to the street) 'and, since this seemed to lead to nothing, I threw a plate into the street, and was overjoyed to see it go to bits so merrily. The von Ochsensteins, who saw how delighted I was and how joyfully I clapped my little hands, called out "Do it again!" I did not hesitate to sling out a pot on to the paving-stones, and then, as they kept crying "Another!", one after another all my little dishes, cooking-pots and pans. My neighbours continued to show their approval and I was highly delighted to be amusing them. But my stock was all used up, and still they cried "Another!" So I ran off straight into the kitchen and fetched the earthenware plates, which made an even finer show as they smashed to bits. And thus I ran backwards and forwards, bringing one plate after another, as I could reach them in turn from the dresser; and, as they were not content with that, I hurled every piece of crockery I could get hold of to the same destruction. Only later did someone come and interfere and put a stop to it all. The damage was done, and to make up for so much broken earthenware there was at least an amusing story, which the rascals who had been its instigators enjoyed to the end of their lives.'

In pre-analytic days it was possible to read this without finding occasion to pause and without feeling surprised, but later on the analytic conscience became active. We had formed definite opinions and expectations about the memories of earliest childhood, and would have liked to claim universal validity for them. It should not be a matter of indifference or entirely without meaning which detail of a child's life had escaped the general oblivion. It might on the contrary be conjectured that what had remained in memory was the most significant element in that whole period of life, whether it had possessed such an importance at the time, or whether it had gained subsequent importance from the influence of later events.

The high value of such childish recollections was, it is true, obvious only in a few cases. Generally they seemed indifferent, worthless even, and it remained at first incomprehensible why just these memories should have resisted amnesia; nor could the person who had preserved them for long years as part of his own store of memories see more in them than any stranger to whom he might relate them. Before their significance could be appreciated, a certain work of interpretation was necessary. This interpretation either showed that their content required to be replaced by some other content, or revealed that they were related to some other unmistakably important experiences and had appeared in their place as what are known as 'screen memories'.[1]

[1] [See Chapter IV of *The Psychopathology of Everyday Life* (1901*b*).]

In every psycho-analytic investigation of a life-history it is always possible to explain the meaning of the earliest childhood memories along these lines. Indeed, it usually happens that the very recollection to which the patient gives precedence, which he relates first, with which he introduces the story of his life, proves to be the most important, the very one that holds the key to the secret pages of his mind.[1] But the little childish episode related in *Dichtung und Wahrheit* does not rise to our expectations. The ways and means that with our patients lead to interpretation are of course not available to us here; the episode does not seem in itself to admit of any traceable connection with important impressions at a later date. A mischievous trick with damaging effects on the household economy, carried out under the spur of outside encouragement, is certainly no fitting headpiece for all that Goethe has to tell us of his richly filled life. An impression of utter innocence and irrelevance clings to this childish memory, and it might be taken as a warning not to stretch the claims of psycho-analysis too far nor to apply it in unsuitable places.

The little problem, therefore, had long since slipped out of my mind, when one day chance brought me a patient in whom a similar childhood memory appeared in a clearer connection. He was a man of twenty-seven, highly educated and gifted, whose life at that time was entirely filled with a conflict with his mother that affected all his interests, and from the effects of which his capacity for love and his ability to lead an independent existence had suffered greatly. This conflict went far back into his childhood; certainly to his fourth year. Before that he had been a very weakly child, always ailing, and yet that sickly period was glorified into a paradise in his memory; for then he had had exclusive, uninterrupted possession of his mother's affection. When he was not yet four, a brother, who is still living, was born, and in his reaction to that disturbing event he became transformed into an obstinate, unmanageable boy, who perpetually provoked his mother's severity. Moreover, he never regained the right path.

When he came to me for treatment—by no means the least reason for his coming was that his mother, a religious bigot, had a horror of psycho-analysis—his jealousy of the younger

[1] [Cf. a footnote of Freud's near the beginning of his case history of the 'Rat Man' (1909*d*), *Standard Ed.*, **10**, 160.]

brother (which had once actually been manifested as a murderous attack on the infant in its cradle) had long been forgotten. He now treated his brother with great consideration; but certain curious fortuitous actions of his (which involved sudden and severe injuries to favourite animals, like his sporting dog or birds which he had carefully reared,) were probably to be understood as echoes of these hostile impulses against the little brother.

Now this patient related that, at about the time of the attack on the baby he so much hated, he had thrown all the crockery he could lay hands on out of the window of their country house into the road—the very same thing that Goethe relates of his childhood in *Dichtung und Wahrheit*! I may remark that my patient was of foreign nationality and was not acquainted with German literature; he had never read Goethe's autobiography.

This communication naturally suggested to me that an attempt might be made to explain Goethe's childish memory on the lines forced upon us by my patient's story. But could the necessary conditions for this explanation be shown to exist in the poet's childhood? Goethe himself, it is true, makes the instigation of the von Ochsenstein brothers responsible for his childish prank. But from his own narrative it can be seen that these grown-up neighbours merely encouraged him to go on with what he was doing. The beginning was on his own initiative, and the reason he gives for this beginning—'since this (the game) seemed to lead to nothing'—is surely, without any forcing of its meaning, a confession that at the time of writing it down and probably for many years previously he was not aware of any adequate motive for his behaviour.

It is well known that Johann Wolfgang and his sister Cornelia were the eldest survivors of a considerable family of very weakly children. Dr. Hanns Sachs has been so kind as to supply me with the following details concerning these brothers and sisters of Goethe's, who died in childhood:

(*a*) Hermann Jakob, baptized Monday, November 27, 1752; reached the age of six years and six weeks; buried January 13, 1759.

(*b*) Katharina Elisabetha, baptized Monday, September 9, 1754; buried Thursday, December 22, 1755. (One year and four months old).

(*c*) Johanna Maria, baptized Tuesday, March 29, 1757, and

buried Saturday, August 11, 1759. (Two years and four months old). (This was doubtless the very pretty and attractive little girl celebrated by her brother.)

(*d*) Georg Adolph, baptized Sunday, June 15, 1760; buried, eight months old, Wednesday, February 18, 1761.

Goethe's next youngest sister, Cornelia Friederica Christiana, was born on December 7, 1750, when he was fifteen months old. This slight difference in age almost excludes the possibility of her having been an object of jealousy. It is known that, when their passions awake, children never develop such violent reactions against the brothers and sisters they find already in existence, but direct their hostility against the newcomers. Nor is the scene we are endeavouring to interpret reconcilable with Goethe's tender age at the time of, or shortly after, Cornelia's birth.

At the time of the birth of the first little brother, Hermann Jakob, Johann Wolfgang was three and a quarter years old. Nearly two years later, when he was about five years old, the second sister was born. Both ages come under consideration in dating the episode of the throwing out of the crockery. The earlier is perhaps to be preferred; and it would best agree with the case of my patient, who was about three and a quarter years old at the birth of his brother.

Moreover, Goethe's brother Hermann Jakob, to whom we are thus led in our attempt at interpretation, did not make so brief a stay in the family nursery as the children born afterwards. One might feel some surprise that the autobiography does not contain a word of remembrance of him.[1] He was over six, and Johann Wolfgang was nearly ten, when he died. Dr. Hitschmann, who was kind enough to place his notes on this subject at my disposal, says:

'*Goethe, too, as a little boy saw a younger brother die without regret.* At least, according to Bettina Brentano his mother gave the following account: "It struck her as very extraordinary that he shed no tears at the death of his younger brother Jakob who was

[1] (*Footnote added* 1924:) I take this opportunity of withdrawing an incorrect statement which should not have been made. In a later passage in this first volume the younger brother *is* mentioned and described. It occurs in connection with memories of the serious illnesses of childhood, from which this brother also suffered 'not a little'. 'He was a delicate child, quiet and self-willed, and we never had much to do with each other. Besides, he hardly survived the years of infancy.'

his playfellow; he seemed on the contrary to feel annoyance at the grief of his parents and sisters. When, later on, his mother asked the young rebel if he had not been fond of his brother, he ran into his room and brought out from under the bed a heap of papers on which lessons and little stories were written, saying that he had done all this to teach his brother." So it seems all the same that the elder brother enjoyed playing father to the younger and showing him his superiority.'

The opinion might thus be formed that the throwing of crockery out of the window was a symbolic action, or, to put it more correctly, a *magic* action, by which the child (Goethe as well as my patient) gave violent expression to his wish to get rid of a disturbing intruder. There is no need to dispute a child's enjoyment of smashing things; if an action is pleasurable in itself, that is not a hindrance but rather an inducement to repeat it in obedience to other purposes as well. It is unlikely, however, that it could have been the pleasure in the crash and the breaking which ensured the childish prank a lasting place in adult memory. Nor is there any objection to complicating the motivation of the action by adding a further factor. A child who breaks crockery knows quite well that he is doing something naughty for which grown-ups will scold him, and if he is not restrained by that knowledge, he probably has a grudge against his parents that he wants to satisfy; he wants to show naughtiness.

The pleasure in breaking and in broken things would be satisfied, too, if the child simply threw the breakable object on the ground. The hurling them out of the window into the street would still remain unexplained. This 'out!' seems to be an essential part of the magic action and to arise directly from its hidden meaning. The new baby must be got rid of—through the window, perhaps because he came in through the window. The whole action would thus be equivalent to the verbal response, already familiar to us, of a child who was told that the stork had brought a little brother. 'The stork can take him away again!' was his verdict.[1]

All the same, we are not blind to the objections—apart from any internal uncertainties—against basing the interpretation of a childhood act on a single parallel. For this reason I had for

[1] [See *The Interpretation of Dreams* (1900*a*), Chapter V (D), *Standard Ed.*, **4**, 251.]

years kept back my theory about the little scene in *Dichtung und Wahrheit*. Then one day I had a patient who began his analysis with the following remarks, which I set down word for word: 'I am the eldest of a family of eight or nine children.[1] One of my earliest recollections is of my father sitting on the bed in his night-shirt, and telling me laughingly that I had a new brother. I was then three and three-quarters years old; that is the difference in age between me and my next younger brother. I know, too, that a short time after (or was it a year before?) [2] I threw a lot of things, brushes—or was it only one brush?—shoes and other things, out of the window into the street. I have a still earlier recollection. When I was two years old, I spent a night with my parents in a hotel bedroom at Linz on the way to the Salzkammergut. I was so restless in the night and made such a noise that my father had to beat me.'

After hearing this statement I threw all doubts to the winds. When in analysis two things are brought out one immediately after the other, as though in one breath, we have to interpret this proximity as a connection of thought. It was, therefore, as if the patient had said, '*Because* I found that I had got a new brother, I shortly afterwards threw these things into the street.' The act of flinging the brushes, shoes and so on, out of the window must be recognized as a reaction to the birth of the brother. Nor is it a matter for regret that in this instance the objects thrown out were not crockery but other things, probably anything the child could reach at the moment.—The hurling out (through the window into the street) thus proves to be the essential thing in the act, while the pleasure in the smashing and the noise, and the class of object on which 'execution is done', are variable and unessential points.

Naturally, the principle of there being a connection of thought must be applied as well to the patient's third childish recollection, which is the earliest, though it was put at the end of the short series. This can easily be done. Evidently the two-year-old child was so restless because he could not bear his

[1] A momentary error of a striking character. It was probably induced by the influence of the intention, which was already showing itself, to get rid of a brother. (Cf. Ferenczi, 1912, 'On Transitory Symptoms during Analysis'.)

[2] This doubt, attaching to the essential point of the communication for purposes of resistance, was shortly afterwards withdrawn by the patient of his own accord.

parents being in bed together. On the journey it was no doubt impossible to avoid the child being a witness of this. The feelings which were aroused at that time in the jealous little boy left him with an embitterment against women which persisted and permanently interfered with the development of his capacity for love.

After making these two observations I expressed the opinion at a meeting of the Vienna Psycho-Analytical Society that occurrences of the same kind might be not infrequent among young children; in response, Frau Dr. von Hug-Hellmuth placed two further observations at my disposal, which I append here.

I

'At the age of about three and a half, little Erich quite suddenly acquired the habit of throwing everything he did not like out of the window. He also did it, however, with things that were not in his way and did not concern him. On his father's birthday—he was three years and four and a half months old—he snatched a heavy rolling-pin from the kitchen, dragged it into the living-room and threw it out of the window of the third-floor flat into the street. Some days later he sent after it the kitchen-pestle, and then a pair of heavy mountaineering boots of his father's, which he had first to take out of the cupboard.[1]

'At that time his mother had a miscarriage, in the seventh or eighth month of pregnancy, and after that the child was "sweet and quiet and so good that he seemed quite changed". In the fifth or sixth month he repeatedly said to his mother, "Mummy, I'll jump on your tummy"—or, "I'll push your tummy in." And shortly before the miscarriage, in October, he said, "If I must have a brother, at least I don't want him till after Christmas." '

II

'A young lady of nineteen told me spontaneously that her earliest recollection was as follows: "I see myself, frightfully naughty, sitting under the table in the dining-room, ready to creep out. My cup of coffee is standing on the table—I can still

[1] 'He always chose heavy objects.'

see the pattern on the china quite plainly—and Granny comes into the room just as I am going to throw it out of the window.

' "For the fact was that no one had been bothering about me, and in the meantime a skin had formed on the coffee, which was always perfectly dreadful to me and still is.

' "On that day my brother, who is two and a half years younger than I am, was born, and so no one had had any time to spare for me.

' "They always tell me that I was insupportable on that day: at dinner I threw my father's favourite glass on the floor, I dirtied my frock several times, and was in the worst temper from morning to night. In my rage I tore a bath-doll to pieces." '

These two cases scarcely call for a commentary. They establish without further analytic effort that the bitterness children feel about the expected or actual appearance of a rival finds expression in throwing objects out of the window and in other acts of naughtiness and destructiveness. In the first case the 'heavy objects' probably symbolized the mother herself, against whom the child's anger was directed so long as the new baby had not yet appeared. The three-and-a-half-year-old boy knew about his mother's pregnancy and had no doubt that she had got the baby in her body. 'Little Hans'[1] and his special dread of heavily loaded carts may be recalled here.[2] In the second case the very youthful age of the child, two and a half years, is noteworthy.

If we now return to Goethe's childhood memory and put in the place it occupies in *Dichtung und Wahrheit* what we believe we have obtained through observations of other children, a

[1] Cf. 'Analysis of a Phobia in a Five-Year-Old Boy', (1909*b*) [*Standard Ed.*, **10**, 91 and 128].

[2] Further confirmation of this pregnancy-symbolism was given me some time ago by a lady of over fifty. She had often been told that as a little child, when she could hardly talk, she used to drag her father to the window in great agitation whenever a heavy furniture-van was passing along the street. In view of other recollections of the houses they had lived in, it became possible to establish that she was then younger than two and three quarter years. At about that time the brother next to her was born, and in consequence of this addition to the family a move was made. At about the same time, she often had an alarming feeling before going to sleep of something uncannily large, that came up to her, and 'her hands got so thick'.

perfectly valid train of thought emerges which we should not otherwise have discovered. It would run thus: 'I was a child of fortune: destiny preserved my life, although I came into the world as though dead. Even more, destiny removed my brother, so that I did not have to share my mother's love with him.' The train of thought [in *Dichtung und Wahrheit*] then goes on to someone else who died in those early days—the grandmother who lived like a quiet friendly spirit in another part of the house.

I have, however, already remarked elsewhere [1] that if a man has been his mother's undisputed darling he retains throughout life the triumphant feeling, the confidence in success, which not seldom brings actual success along with it. And Goethe might well have given some such heading to his autobiography as: 'My strength has its roots in my relation to my mother.'

[1] [In a footnote added in 1911 to Chapter VI (E) of *The Interpretation of Dreams* (1900*a*), *Standard Ed.*, **5**, 398*n*.]

LINES OF ADVANCE IN PSYCHO-ANALYTIC THERAPY
(1919 [1918])

WEGE DER PSYCHOANALYTISCHEN THERAPIE

(*a*) German Editions:

1919 *Int. Z. Psychoanal.*, **5** (2), 61–8.
1922 *S.K.S.N.*, **5**, 146–58.
1924 *Technik und Metapsychol.*, 136–47.
1925 *G.S.*, **6**, 136–47.
1931 *Neurosenlehre und Technik*, 411–22.
1947 *G.W.*, **12**, 183–94.

(*b*) English Translation:

'Turnings in the Ways of Psycho-Analytic Therapy'
1924 *C.P.*, **2**, 392–402. (Tr. Joan Riviere.)

The present translation, with a modified title, is based on the one published in 1924.

This address was read by Freud before the Fifth International Psycho-Analytical Congress, held at Budapest on September 28 and 29, 1918, shortly before the end of the first World War. It was written during the summer before the Congress, while he was staying with Anton von Freund (see p. 167, footnote 1) at his house in Steinbruch, a suburb of Budapest. The paper, in which the main stress is on the 'active' methods chiefly associated later with the name of Ferenczi, was the last of Freud's purely technical works before the two which he published nearly twenty years later (1937*c* and 1937*d*), towards the end of his life. He had already foreshadowed these 'active' methods in his address at the Nuremberg Congress (1910*d*).

LINES OF ADVANCE IN PSYCHO-ANALYTIC THERAPY

GENTLEMEN,—As you know, we have never prided ourselves on the completeness and finality of our knowledge and capacity. We are just as ready now as we were earlier to admit the imperfections of our understanding, to learn new things and to alter our methods in any way that can improve them.

Now that we are met together once more after the long and difficult years of separation that we have lived through, I feel drawn to review the position of our therapeutic procedure—to which, indeed, we owe our place in human society—and to take a survey of the new directions in which it may develop.

We have formulated our task as physicians thus: to bring to the patient's knowledge the unconscious, repressed impulses existing in him, and, for that purpose, to uncover the resistances that oppose this extension of his knowledge about himself. Does the uncovering of these resistances guarantee that they will also be overcome? Certainly not always; but our hope is to achieve this by exploiting the patient's transference to the person of the physician, so as to induce him to adopt our conviction of the inexpediency of the repressive process established in childhood and of the impossibility of conducting life on the pleasure principle. I have set out elsewhere [1] the dynamic conditions prevailing in the fresh conflict through which we lead the patient and which we substitute in him for his previous conflict—that of his illness. I have nothing at the moment to alter in that account.

The work by which we bring the repressed mental material into the patient's consciousness has been called by us psycho-analysis. Why 'analysis'—which means breaking up or separating out, and suggests an analogy with the work carried out by chemists on substances which they find in nature and bring into their laboratories? Because in an important respect there really is an analogy between the two. The patient's symptoms

[1] [Cf. Freud's technical paper 'Recollecting, Repeating and Working Through' (1914*g*) and Lecture XXVII of his *Introductory Lectures* (1916–17).]

and pathological manifestations, like all his mental activities, are of a highly composite kind; the elements of this compound are at bottom motives, instinctual impulses. But the patient knows nothing of these elementary motives or not nearly enough. We teach him to understand the way in which these highly complicated mental formations are compounded; we trace the symptoms back to the instinctual impulses which motivate them; we point out to the patient these instinctual motives, which are present in his symptoms and of which he has hitherto been unaware,—just as a chemist isolates the fundamental substance, the chemical 'element', out of the salt in which it had been combined with other elements and in which it was unrecognizable. In the same way, as regards those of the patient's mental manifestations that were not considered pathological, we show him that he was only to a certain extent conscious of their motivation—that other instinctual impulses of which he had remained in ignorance had co-operated in producing them.

Again, we have thrown light on the sexual impulsions in man by separating them into their component elements; and when we interpret a dream we proceed by ignoring the dream as a whole and starting associations from its single elements.

This well-founded comparison of medical psycho-analytic activity with a chemical procedure might suggest a new direction for our therapy. We have *analysed* the patient—that is, separated his mental processes into their elementary constituents and demonstrated these instinctual elements in him singly and in isolation; what could be more natural than to expect that we should also help him to make a new and a better combination of them? You know that this demand has actually been put forward. We have been told that after an analysis of a sick mind a synthesis of it must follow. And, close upon this, concern has been expressed that the patient might be given too much analysis and too little synthesis; and there has then followed a move to put all the weight on this synthesis as the main factor in the psychotherapeutic effect, to see in it a kind of restoration of something that had been destroyed—destroyed, as it were, by vivisection.

But I cannot think, Gentlemen, that any new task is set us by this psycho-synthesis. If I allowed myself to be frank and uncivil I should say it was nothing but an empty phrase. I will limit myself to remarking that it is merely pushing a comparison so far that it ceases to have any meaning, or, if you prefer, that it is an unjustifiable exploitation of a name. A name, however, is only a label applied to distinguish a thing from other similar things, not a syllabus, a description of its content or a definition. And the two objects compared need only coincide at a single point and may be entirely different from each other in everything else. What is psychical is something so unique and peculiar to itself that no one comparison can reflect its nature. The work of psycho-analysis suggests analogies with chemical analysis, but it does so just as much with the intervention of a surgeon or the manipulations of an orthopaedist or the influence of an educator. The comparison with chemical analysis has its limitation: for in mental life we have to deal with trends that are under a compulsion towards unification and combination. Whenever we succeed in analysing a symptom into its elements, in freeing an instinctual impulse from one nexus, it does not remain in isolation, but immediately enters into a new one.[1]

In actual fact, indeed, the neurotic patient presents us with a torn mind, divided by resistances. As we analyse it and remove the resistances, it grows together; the great unity which we call his ego fits into itself all the instinctual impulses which before had been split off and held apart from it.[2] The psycho-synthesis is thus achieved during analytic treatment without our intervention, automatically and inevitably. We have created the conditions for it by breaking up the symptoms into their elements and by removing the resistances. It is not true that something in the patient has been divided into its components and is now quietly waiting for us to put it somehow together again.

Developments in our therapy, therefore, will no doubt proceed along other lines; first and foremost, along the one which

[1] After all, something very similar occurs in chemical analysis. Simultaneously with the isolation of the various elements induced by the chemist, syntheses which are no part of his intention come about, owing to the liberation of the elective affinities of the substances concerned.

[2] [The synthetic function of the ego is discussed at greater length in Chapter III of *Inhibitions, Symptoms and Anxiety* (1926*d*).]

Ferenczi, in his paper 'Technical Difficulties in an Analysis of Hysteria' (1919),[1] has lately termed 'activity' on the part of the analyst.

Let us at once agree upon what we mean by this activity. We have defined our therapeutic task as consisting of two things: making conscious the repressed material and uncovering the resistances. In that we are active enough, to be sure. But are we to leave it to the patient to deal alone with the resistances we have pointed out to him? Can we give him no other help in this besides the stimulus he gets from the transference? Does it not seem natural that we should help him in another way as well, by putting him into the mental situation most favourable to the solution of the conflict which is our aim? After all, what he can achieve depends, too, on a combination of external circumstances. Should we hesitate to alter this combination by intervening in a suitable manner? I think activity of such a kind on the part of the analysing physician is unobjectionable and entirely justified.

You will observe that this opens up a new field of analytic technique the working over of which will require close application and which will lead to quite definite rules of procedure. I shall not attempt to-day to introduce you to this new technique, which is still in the course of being evolved, but will content myself with enunciating a fundamental principle which will probably dominate our work in this field. It runs as follows: *Analytic treatment should be carried through, as far as is possible, under privation—in a state of abstinence.*[2]

How far it is possible to show that I am right in this must be left to a more detailed discussion. By abstinence, however, is not to be understood doing without any and every satisfaction—that would of course not be practicable; nor do we mean what it popularly connotes, refraining from sexual intercourse; it means something else which has far more to do with the dynamics of falling ill and recovering.

You will remember that it was a *frustration* that made the patient ill, and that his symptoms serve him as substitutive

[1] [According to a statement by Ferenczi in the same paper, and to another in a later one (Ferenczi, 1921), the idea of this was based on an oral suggestion originally made to him by Freud himself.]

[2] [Freud had already mentioned this principle in connection with 'transference-love' (1915*a*).]

satisfactions.[1] It is possible to observe during the treatment that every improvement in his condition reduces the rate at which he recovers and diminishes the instinctual force impelling him towards recovery. But this instinctual force is indispensible; reduction of it endangers our aim—the patient's restoration to health. What, then, is the conclusion that forces itself inevitably upon us? Cruel though it may sound, we must see to it that the patient's suffering, to a degree that is in some way or other effective, does not come to an end prematurely. If, owing to the symptoms having been taken apart and having lost their value, his suffering becomes mitigated, we must re-instate it elsewhere in the form of some appreciable privation; otherwise we run the danger of never achieving any improvements except quite insignificant and transitory ones.

As far as I can see, the danger threatens from two directions in especial. On the one hand, when the illness has been broken down by the analysis, the patient makes the most assiduous efforts to create for himself in place of his symptoms new substitutive satisfactions, which now lack the feature of suffering. He makes use of the enormous capacity for displacement possessed by the now partly liberated libido, in order to cathect with libido and promote to the position of substitutive satisfactions the most diverse kinds of activities, preferences and habits, not excluding some that have been his already. He continually finds new distractions of this kind, into which the energy necessary to carrying on the treatment escapes, and he knows how to keep them secret for a time. It is the analyst's task to detect these divergent paths and to require him every time to abandon them, however harmless the activity which leads to satisfaction may be in itself. The half-recovered patient may also enter on less harmless paths—as when, for instance, if he is a man, he seeks prematurely to attach himself to a woman. It may be observed, incidently, that unhappy marriage and physical infirmity are the two things that most often supersede a neurosis. They satisfy in particular the sense of guilt (need for punishment) which makes many patients cling so fast to their neuroses. By a foolish choice in marriage they punish themselves; they regard a long organic illness as a punishment by fate and thereafter often cease to keep up their neurosis.

[1] [See the opening pages of 'Types of Onset of Neurosis' (Freud, 1912*c*).]

In all such situations activity on the part of the physician must take the form of energetic opposition to premature substitutive satisfactions. It is easier for him, however, to prevent the *second* danger which jeopardizes the propelling force of the analysis, though it is not one to be under-estimated. The patient looks for his substitutive satisfactions above all in the treatment itself, in his transference-relationship with the physician; and he may even strive to compensate himself by this means for all the other privations laid upon him. Some concessions must of course be made to him, greater or less, according to the nature of the case and the patient's individuality. But it is not good to let them become too great. Any analyst who out of the fullness of his heart, perhaps, and his readiness to help, extends to the patient all that one human being may hope to receive from another, commits the same economic error as that of which our non-analytic institutions for nervous patients are guilty. Their one aim is to make everything as pleasant as possible for the patient, so that he may feel well there and be glad to take refuge there again from the trials of life. In so doing they make no attempt to give him more strength for facing life and more capacity for carrying out his actual tasks in it. In analytic treatment all such spoiling must be avoided. As far as his relations with the physician are concerned, the patient must be left with unfulfilled wishes in abundance. It is expedient to deny him precisely those satisfactions which he desires most intensely and expresses most importunately.

I do not think I have exhausted the range of desirable activity on the part of the physician in saying that a condition of privation is to be kept up during the treatment. Activity in another direction during analytic treatment has already, as you will remember, been a point at issue between us and the Swiss school.[1] We refused most emphatically to turn a patient who puts himself into our hands in search of help into our private property, to decide his fate for him, to force our own ideals upon him, and with the pride of a Creator to form him in our own image and see that it is good. I still adhere to this refusal, and I think that this is the proper place for the medical discretion which we have had to ignore in other connections. I have learnt by experience, too, that such a far-reaching activity

[1] [Cf. the later part of Section III of Freud's 'History of the Psycho-Analytic Movement' (1914*d*).]

towards patients is not in the least necessary for therapeutic purposes. For I have been able to help people with whom I had nothing in common—neither race, education, social position nor outlook upon life in general—without affecting their individuality. At the time of the controversy I have just spoken of, I had the impression, to be sure, that the objections of our spokesmen—I think it was Ernest Jones who took the chief part[1]—were too harsh and uncompromising. We cannot avoid taking some patients for treatment who are so helpless and incapable of ordinary life that for them one has to combine analytic with educative influence; and even with the majority, occasions now and then arise in which the physician is bound to take up the position of teacher and mentor. But it must always be done with great caution, and the patient should be educated to liberate and fulfil his own nature, not to resemble ourselves.

Our honoured friend, J. J. Putnam, in the land of America which is now so hostile to us, must forgive us if we cannot accept his proposal either—namely that psycho-analysis should place itself in the service of a particular philosophical outlook on the world and should urge this upon the patient for the purpose of ennobling his mind. In my opinion, this is after all only to use violence, even though it is overlaid with the most honourable motives.[2]

Lastly, another quite different kind of activity is necessitated by the gradually growing appreciation that the various forms of disease treated by us cannot all be dealt with by the same technique. It would be premature to discuss this in detail, but I can give two examples of the way in which a new kind o activity comes into question. Our technique grew up in the treatment of hysteria and is still directed principally to the cure of that affection. But the phobias have already made it necessary for us to go beyond our former limits. One can hardly master a phobia if one waits till the patient lets the analysis influence him to give it up. He will never in that case bring into the analysis the material indispensable for a convincing

[1] [This may be a reference to the paper read by Ernest Jones at the Fourth (Munich) International Psycho-Analytical Congress held in 1913 (Jones, 1914).]

[2] [Some further comments on Putnam's psycho-analytic views will be found in Freud's Preface to Putnam's *Addresses on Psycho-Analysis* (Freud, 1921*a*).—See also below, p. 271.]

resolution of the phobia. One must proceed differently. Take the example of agoraphobia; there are two classes of it, one mild, the other severe. Patients belonging to the first class suffer from anxiety when they go into the street by themselves, but they have not yet given up going out alone on that account; the others protect themselves from the anxiety by altogether ceasing to go about alone. With these last one succeeds only when one can induce them by the influence of the analysis to behave like phobic patients of the first class—that is, to go into the street and to struggle with their anxiety while they make the attempt. One starts, therefore, by moderating the phobia so far; and it is only when that has been achieved at the physician's demand that the associations and memories come into the patient's mind which enable the phobia to be resolved.

In severe cases of obsessive acts a passive waiting attitude seems even less indicated. Indeed in general these cases incline to an 'asymptotic' process of recovery, an interminable protraction of the treatment. Their analysis is always in danger of bringing to light a great deal and changing nothing. I think there is little doubt that here the correct technique can only be to wait until the treatment itself has become a compulsion, and then with this counter-compulsion forcibly to suppress the compulsion of the disease. You will understand, however, that these two instances I have given you are only samples of the new developments towards which our therapy is tending.[1]

And now in conclusion I will cast a glance at a situation which belongs to the future—one that will seem fantastic to many of you, but which I think, nevertheless, deserves that we should be prepared for it in our minds. You know that our therapeutic activities are not very far-reaching. There are only a handful of us, and even by working very hard each one can devote himself in a year to only a small number of patients. Compared to the vast amount of neurotic misery which there is in the world, and perhaps need not be, the quantity we can do away with is almost negligible. Besides this, the necessities of our existence limit our work to the well-to-do classes, who are accustomed to choose their own physicians and whose choice is diverted away from psycho-analysis by all kinds of

[1] [Cf. the technical device described in the first section of the 'Wolf Man' analysis (1918*b*), p. 11 above.]

prejudices. At present we can do nothing for the wider social strata, who suffer extremely seriously from neuroses.

Now let us assume that by some kind of organization we succeeded in increasing our numbers to an extent sufficient for treating a considerable mass of the population. On the other hand, it is possible to foresee that at some time or other the conscience of society will awake and remind it that the poor man should have just as much right to assistance for his mind as he now has to the life-saving help offered by surgery; and that the neuroses threaten public health no less than tuberculosis, and can be left as little as the latter to the impotent care of individual members of the community. When this happens, institutions or out-patient clinics will be started, to which analytically-trained physicians will be appointed, so that men who would otherwise give way to drink, women who have nearly succumbed under their burden of privations, children for whom there is no choice but between running wild or neurosis, may be made capable, by analysis, of resistance and of efficient work. Such treatments will be free. It may be a long time before the State comes to see these duties as urgent. Present conditions may delay its arrival even longer. Probably these institutions will first be started by private charity. Some time or other, however, it must come to this.[1]

We shall then be faced by the task of adapting our technique to the new conditions. I have no doubt that the validity of our psychological assumptions will make its impression on the uneducated too, but we shall need to look for the simplest and most easily intelligible ways of expressing our theoretical doctrines. We shall probably discover that the poor are even less ready to part with their neuroses than the rich, because the hard life that awaits them if they recover offers them no attraction, and illness gives them one more claim to social help. Often, perhaps, we may only be able to achieve anything by combining mental assistance with some material support, in the manner of the Emperor Joseph.[2] It is very probable, too, that

[1] [At the time at which this address was delivered Anton von Freund was planning the foundation of an Institute of the kind suggested here. See Freud's obituary of von Freund (1920*c*).]

[2] [The Emperor Joseph II of Austria (1741–1790), about whose unconventional methods of philanthropy many legends were current. He is referred to in the same connection in one of Freud's earlier technical papers (1913*c*).]

the large-scale application of our therapy will compel us to alloy the pure gold of analysis freely with the copper of direct suggestion; and hypnotic influence, too, might find a place in it again, as it has in the treatment of war neuroses.[1] But, whatever form this psychotherapy for the people may take, whatever the elements out of which it is compounded, its most effective and most important ingredients will assuredly remain those borrowed from strict and untendentious psycho-analysis.

[1] [The treatment of war neuroses was a main topic at the Congress before which this address was given. (See p. 206.)]

ON THE TEACHING OF PSYCHO-ANALYSIS IN UNIVERSITIES
(1919 [1918])

KELL-E AZ EGYETEMEN A PSYCHOANALYSIST TANITANI?

(*a*) German Editions:

(1918 Probable date of composition.)

(1919 *Gyógyászat*, **59** (13), 192. In a Hungarian translation.)

(*b*) English Translation:

'On the Teaching of Psycho-Analysis in Universities'

No trace can be found of the original German text.

This paper was first published in a Hungarian translation (probably made by Ferenczi) in the Budapest medical periodical *Gyógyászat*, on March 30, 1919. The Hungarian title means literally: 'Should psycho-analysis be taught at the University?'. The paper seems to have been one of a series, by different writers, dealing with reforms in medical education. It is likely that Freud wrote it in the autumn of 1918, at about the time of the Fifth International Psycho-Analytical Congress in Budapest. There was then a considerable agitation among the medical students at Budapest for the inclusion of psycho-analysis in their curriculum. In March, 1919, when a Bolshevik government took temporary control in Hungary, Ferenczi was in fact installed as Professor of Psycho-Analysis at the University.—The rediscovery of the paper is due to the energy of Dr. Ludovico Rosenthal of Buenos Aires, and we are indebted to him for putting a photostat of the original publication at our disposal. The present translation from the Hungarian is based on one made by J. F. O'Donovan and Ludovico Rosenthal. It has been revised with the assistance of Dr. Michael Balint. Readers will understand that this is at best only a third-hand version of Freud's actual words.

ON THE TEACHING OF PSYCHO-ANALYSIS IN UNIVERSITIES

The question of the advisability of teaching psycho-analysis in Universities may be considered from two points of view: that of psycho-analysis and that of the University.

(1) The inclusion of psycho-analysis in the University curriculum would no doubt be regarded with satisfaction by every psycho-analyst. At the same time it is clear that the psycho-analyst can dispense entirely with the University without any loss to himself. For what he needs in the matter of theory can be obtained from the literature of the subject and, going more deeply, at the scientific meetings of the psycho-analytic societies as well as by personal contact with their more experienced members. As regards practical experience, apart from what he gains from his own personal analysis, he can acquire it by carrying out treatments, provided that he can get supervision and guidance from recognized psycho-analysts.

The fact that an organization of this kind exists is actually due to the exclusion of psycho-analysis from Universities. And it is therefore evident that these arrangements will continue to perform an effective function so long as this exclusion persists.

(2) So far as the Universities are concerned, the question depends on their deciding whether they are willing to attribute any value at all to psycho-analysis in the training of physicians and scientists. If so, the further problem remains of how it is to be incorporated into the regular educational framework.

The importance of psycho-analysis for the whole of medical and academic training is based on the following facts:

(*a*) This training has been quite rightly criticized during the last few decades for the one-sided way in which it directs the student into the fields of anatomy, physics and chemistry, while failing, on the other hand, to make plain to him the significance of mental factors in the different vital functions as well as in illnesses and their treatment. This short-coming in medical education makes itself felt later as a flagrant blind spot in the physician. This will not only show itself in his lack of interest in the most absorbing problems of human life, whether healthy or diseased, but will also render him unskilful in his treatment of patients, so that even quacks and 'healers' will have a greater effect on them than he does.

This obvious deficiency led some time ago to the inclusion in the University curriculum of courses of lectures on medical psychology. But so long as these lectures were based on academic psychology or on experimental psychology (which deals only with questions of detail), they were unable to meet the requirements of the student's training; nor could they bring him any nearer to the problems of life in general or to those of his profession. For these reasons the place occupied by this kind of medical psychology in the curriculum proved insecure.

A course of lectures on psycho-analysis, on the other hand, would certainly answer these requirements. Before coming to psycho-analysis proper, an introductory course would be needed, which would deal in detail with the relations between mental and physical life—the basis of all kinds of psychotherapy—, would describe the various kinds of suggestive procedures, and would finally show how psycho-analysis constitutes the outcome and culmination of all the earlier methods of mental treatment. Psycho-analysis, in fact, more than any other system, is fitted for teaching psychology to the medical student.

(*b*) Another of the functions of psycho-analysis should be to afford a preparation for the study of psychiatry. This, in its present shape, is exclusively descriptive in character; it merely teaches the student to recognize a series of pathological entities, enabling him to distinguish which are incurable and which are dangerous to the community. Its sole connection with the other branches of medical science lies in organic aetiology—that is, in its anatomical findings; but it offers not the slightest understanding of the facts observed. Such an understanding can be furnished only by a depth-psychology.

In America, according to the best of my information, it has already been recognized that psycho-analysis (the first attempt at a depth-psychology) has made successful inroads into this unexplored region of psychiatry. Many medical schools in that country, accordingly, have already organized courses of psycho-analysis as an introduction to psychiatry.

The teaching of psycho-analysis would have to proceed in

two stages: an elementary course, designed for all medical students, and a course of specialized lectures for psychiatrists.

(*c*) In the investigation of mental processes and intellectual functions, psycho-analysis pursues a specific method of its own. The application of this method is by no means confined to the field of psychological disorders, but extends also to the solution of problems in art, philosophy and religion. In this direction it has already yielded several new points of view and thrown valuable light on such subjects as the history of literature, on mythology, on the history of civilizations and on the philosophy of religion. Thus the general psycho-analytic course should be thrown open to the students of these branches of learning as well. The fertilizing effects of psycho-analytic thought on these other disciplines would certainly contribute greatly towards forging a closer link, in the sense of a *universitas literarum*, between medical science and the branches of learning which lie within the sphere of philosophy and the arts.

To sum up, it may be asserted that a University stands only to gain by the inclusion in its curriculum of the teaching of psycho-analysis. That teaching, it is true, can only be given in a dogmatic and critical manner, by means of theoretical lectures; for these lectures will allow only a very restricted opportunity for carrying out experiments or for practical demonstrations. For the purposes of research, it should be sufficient for teachers of psycho-analysis to have access to an out-patient department for the supply of the necessary material in the form of 'neurotic' patients. For psycho-analytic psychiatry, a mental in-patient department would also have to be available.

Consideration, lastly, must be given to the objection that, along these lines, the medical student will never learn psycho-analysis proper. This is indeed true, if we have in mind the actual practice of psycho-analysis. But for the purposes we have in view it will be enough if he learns something *about* psycho-analysis and something *from* it. After all, University training does not equip the medical student to be a skilled surgeon; and no one who chooses surgery as a profession can avoid further training in the form of several years of work in a surgical department of a hospital.

'A CHILD IS BEING BEATEN'
A CONTRIBUTION TO THE STUDY OF THE ORIGIN OF SEXUAL PERVERSIONS
(1919)

EDITOR'S NOTE

'EIN KIND WIRD GESCHLAGEN'

BEITRAG ZUR KENNTNIS DER ENTSTEHUNG SEXUELLER PERVERSIONEN

(*a*) German Editions:

1919 *Int. Z. Psychoanal.*, **5** (3), 151–72.
1922 *S.K.S.N.*, **5**, 195–228.
1924 *G.S.*, **5**, 344–75.
1926 *Psychoanalyse der Neurosen*, 50–84.
1931 *Sexualtheorie und Traumlehre*, 124–55.
1947 *G.W.*, **12**, 197–226.

(*b*) English Translation:

' "A Child is being Beaten"
A Contribution to the Study of the Origin of Sexual Perversions'

1920 *Int. J. Psycho-Anal.*, **1**, 371–95. (Tr. A. and J. Strachey.)
1924 *C.P.*, **2**, 172–201. (Same translators.)

The present translation is a corrected version of the one published in 1924.

In a letter to Ferenczi of January 24, 1919, Freud announced that he was writing a paper on masochism. The paper was finished and given its present title by the middle of March, 1919, and it was published in the summer of the same year.

The greater part of the paper consists of a very detailed clinical enquiry into a particular kind of perversion. Freud's findings throw special light on the problem of masochism; and, as the sub-title implies, the paper was also designed to extend our knowledge of the perversions in general. From this point of view, it may be regarded as a supplement to the first of Freud's *Three Essays on the Theory of Sexuality* (1905*d*).

In addition to this, however, the paper includes a discussion, to which Freud attached considerable importance, of the motives which cause repression to be put into operation, with special reference to two theories on the subject, proposed respectively by Fliess and Adler (cf. pp. 200–4). The *mechanism* of repression is exhaustively discussed in two of Freud's metapsychological papers—in 'Repression' (1915*d*) and in Section IV of 'The Unconscious' (1915*e*); but the question of the *motives* leading to repression, though it is touched upon in the last section of the analysis of the 'Wolf Man' (1918*b*), p. 110 f. of this volume, is nowhere examined more fully than in the present paper. The problem was, of course, one which had interested and also puzzled Freud from very early days, and there are many references to it in the Fliess correspondence (1950*a*). At the very end of his life Freud returned to it once more, in the last section of his 'Analysis Terminable and Interminable' (1937*c*), where he discussed the theories of Fliess and Adler once again.

'A CHILD IS BEING BEATEN'

A CONTRIBUTION TO THE STUDY OF THE ORIGIN OF SEXUAL PERVERSIONS

I

It is surprising how often people who seek analytic treatment for hysteria or an obsessional neurosis confess to having indulged in the phantasy: 'A child is being beaten.' Very probably there are still more frequent instances of it among the far greater number of people who have not been obliged to come to analysis by manifest illness.

The phantasy has feelings of pleasure attached to it, and on their account the patient has reproduced it on innumerable occasions in the past or may even still be doing so. At the climax of the imaginary situation there is almost invariably a masturbatory satisfaction—carried out, that is to say, on the genitals. At first this takes place voluntarily, but later on it does so in spite of the patient's efforts, and with the characteristics of an obsession.

It is only with hesitation that this phantasy is confessed to. Its first appearance is recollected with uncertainty. The analytic treatment of the topic is met by unmistakable resistance. Shame and a sense of guilt are perhaps more strongly excited in this connection than when similar accounts are given of memories of the beginning of sexual life.

Eventually it becomes possible to establish that the first phantasies of the kind were entertained very early in life: certainly before school age, and not later than in the fifth or sixth year. When the child was at school and saw other children being beaten by the teacher, then, if the phantasies had become dormant, this experience called them up again, or, if they were still present, it reinforced them and noticeably modified their content. From that time forward it was 'an indefinite number' of children that were being beaten. The influence of the school was so clear that the patients concerned were at first tempted to trace back their beating-phantasies exclusively to these impressions of school life, which dated from later than their sixth year. But it was never possible for them to maintain that position; the phantasies had already been in existence before.

Though in the higher forms at school the children were no longer beaten, the influence of such occasions was replaced and more than replaced by the effects of reading, of which the importance was soon to be felt. In my patients' *milieu* it was almost always the same books whose contents gave a new stimulus to the beating-phantasies: those accessible to young people, such as what was known as the '*Bibliothèque rose*'[1], *Uncle Tom's Cabin*, etc. The child began to compete with these works of fiction by producing his own phantasies and by constructing a wealth of situations and institutions, in which children were beaten, or were punished and disciplined in some other way, because of their naughtiness and bad behaviour.

This phantasy—'a child is being beaten'—was invariably cathected with a high degree of pleasure and had its issue in an act of pleasurable auto-erotic satisfaction. It might therefore be expected that the sight of another child being beaten at school would also be a source of similar enjoyment. But as a matter of fact this was never so. The experience of real scenes of beating at school produced in the child who witnessed them a peculiarly excited feeling which was probably of a mixed character and in which repugnance had a large share. In a few cases the real experience of the scenes of beating was felt to be intolerable. Moreover, it was always a condition of the more sophisticated phantasies of later years that the punishment should do the children no serious injury.

The question was bound to arise of what relation there might be between the importance of the beating-phantasies and the part that real corporal punishment might have played in the child's bringing up at home. It was impossible, on account of the one-sidedness of the material, to confirm the first suspicion that the relation was an inverse one. The individuals from whom the data for these analyses were derived very seldom beaten in their childhood, or were at all events not brought up by the help of the rod. Naturally, however, each of these children was bound to have become aware at one time or another of the superior physical strength of its parents or educators; the fact

[1] [A well-known series of books by Mme. de Ségur, of which *Les Malheurs de Sophie* was perhaps the most popular.]

that in every nursery the children themselves at times come to blows requires no special emphasis.

As regards the early and simple phantasies which could not be obviously traced to the influence of school impressions or of scenes taken from books, further information would have been welcome. Who was the child that was being beaten? The one who was himself producing the phantasy or another? Was it always the same child or as often as not a different one? Who was it that was beating the child? A grown-up person? And if so, who? Or did the child imagine that he himself was beating another one? Nothing could be ascertained that threw any light upon all these questions—only the hesitant reply: 'I know nothing more about it: a child is being beaten.'

Enquiries as to the sex of the child that was being beaten met with more success, but none the less brought no enlightenment. Sometimes the answer was: 'Always boys', or 'Only girls'; more often it was: 'I don't know', or 'It doesn't matter which'. But the point to which the questions were directed, the discovery of some constant relation between the sex of the child producing the phantasy and that of the child that was being beaten, was never established. Now and again another characteristic detail of the content of the phantasy came to light: 'A small child is being beaten on its naked bottom.'

In these circumstances it was impossible at first even to decide whether the pleasure attaching to the beating-phantasy was to be described as sadistic or masochistic.

II

A phantasy of this kind, arising, perhaps from accidental causes, in early childhood and retained for the purpose of auto-erotic satisfaction, can, in the light of our present knowledge, only be regarded as a primary trait of perversion. One of the components of the sexual function has, it seems, developed in advance of the rest, has made itself prematurely independent, has undergone fixation and in consequence been withdrawn from the later processes of development, and has in this way given evidence of a peculiar and abnormal constitution in the individual. We know that an infantile perversion of this sort need not persist for a whole lifetime; later on it can be subjected to repression, be replaced by a reaction-formation, or be transformed by sublimation. (It is possible that sublimation arises out of some special process [1] which would be held back by repression.) But if these processes do not take place, then the perversion persists to maturity; and whenever we find a sexual aberration in adults—perversion, fetishism, inversion—we are justified in expecting that anamnestic investigation will reveal an event such as I have suggested, leading to a fixation in childhood. Indeed, long before the days of psycho-analysis, observers like Binet were able to trace the strange sexual aberrations of maturity back to similar impressions and to precisely the same period of childhood, namely, the fifth or sixth year.[2] But at this point the enquiry was confronted with the limitations of our knowledge; for the impressions that brought about the fixation were without any traumatic force. They were for the most part commonplace and unexciting to other people. It was impossible to say why the sexual impulse had undergone fixation particularly upon them. It was possible, however, to look for their significance in the fact that they offered an occasion for fixation (even though it was an accidental one) to precisely that component which was prematurely developed and ready to press forward. We had in any case to be prepared to come to a provisional end somewhere or other in tracing back the train of causal connection; and the congenital constitution seemed exactly to correspond with what was required for a stopping-place of that kind.

If the sexual component which has broken loose prematurely is the sadistic one, then we may expect, on the basis of knowledge derived from other sources, that its subsequent repression will result in a disposition to an obsessional neurosis.[3] This expectation cannot be said to be contradicted by the results of enquiry. The present short paper is based on the exhaustive study of six cases (four female and two male). Of these, two were cases of obsessional neurosis; one extremely severe and incapacitating, the other of moderate severity and quite well accessible to influence. There was also a third case which at all

[1] [This may be related to the theory of sublimation touched upon in Chapter III of *The Ego and the Id* (1923*b*).]

[2] [This observation of Binet's (1888) was mentioned by Freud in his *Three Essays* (1905*d*) and commented upon in a footnote added to that work in 1920 (*Standard Ed.*, **7**, 154).]

[3] [See 'The Predisposition to Obsessional Neurosis' (1913*i*).]

events exhibited clearly marked individual traits of obsessional neurosis. The fourth case, it must be admitted, was one of straightforward hysteria, with pains and inhibitions; and the fifth patient, who had come to be analysed merely on account of indecisiveness in life, would not have been classified at all by coarse clinical diagnosis, or would have been dismissed as 'psychasthenic'.[1] There is no need for feeling disappointed over these statistics. In the first place, we know that not every disposition is necessarily developed into a disorder; in the second place, we ought to be content to explain the facts before us, and ought as a rule to avoid the additional task of making it clear why something has *not* taken place.

The present state of our knowledge would allow us to make our way so far and no further towards the comprehension of beating-phantasies. In the mind of the analytic physician, it is true, there remains an uneasy suspicion that this is not a final solution of the problem. He is obliged to admit to himself that to a great extent these phantasies subsist apart from the rest of the content of a neurosis, and find no proper place in its structure. But impressions of this kind, as I know from my own experience, are only too willingly put on one side.

III

Strictly considered—and why should this question not be considered with all possible strictness?—analytic work deserves to be recognized as genuine psycho-analysis only when it has succeeded in removing the amnesia which conceals from the adult his knowledge of his childhood from its beginning (that is, from about the second to the fifth year). This cannot be said among analysts too emphatically or repeated too often. The motives for disregarding this reminder are, indeed, intelligible. It would be desirable to obtain practical results in a shorter period and with less trouble. But at the present time theoretical knowledge is still far more important to all of us than therapeutic success, and anyone who neglects childhood analysis is bound to fall into the most disastrous errors. The emphasis which is laid here upon the importance of the earliest experiences does not imply any underestimation of the influence of later ones. But the later impressions of life speak loudly enough through

[1] [Nothing is said here of the sixth case.]

the mouth of the patient, while it is the physician who has to raise his voice on behalf of the claims of childhood.

It is in the years of childhood between the ages of two and four or five that the congenital libidinal factors are first awakened by actual experiences and become attached to certain complexes. The beating-phantasies which are now under discussion show themselves only towards the end of this period or after its termination. So it may quite well be that they have an earlier history, that they go through a process of development, that they represent an end-product and not an initial manifestation.

This suspicion is confirmed by analysis. A systematic application of it shows that beating-phantasies have a historical development which is by no means simple, and in the course of which they are changed in most respects more than once—as regards their relation to the author of the phantasy, and as regards their object, their content and their significance.

In order to make it easier to follow these transformations in beating-phantasies I shall now venture to confine my descriptions to the female cases, which, since they are four as against two, in any case constitute the greater part of my material. Moreover, beating-phantasies in men are connected with another subject, which I shall leave on one side in this paper.[1] In my description I shall be careful to avoid being more schematic than is inevitable for the presentation of an average case. If then on further observation a greater complexity of circumstances should come to light, I shall nevertheless be sure of having before us a typical occurrence, and one, moreover, that is not of an uncommon kind.

The first phase of beating-phantasies among girls, then, must belong to a very early period of childhood. Some features remain curiously indefinite, as though they were a matter of indifference. The scanty information given by the patients in their first statement, 'a child is being beaten', seems to be justified in respect to this phase. But another of their features can be established with certainty, and to the same effect in every case. The child being beaten is never the one producing the phantasy, but is invariably another child, most often a brother or a sister

[1] [Freud does in fact discuss beating-phantasies in men below (p. 196 ff.). Their specifically feminine basis is what he probably has in mind in speaking of 'another subject'.]

if there is any. Since this other child may be a boy or a girl, there is no constant relation between the sex of the child producing the phantasy and that of the child being beaten. The phantasy, then, is certainly not masochistic. It would be tempting to call it sadistic, but one cannot neglect the fact that the child producing the phantasy is never doing the beating herself. The actual identity of the person who does the beating remains obscure at first. Only this much can be established: it is not a child but an adult. Later on this indeterminate grown-up person becomes recognizable clearly and unambiguously as the (girl's) *father*.

This first phase of the beating-phantasy is therefore completely represented by the phrase: '*My father is beating the child.*' I am betraying a great deal of what is to be brought forward later when instead of this I say: 'My father is beating the child *whom I hate.*' Moreover, one may hesitate to say whether the characteristics of a 'phantasy' can yet be ascribed to this first step towards the later beating-phantasy. It is perhaps rather a question of recollections of events which have been witnessed, or of desires which have arisen on various occasions. But these doubts are of no importance.

Profound transformations have taken place between this first phase and the next. It is true that the person beating remains the same (that is, the father); but the child who is beaten has been changed into another one and is now invariably the child producing the phantasy. The phantasy is accompanied by a high degree of pleasure, and has now acquired a significant content, with the origin of which we shall be concerned later. Now, therefore, the wording runs: '*I am being beaten by my father.*' It is of an unmistakably masochistic character.

This second phase is the most important and the most momentous of all. But we may say of it in a certain sense that it has never had a real existence. It is never remembered, it has never succeeded in becoming conscious. It is a construction of analysis, but it is no less a necessity on that account.

The third phase once more resembles the first. It has the wording which is familiar to us from the patient's statement. The person beating is never the father, but is either left undetermined just as in the first phase, or turns in a characteristic way into a representative of the father, such as a teacher. The figure of the child who is producing the beating-phantasy no longer itself appears in it. In reply to pressing enquiries the patients only declare: 'I am probably looking on.' Instead of the one child that is being beaten, there are now a number of children present as a rule. Most frequently it is boys who are being beaten (in girls' phantasies), but none of them is personally known to the subject. The situation of being beaten, which was originally simple and monotonous, may go through the most complicated alterations and elaborations; and punishments and humiliations of another kind may be substituted for the beating itself. But the essential characteristic which distinguishes even the simplest phantasies of this phase from those of the first, and which establishes the connection with the intermediate phase, is this: the phantasy now has strong and unambiguous sexual excitement attached to it, and so provides a means for masturbatory satisfaction. But this is precisely what is puzzling. By what path has the phantasy of strange and unknown boys being beaten (a phantasy which has by this time become sadistic) found its way into the permanent possession of the little girl's libidinal trends?

Nor can we conceal from ourselves that the interrelations and sequence of the three phases of the beating-phantasy, as well as all its other peculiarities, have so far remained quite unintelligible.

IV

If the analysis is carried through the early period to which the beating-phantasies are referred and from which they are recollected, it shows us the child involved in the agitations of its parental complex.

The affections of the little girl are fixed on her father, who has probably done all he could to win her love, and in this way has sown the seeds of an attitude of hatred and rivalry towards her mother. This attitude exists side by side with a current of affectionate dependence on her, and as years go on it may be destined to come into consciousness more and more clearly and forcibly, or else to give an impetus to an excessive reaction of devotion to her. But it is not with the girl's relation to her mother that the beating-phantasy is connected. There are other children in the nursery, only a few years older or younger, who are disliked on all sorts of other grounds, but chiefly because the parents' love has to be shared with them, and for this reason they are repelled with all the wild energy characteristic of the emotional life of those years. If the child in question is a younger brother or sister (as in three of my four cases) it is despised as well as hated; yet it attracts to itself the share of affection which the blinded parents are always ready to give the youngest child, and this is a spectacle the sight of which cannot be avoided. One soon learns that being beaten, even if it does not hurt very much, signifies a deprivation of love and a humiliation. And many children who believed themselves securely enthroned in the unshakable affection of their parents have by a single blow been cast down from all the heavens of their imaginary omnipotence. The idea of the father beating this hateful child is therefore an agreeable one, quite apart from whether he has actually been seen doing so. It means: 'My father does not love this other child, *he loves only me*.'

This then is the content and meaning of the beating-phantasy in its first phase. The phantasy obviously gratifies the child's jealousy and is dependent upon the erotic side of its life, but is also powerfully reinforced by the child's egoistic interests. Doubt remains, therefore, whether the phantasy ought to be described as purely 'sexual', nor can one venture to call it 'sadistic'.

As is well known, all the signs on which we are accustomed to base our distinctions tend to lose their clarity as we come nearer to the source. So perhaps we may say in terms recalling the prophecy made by the Three Witches to Banquo: 'Not clearly sexual, not in itself sadistic, but yet the stuff from which both will later come.' In any case, however, there is no ground for suspecting that in this first phase the phantasy is already at the service of an excitation which involves the genitals and finds its outlet in a masturbatory act.

It is clear that the child's sexual life has reached the stage of genital organization, now that its incestuous love has achieved this premature choice of an object. This can be demonstrated more easily in the case of boys, but is also indisputable in the case of girls. Something like a premonition of what are later to be the final and normal sexual aims governs the child's libidinal trends. We may justly wonder why this should be so, but we may regard it as a proof of the fact that the genitals have already begun playing their part in the process of excitation. With boys the wish to beget a child from their mother is never absent, with girls the wish to have a child by their father is equally constant; and this in spite of their being completely incapable of forming any clear idea of the means for fulfilling these wishes. The child seems to be convinced that the genitals have something to do with the matter, even though in its constant brooding it may look for the essence of the presumed intimacy between its parents in relations of another sort, such as in their sleeping together, micturating in each other's presence, etc.; and material of the latter kind can be more easily apprehended in verbal images than the mystery that is connected with the genitals.

But the time comes when this early blossoming is nipped by the frost. None of these incestuous loves can avoid the fate of repression. They may succumb to it on the occasion of some discoverable external event which leads to disillusionment—such as unexpected slights, the unwelcome birth of a new brother or sister (which is felt as faithlessness), etc.; or the same thing may happen owing to internal conditions apart from any such events, perhaps simply because their yearning remains unsatisfied too long. It is unquestionably true that such events are not the *effective* causes, but that these love-affairs are bound to come to grief sooner or later, though we cannot say on what particular stumbling block. Most probably they pass away because their time is over, because the children have entered upon a new phase of development in which they are compelled to recapitulate from the history of mankind the repression of an incestuous object-choice, just as at an earlier stage they were obliged to effect an object-choice of that very sort.[1] In the new phase no mental product of the incestuous love-impulses that is present unconsciously is taken over by consciousness; and anything that has already come into consciousness is expelled from it. At the same time as this process of repression takes place, a sense of guilt appears. This is also of unknown origin, but there is no doubt whatever that it is connected with the incestuous wishes, and that it is justified by the persistence of those wishes in the unconscious.[2]

[1] Compare the part played by Fate in the myth of Oedipus.

[2] [*Footnote added* 1924:] See the continuation of this line of thought in 'The Dissolution of the Oedipus Complex' (1924*d*).

The phantasy of the period of incestuous love had said: 'He (my father) loves only me, and not the other child, for he is beating it.' The sense of guilt can discover no punishment more severe than the reversal of this triumph: 'No, he does not love you, for he is beating you.' In this way the phantasy of the second phase, that of being beaten by her father, is a direct expression of the girl's sense of guilt, to which her love for her father has now succumbed. The phantasy, therefore, has become masochistic. So far as I know, this is always so; a sense of guilt is invariably the factor that transforms sadism into masochism. But this is certainly not the whole content of masochism. The sense of guilt cannot have won the field alone; a share must also fall to the love-impulse. We must remember that we are dealing with children in whom the sadistic component was able for constitutional reasons to develop prematurely and in isolation. We need not abandon this point of view. It is precisely such children who find it particularly easy to hark back to the pregenital, sadistic-anal organization of their sexual life. If the genital organization, when it has scarcely been effected, is met by repression, the result is not only that every psychical representation of the incestuous love becomes unconscious, or remains so, but there is another result as well: a regressive debasement of the genital organization itself to a lower level. 'My father loves me' was meant in a genital sense; owing to the regression it is turned into 'My father is beating me (I am being beaten by my father)'. This being beaten is now a convergence of the sense of guilt and sexual love. *It is not only the punishment for the forbidden genital relation, but also the regressive substitute for that relation*, and from this latter source it derives the libidinal excitation which is from this time forward attached to it, and which finds its outlet in masturbatory acts. Here for the first time we have the essence of masochism.

This second phase—the child's phantasy of being itself beaten by its father—remains unconscious as a rule, probably in consequence of the intensity of the repression. I cannot explain why nevertheless in one of my six cases, that of a male, it was consciously remembered. This man, now grown up, had preserved the fact clearly in his memory that he used to employ the idea of being beaten by his mother for the purpose of masturbation, though to be sure he soon substituted for his own mother the mothers of his school-fellows or other women who in some way resembled her. It must not be forgotten that when a boy's incestuous phantasy is transformed into the corresponding masochistic one, one more reversal has to take place than in the case of a girl, namely the substitution of passivity for activity; and this additional degree of distortion may save the phantasy from having to remain unconscious as a result of repression. In this way the sense of guilt would be satisfied by regression instead of by repression. In the female cases the sense of guilt, in itself perhaps more exacting, could be appeased only by a combination of the two.

In two of my four female cases an elaborate superstructure of day-dreams, which was of great significance for the life of the person concerned, had grown up over the masochistic beating-phantasy. The function of this superstructure was to make possible a feeling of satisfied excitation, even though the masturbatory act was abstained from. In one of these cases the content—being beaten by the father—was allowed to venture again into consciousness, so long as the subject's own ego was made unrecognizable by a thin disguise. The hero of these stories was invariably beaten (or later only punished, humiliated, etc.) by his father.

I repeat, however, that as a rule the phantasy remains unconscious, and can only be reconstructed in the course of the analysis. This fact perhaps vindicates patients who say they remember that with them masturbation made its appearance before the third phase of the beating-phantasy (shortly to be discussed), and that this phase was only a later addition, made perhaps under the impression of scenes at school. Every time I have given credit to these statements I have felt inclined to assume that the masturbation was at first under the dominance of unconscious phantasies and that conscious ones were substituted for them later.

I look upon the beating-phantasy in its familiar third phase, which is its final form, as a substitute of this sort. Here the child who produces the phantasy appears almost as a spectator, while the father persists in the shape of a teacher or some other person in authority. The phantasy, which now resembles that of the first phase, seems to have become sadistic once more. It appears as though in the phrase, 'My father is beating the child, he loves only me', the stress has been shifted back on to the first part after the second part has undergone repression.

But only the *form* of this phantasy is sadistic; the satisfaction which is derived from it is masochistic. Its significance lies in the fact that it has taken over the libidinal cathexis of the repressed portion and at the same time the sense of guilt which is attached to the content of that portion. All of the many unspecified children who are being beaten by the teacher are, after all, nothing more than substitutes for the child itself.

We find here for the first time, too, something like a constancy of sex in the persons who play a part in the phantasy. The children who are being beaten are almost invariably boys, in the phantasies of boys just as much as in those of girls. This characteristic is naturally not to be explained by any rivalry between the sexes, as otherwise of course in the phantasies of boys it would be girls who would be being beaten; and it has nothing to do with the sex of the child who was hated in the first phase. But it points to a complication in the case of girls. When they turn away from their incestuous love for their father, with its genital significance, they easily abandon their feminine role. They spur their 'masculinity complex' (Van Ophuijsen, 1917) into activity, and from that time forward only want to be boys. For that reason the whipping-boys who represent them are boys too. In both the cases of day-dreaming —one of which almost rose to the level of a work of art—the heroes were always young men; indeed women used not to come into these creations at all, and only made their first appearance after many years, and then in minor parts.

V

I hope I have brought forward my analytic observations in sufficient detail, and I should only like to add that the six cases I have mentioned so often do not exhaust my material. Like other analysts, I have at my disposal a far larger number of cases which have been investigated less thoroughly. These observations can be made use of along various lines: for elucidating the genesis of the perversions in general and of masochism in particular, and for estimating the part played by difference of sex in the dynamics of neurosis.

The most obvious result of such a discussion is its application to the origin of the perversions. The view which brought into the foreground in this connection the constitutional reinforcement or premature growth of a single sexual component is not shaken, indeed; but it is seen not to comprise the whole truth. The perversion is no longer an isolated fact in the child's sexual life, but falls into its place among the typical, not to say normal, processes of development which are familiar to us. It is brought into relation with the child's incestuous love-object, with its Oedipus complex. It first comes into prominence in the sphere of this complex, and after the complex has broken down it remains over, often quite by itself, the inheritor of the charge of libido from that complex and weighed down by the sense of guilt that was attached to it. The abnormal sexual constitution, finally, has shown its strength by forcing the Oedipus complex into a particular direction, and by compelling it to leave an unusual residue behind.

A perversion in childhood, as is well known, may become the basis for the construction of a perversion having a similar sense and persisting throughout life, one which consumes the subject's whole sexual life. On the other hand the perversion may be broken off and remain in the background of a normal sexual development, from which, however, it continues to withdraw a certain amount of energy. The first of these alternatives was already known before the days of analysis. Analytic investigation, however, of such fully-developed cases almost bridges the gulf between the two. For we find often enough with these perverts that they too made an attempt at developing normal sexual activity, usually at the age of puberty; but their attempt had not enough force in it and was abandoned in the face of the first obstacles which inevitably arise, whereupon they fell back upon their infantile fixation once and for all.

It would naturally be important to know whether the origin of infantile perversions from the Oedipus complex can be asserted as a general principle. While this cannot be decided without further investigation, it does not seem impossible. When we recall the anamneses which have been obtained in adult cases of perversion we cannot fail to notice that the decisive impression, the 'first experience', of all these perverts, fetishists, etc., is scarcely ever referred back to a time earlier than the sixth year. At this time, however, the dominance of the Oedipus complex is already over; the experience which is recalled, and which has been effective in such a puzzling way, may very well have represented the legacy of that complex. The connections between the experience and the complex which is by this time repressed are bound to remain obscure so long as analysis has not thrown any light on the time before the first 'pathogenic' impression. So it may be imagined how little value is to be attached, for instance, to an assertion that a case of homosexuality is congenital, when the ground given for this belief is that ever since his eighth or sixth year the person in question has felt inclinations only towards his own sex.

If, however, the derivation of perversions from the Oedipus complex can be generally established, our estimate of its importance will have gained added strength. For in our opinion the Oedipus complex is the actual nucleus of neuroses, and the infantile sexuality which culminates in this complex is the true determinant of neuroses. What remains of the complex in the unconscious represents the disposition to the later development of neuroses in the adult. In this way the beating-phantasy and other analogous perverse fixations would also only be precipitates of the Oedipus complex, scars, so to say, left behind after the process has ended, just as the notorious 'sense of inferiority' corresponds to a narcissistic scar of the same sort. In taking this view of the matter I must express my unreserved agreement with Marcinowski (1918), who has recently put it forward most happily. As is well known, this neurotic delusion of inferiority is only a partial one, and is completely compatible with the existence of a self-overvaluation derived from other sources. The origin of the Oedipus complex itself, and the destiny which compels man, probably alone among all animals, to begin his sexual life twice over, first like all other creatures in his early childhood, and then after a long interruption once more at the age of puberty—all the problems that are connected with man's 'archaic heritage'—have been discussed by me elsewhere, and I have no intention of going into them in this place.[1]

Little light is thrown upon the genesis of masochism by our discussion of the beating-phantasy. To begin with, there seems to be a confirmation of the view that masochism is not the

[1] [Freud had discussed these questions at length, not long before, in his *Introductory Lectures* (1916–17), especially in Lectures XXI and XXIII. Cf. also below, pp. 261–2.]

manifestation of a primary instinct, but originates from sadism which has been turned round upon the self—that is to say, by means of regression from an object to the ego.[1] Instincts with a passive aim must be taken for granted as existing, especially among women. But passivity is not the whole of masochism. The characteristic of unpleasure belongs to it as well,—a bewildering accompaniment to the satisfaction of an instinct. The transformation of sadism into masochism appears to be due to the influence of the sense of guilt which takes part in the act of repression. Thus repression is operative here in three ways: it renders the consequences of the genital organization unconscious, it compels that organization itself to regress to the earlier sadistic-anal stage, and it transforms the sadism of this stage into masochism, which is passive and again in a certain sense narcissistic. The second of these three effects is made possible by the weakness of the genital organization, which must be presupposed in these cases. The third becomes necessary because the sense of guilt takes as much objection to sadism as to incestuous object-choice genitally conceived. Again, the analyses do not tell us the origin of the sense of guilt itself. It seems to be brought along by the new phase upon which the child is entering, and, if it afterwards persists, it seems to correspond to a scar-like formation which is similar to the sense of inferiority. According to our present orientation in the structure of the ego, which is as yet uncertain, we should assign it to the agency in the mind which sets itself up as a critical conscience over against the rest of the ego, which produces Silberer's functional phenomenon in dreams, and which cuts itself loose from the ego in delusions of being watched.[2]

We may note too in passing that the analysis of the infantile perversion dealt with here is also of help in solving an old riddle—one which, it is true, has always troubled those who have not accepted psycho-analysis more than analysts themselves. Yet quite recently even Bleuler regarded it as a remarkable and inexplicable fact that neurotics make masturba-

[1] Cf. 'Instincts and their Vicissitudes' (1915*c*).—[In *Beyond the Pleasure Principle* (1920*g*), *Standard Ed.*, **18**, 54–5, Freud suggested that there might after all be a primary masochism.]

[2] [See Part III of Freud's paper on narcissism (1914*c*). This agency was, of course, later described as the 'super-ego'. Cf. Chapter III of *The Ego and the Id* (1923*b*).]

tion the central point of their sense of guilt. We have long assumed that this sense of guilt relates to the masturbation of early childhood and not to that of puberty, and that in the main it is to be connected not with the act of masturbation but with the phantasy which, although unconscious, lies at its root—that is to say, with the Oedipus complex.[1]

As regards the third and apparently sadistic phase of the beating-phantasy, I have already [pp. 190–1] discussed the significance that it gains as the vehicle of the excitation impelling towards masturbation; and I have shown how it arouses activities of the imagination which on the one hand continue the phantasy along the same line, and on the other hand neutralize it through compensation. Nevertheless the second phase, the unconscious and masochistic one, in which the child itself is being beaten by its father, is incomparably the more important. This is not only because it continues to operate through the agency of the phase that takes its place; we can also detect effects upon the character, which are directly derived from its unconscious form. People who harbour phantasies of this kind develop a special sensitiveness and irritability towards anyone whom they can include in the class of fathers. They are easily offended by a person of this kind, and in that way (to their own sorrow and cost) bring about the realization of the imagined situation of being beaten by their father. I should not be surprised if it were one day possible to prove that the same phantasy is the basis of the delusional litigiousness of paranoia.

VI

It would have been quite impossible to give a clear survey of infantile beating-phantasies if I had not limited it, except in one or two connections, to the state of things in females. I will briefly recapitulate my conclusions. The little girl's beating-phantasy passes through three phases, of which the first and third are consciously remembered, the middle one remaining unconscious. The two conscious phases appear to be sadistic, whereas the middle and unconscious one is undoubtedly of a masochistic nature; its content consists in the child's being beaten by her father, and it carries with it the libidinal charge

[1] [See for example a discussion in the 'Rat Man' case history (1909*d*), *Standard Ed.*, **10**, 202 ff.]

and the sense of guilt. In the first and third phantasies the child who is being beaten is always someone other than the subject; in the middle phase it is always the child herself; in the third phase it is almost invariably only boys who are being beaten. The person who does the beating is from the first her father, replaced later on by a substitute taken from the class of fathers. The unconscious phantasy of the middle phase had primarily a genital significance and developed by means of repression and regression out of an incestuous wish to be loved by the father. Another fact, though its connection with the rest does not appear to be close, is that between the second and third phases the girls change their sex, for in the phantasies of the latter phase they turn into boys.

I have not been able to get so far in my knowledge of beating-phantasies in boys, perhaps because my material was unfavourable. I naturally expected to find a complete analogy between the state of things in the case of boys and in that of girls, the mother taking the father's place in the phantasy. This expectation seemed to be fulfilled; for the content of the boy's phantasy which was taken to be the corresponding one was actually his being beaten by his mother (or later on by a substitute for her). But this phantasy, in which the boy's own self was retained as the person who was being beaten, differed from the second phase in girls in that it was able to become conscious. If on this account, however, we attempt to draw a parallel between it and the *third* phase of the girl's phantasy, a new difference is found, for the figure of the boy himself is not replaced by a number of unknown, and unspecified children, least of all by a number of girls. Therefore the expectation of there being a complete parallel was mistaken.

My male cases with an infantile beating-phantasy comprised only a few who did not exhibit some other gross injury to their sexual activities; again they included a fairly large number of persons who would have to be described as true masochists in the sense of being sexual perverts. They were either people who obtained their sexual satisfaction exclusively from masturbation accompanied by masochistic phantasies; or they were people who had succeeded in combining masochism with their genital activity in such a way that, along with masochistic performances and under similar conditions, they were able to bring about erection and emission or to carry out normal intercourse.

In addition to this there was the rarer case in which a masochist is interfered with in his perverse activities by the appearance of obsessional ideas of unbearable intensity. Now perverts who can obtain satisfaction do not often have occasion to come for analysis. But as regards the three classes of masochists that have been mentioned there may be strong motives to induce them to go to an analyst. The masochist masturbator finds that he is absolutely impotent if after all he does attempt intercourse with a woman; and the man who has hitherto effected intercourse with the help of a masochistic idea or performance may suddenly make the discovery that the alliance which was so convenient for him has broken down, his genital organs no longer reacting to the masochistic stimulus. We are accustomed confidently to promise recovery to psychically impotent patients who come to us for treatment; but we ought to be more guarded in making this prognosis so long as the dynamics of the disturbance are unknown to us. It comes as a disagreeable surprise if the analysis reveals the cause of the 'merely psychical' impotence to be a typically masochistic attitude, perhaps deeply embedded since infancy.

As regards these masochistic men, however, a discovery is made at this point which warns us not to pursue the analogy between their case and that of women any further at present, but to judge each independently. For the fact emerges that in their masochistic phantasies, as well as in the performances they go through for their realization, they invariably transfer themselves into the part of a woman; that is to say, their masochistic attitude coincides with a *feminine* one. This can easily be demonstrated from details of the phantasies; but many patients are even aware of it themselves, and give expression to it as a subjective conviction. It makes no difference if in a fanciful embellishment of the masochistic scene they keep up the fiction that a mischievous boy, or page, or apprentice is going to be punished. On the other hand the persons who administer chastisement are always women, both in the phantasies and the performances. This is confusing enough; and the further question must be asked whether this feminine attitude already forms the basis of the masochistic element in the *infantile* beating-phantasy.[1]

[1] [*Footnote added* 1924:] Further remarks on this subject will be found in 'The Economic Problem of Masochism' (1924*c*).

Let us therefore leave aside consideration of the state of things in cases of adult masochism, which it is so hard to clear up, and turn to the infantile beating-phantasy in the male sex. Analysis of the earliest years of childhood once more allows us to make a surprising discovery in this field. The phantasy which has as its content being beaten by the mother, and which is conscious or can become so, is not a primary one. It possesses a preceding stage which is invariably unconscious and has as its content: '*I am being beaten by my father.*' This preliminary stage, then, really corresponds to the second phase of the phantasy in the girl. The familiar and conscious phantasy: 'I am being beaten by my mother', takes the place of the third phase in the girl, in which, as has been mentioned already, unknown boys are the objects that are being beaten. I have not been able to demonstrate among boys a preliminary stage of a sadistic nature that could be set beside the first phase of the phantasy in girls, but I will not now express any final disbelief in its existence, for I can readily see the possibility of meeting with more complicated types.

In the male phantasy—as I shall call it briefly, and, I hope, without any risk of being misunderstood—the being beaten also stands for being loved (in a genital sense), though this has been debased to a lower level owing to regression. So the original form of the unconscious male phantasy was not the provisional one that we have hitherto given: 'I am being beaten by my father', but rather: '*I am loved by my father*'. The phantasy has been transformed by the processes with which we are familiar into the conscious phantasy: '*I am being beaten by my mother*'. The boy's beating-phantasy is therefore passive from the very beginning, and is derived from a feminine attitude towards his father. It corresponds with the Oedipus complex just as the female one (that of the girl) does; only the parallel relation which we expected to find between the two must be given up in favour of a common character of another kind. *In both cases the beating-phantasy has its origin in an incestuous attachment to the father.*[1]

It will help to make matters clearer if at this point I enumerate the other similarities and differences between beating-phantasies in the two sexes. In the case of the girl the un-

[1] [A beating-phantasy plays some little part in the analysis of the 'Wolf Man' (1918*b*). See above, pp. 26 and 47.]

conscious masochistic phantasy starts from the normal Oedipus attitude; in that of the boy it starts from the inverted attitude, in which the father is taken as the object of love. In the case of the girl the phantasy has a preliminary stage (the first phase), in which the beating bears no special significance and is performed upon a person who is viewed with jealous hatred. Both of these features are absent in the case of the boy, but this particular difference is one which might be removed by more fortunate observation. In her transition to the conscious phantasy [the third phase] which takes the place of the unconscious one, the girl retains the figure of her father, and in that way keeps unchanged the sex of the person beating; but she changes the figure and sex of the person being beaten, so that eventually a man is beating male children. The boy, on the contrary, changes the figure and sex of the person beating, by putting his mother in the place of his father; but he retains his own figure, with the result that the person beating and the person being beaten are of opposite sexes. In the case of the girl what was originally a masochistic (passive) situation is transformed into a sadistic one by means of repression, and its sexual quality is almost effaced. In the case of the boy the situation remains masochistic, and shows a greater resemblance to the original phantasy with its genital significance, since there is a difference of sex between the person beating and the person being beaten. The boy evades his homosexuality by repressing and remodelling his unconscious phantasy: and the remarkable thing about his later conscious phantasy is that it has for its content a feminine attitude without a homosexual object-choice. By the same process, on the other hand, the girl escapes from the demands of the erotic side of her life altogether. She turns herself in phantasy into a man, without herself becoming active in a masculine way, and is no longer anything but a spectator of the event which takes the place of a sexual act.

We are justified in assuming that no great change is effected by the *repression* of the original unconscious phantasy. Whatever is repressed from consciousness or replaced in it by something else remains intact and potentially operative in the unconscious. The effect of *regression* to an earlier stage of the sexual organization is quite another matter. As regards this we are led to believe that the state of things changes in the unconscious as well. Thus in both sexes the masochistic phantasy of being beaten by the father, though not the passive phantasy of being loved by him, lives on in the unconscious after repression has taken place. There are, besides, plenty of indications that the repression has only very incompletely attained its object. The boy, who has tried to escape from a homosexual object-choice, and who has not changed his sex, nevertheless feels like a woman in his conscious phantasies, and endows the women who are beating him with masculine attributes and characteristics. The girl, who has even renounced her sex, and who has on the whole accomplished a more thoroughgoing work of repression, nevertheless does not become freed from her father; she does not venture to do the beating herself; and since she has herself become a boy, it is principally boys whom she causes to be beaten.

I am aware that the differences that I have here described between the two sexes in regard to the nature of the beating-phantasy have not been cleared up sufficiently. But I shall not attempt to unravel these complications by tracing out their dependence on other factors, as I do not consider that the material for observation is exhaustive. So far as it goes, however, I should like to make use of it as a test for two theories. These theories stand in opposition to each other, though both of them deal with the relation between repression and sexual character, and each, according to its own view, represents the relation as a very intimate one. I may say at once that I have always regarded both theories as incorrect and misleading.

The first of these theories is anonymous. It was brought to my notice many years ago by a colleague with whom I was at that time on friendly terms.[1] The theory is so attractive on account of its bold simplicity that the only wonder is that it should not have found its way into the literature of the subject except in a few scattered allusions. It is based on the fact of the bisexual constitution of human beings, and asserts that the motive force of repression in each individual is a struggle between the two sexual characters. The dominant sex of the person, that which is the more strongly developed, has repressed the mental representation of the subordinated sex into the

[1] [Near the end of Freud's 'Analysis Terminable and Interminable (1937*c*), where he refers back to the present passage, he attributes this theory to Wilhelm Fliess.]

unconscious. Therefore the nucleus of the unconscious (that is to say, the repressed) is in each human being that side of him which belongs to the opposite sex. Such a theory as this can only have an intelligible meaning if we assume that a person's sex is to be determined by the formation of his genitals; for otherwise it would not be certain which is a person's stronger sex and we should run the risk of reaching from the results of our enquiry the very fact which has to serve as its point of departure. To put the theory briefly: with men, what is unconscious and repressed can be brought down to feminine instinctual impulses; and conversely with women.

The second theory is of more recent origin.[1] It is in agreement with the first one in so far as it too represents the struggle between the two sexes as being the decisive cause of repression. In other respects it comes into conflict with the former theory; moreover, it looks for support to sociological rather than biological sources. According to this theory of the 'masculine protest', formulated by Alfred Adler, every individual makes efforts not to remain on the inferior 'feminine line [of development]' and struggles towards the 'masculine line', from which satisfaction can alone be derived. Adler makes the masculine protest responsible for the whole formation both of character and of neuroses. Unfortunately he makes so little distinction between the two processes, which certainly have to be kept separate, and sets altogether so little store in general by the fact of repression, that to attempt to apply the doctrine of the masculine protest to repression brings with it the risk of misunderstanding. In my opinion such an attempt could only lead us to infer that the masculine protest, the desire to break away from the feminine line, was in every case the motive force of repression. The repressing agency, therefore, would always be a masculine instinctual impulse, and the repressed would be a feminine one. But symptoms would also be the result of a feminine impulse, for we cannot discard the characteristic feature of symptoms—that they are substitutes for the repressed, substitutes that have made their way out in spite of repression.

Now let us take these two theories, which may be said to have in common a sexualization of the process of repression,

[1] [Adler's theory of repression was discussed briefly in the case history of the 'Wolf Man' (1918*b*), p. 110 f. above.]

and test them by applying them to the example of the beating-phantasies which we have been studying. The original phantasy, 'I am being beaten by my father', corresponds, in the case of the boy, to a feminine attitude, and is therefore an expression of that part of his disposition which belongs to the opposite sex. If this part of him undergoes repression, the first theory seems shown to be correct; for this theory set it up as a rule that what belongs to the opposite sex is identical with the repressed. It scarcely answers to our expectations, it is true, when we find that the conscious phantasy, which arises after repression has been accomplished, nevertheless exhibits the feminine attitude once more, though this time directed towards the mother. But we will not go into such doubtful points, when the whole question can be so quickly decided. There can be no doubt that the original phantasy in the case of the girl, 'I am being beaten (i.e. I am loved) by my father', represents a feminine attitude, and corresponds to her dominant and manifest sex; according to the theory, therefore, it ought to escape repression, and there would be no need for its becoming unconscious. But as a matter of fact it does become unconscious, and is replaced by a conscious phantasy which disavows the girl's manifest sexual character. The theory is therefore useless as an explanation of beating-phantasies, and is contradicted by the facts. It might be objected that it is precisely in unmanly boys and unwomanly girls that these beating-phantasies appeared and went through these vicissitudes; or that it was a trait of femininity in the boy and of masculinity in the girl which must be made responsible for the production of a passive phantasy in the boy, and its repression in the girl. We should be inclined to agree with this view, but it would not be any the less impossible to defend the supposed relation between manifest sexual character and the choice of what is destined for repression. In the last resort we can only see that both in male and female individuals masculine as well as feminine instinctual impulses are found, and that each can equally well undergo repression and so become unconscious.

The theory of the masculine protest seems to maintain its ground very much better on being tested in regard to the beating-phantasies. In the case of both boys and girls the beating-phantasy corresponds with a feminine attitude—one, that is, in which the individual is lingering on the 'feminine line'—and both sexes hasten to get free from this attitude by repressing the phantasy. Nevertheless, it seems to be only with the girl that the masculine protest is attended with complete success, and in that instance, indeed, an ideal example is to be found of the operation of the masculine protest. With the boy the result is not entirely satisfactory; the feminine line is not given up, and the boy is certainly not 'on top' in his conscious masochistic phantasy. It would therefore agree with the expectations derived from the theory if we were to recognize that this phantasy was a symptom which had come into existence through the failure of the masculine protest. It is a disturbing fact, to be sure, that the girl's phantasy, which owes its origin to the forces of repression, also has the value and meaning of a symptom. In this instance, where the masculine protest has completely achieved its object, surely the determining condition for the formation of a symptom must be absent.

Before we are led by this difficulty to a suspicion that the whole conception of the masculine protest is inadequate to meet the problem of neuroses and perversions, and that its application to them is unfruitful, we will for a moment leave the passive beating-phantasies and turn our attention to other instinctual manifestations of infantile sexual life—manifestations which have equally undergone repression. No one can doubt that there are also wishes and phantasies which keep to the masculine line from their very nature, and which are the expression of masculine instinctual impulses—sadistic tendencies, for instance, or a boy's lustful feelings towards his mother arising out of the normal Oedipus complex. It is no less certain that these impulses, too, are overtaken by repression. If the masculine protest is to be taken as having satisfactorily explained the repression of passive phantasies (which later become masochistic), then it becomes for that very reason totally inapplicable to the opposite case of active phantasies. That is to say, the doctrine of the masculine protest is altogether incompatible with the fact of repression. Unless we are prepared to throw away all that has been acquired in psychology since Breuer's first cathartic treatment and through its agency, we cannot expect that the principle of the masculine protest will acquire any significance in the elucidation of the neuroses and perversions.

The theory of psycho-analysis (a theory based on observation) holds firmly to the view that the motive forces of repression must not be sexualized. Man's archaic heritage forms the nucleus of the unconscious mind; and whatever part of that heritage has to be left behind in the advance to later phases of development, because it is unserviceable or incompatible with what is new and harmful to it, falls a victim to the process of repression. This selection is made more successfully with one group of instincts than with the other. In virtue of special circumstances which have often been pointed out already,[1] the latter group, that of the sexual instincts, are able to defeat the intentions of repression, and to enforce their representation by substitutive formations of a disturbing kind. For this reason infantile sexuality, which is held under repression, acts as the chief motive force in the formation of symptoms; and the essential part of its content, the Oedipus complex, is the nuclear complex of neuroses. I hope that in this paper I have raised an expectation that the sexual aberrations of childhood, as well as those of mature life, are ramifications of the same complex.

[1] [See for instance Freud's paper 'Formulations on the Two Principles of Mental Functioning' (1911*b*).]

INTRODUCTION TO *PSYCHO-ANALYSIS AND THE WAR NEUROSES* (1919)

INTRODUCTION TO *ZUR PSYCHOANALYSE DER KRIEGSNEUROSEN*

(*a*) GERMAN EDITIONS:

1919 Leipzig and Vienna: Internationaler Psychoanalytischer Verlag. 3–7.

1928 *G.S.*, **11**, 252–5.

1931 *Neurosenlehre und Technik*, 310–15.

1947 *G.W.*, **12**, 321–4.

(*b*) ENGLISH TRANSLATIONS:

Introduction to *Psycho-Analysis and the War Neuroses*

1921 London, Vienna and New York: International Psycho-Analytical Press. 1–4.

1950 *C.P.*, **5**, 83–7. (Tr. J. Strachey.) (Under the title 'Psycho-Analysis and War Neuroses'.)

It seems probable that the translation published in 1921 was by Ernest Jones. The present translation is a slightly corrected version of the one published in 1950.

The proceedings at the Fifth International Psycho-Analytical Congress, held at Budapest on September 28 and 29, 1918, at which Freud read the paper on p. 159 ff. above, also included a symposium on 'The Psycho-Analysis of War Neuroses', which was opened with three papers read respectively by Sándor Ferenczi, Karl Abraham and Ernst Simmel. These three papers, together with another on the same topic by Ernest Jones, which had been read in London before the Royal Society of Medicine on April 9, 1918, were published a year later in a small volume, the first to be issued by the newly founded Internationaler Psychoanalytischer Verlag (see below, p. 267). They were there preceded by the present short introduction by Freud. In the original English translation, but not in any of the German editions, this introduction is dated 'Spring, 1919'.

Freud returned to the subject of the treatment of war neuroses in a Memorandum presented by him to a Commission set up by the Austrian War Ministry in the following year (Freud 1955*c* [1920]). This is printed as an appendix to this paper.

INTRODUCTION TO *PSYCHO-ANALYSIS AND THE WAR NEUROSES*

This small book on the war neuroses—the opening volume of our *Internationale Psychoanalytische Bibliothek*—deals with a subject which until recently enjoyed the advantage of being in the greatest degree topical. When it came up for discussion at the Fifth Psycho-Analytical Congress, which was held in Budapest in September, 1918, official representatives from the highest quarters of the Central European Powers were present as observers at the papers and other proceedings. The hopeful result of this first contact was that the establishment of psycho-analytic Centres was promised, at which analytically trained physicians would have leisure and opportunity for studying the nature of these puzzling disorders and the therapeutic effect exercised on them by psycho-analysis. Before these proposals could be put into effect, the war came to an end, the state organizations collapsed and interest in the war neuroses gave place to other concerns. It is, however, a significant fact that, when war conditions ceased to operate, the greater number of the neurotic disturbances brought about by the war simultaneously vanished. The opportunity for a thorough investigation of these affections was thus unluckily lost—though, we must add, the early recurrence of such an opportunity is not a thing to be desired.

But this episode, though it is now closed, was not without an important influence on the spread of psycho-analysis. Medical men who had hitherto held back from any approach to psycho-analytic theories were brought into closer contact with them when, in the course of their duties as army doctors, they were obliged to deal with war neuroses. The reader will be able to gather from Ferenczi's paper with what hesitations and under what disguises these closer contacts were made. Some of the factors which psycho-analysis had recognized and described long before as being at work in peace-time neuroses—the psychogenic origin of the symptoms, the importance of *unconscious* instinctual impulses, the part played in dealing with mental conflicts by the primary gain from being ill ('the flight into illness')—were observed to be present equally in the war neuroses and were accepted almost universally. Simmel's studies show, too, what successes could be achieved by treating war neurotics by the method of catharsis, which, as we know, was the first step towards the psycho-analytic technique.

There is, however, no need to consider that these approaches to psycho-analysis imply any reconciliation or any appeasement of opposition. Suppose someone has hitherto rejected the whole of a complex of interdependent propositions, but now suddenly finds himself in a position to convince himself of the truth of one portion of the whole. It might be thought that he will begin to hesitate about his opposition in general and permit himself some degree of deferent expectation that the other portion, about which he has had no personal experience and can consequently form no judgement of his own, may also turn out to be true. This other portion of psycho-analytic theory, with which the study of the war neuroses did not come into contact, is to the effect that the motive forces which are expressed in the formation of symptoms are sexual and that neuroses arise from a conflict between the ego and the sexual instincts which it repudiates. ('Sexuality' in this context is to be understood in the extended sense in which it is used in psycho-analysis and is not to be confused with the narrower concept of 'genitality'.) Now it is quite true, as Ernest Jones remarks in his contribution to this volume, that this portion of the theory has not yet been proved to apply to the war neuroses. The work that might prove it has not yet been taken in hand. It may be that the war neuroses are altogether unsuitable material for the purpose. But the opponents of psycho-analysis, whose dislike of sexuality is evidently stronger than their logic, have been in a hurry to proclaim that the investigation of the war neuroses has finally disproved this portion of psycho-analytic theory. They have been guilty here of a slight confusion. If the investigation of the war neuroses (and a very superficial one at that) has *not shown* that the sexual theory of the neuroses is *correct*, that is something very different from its *showing* that that theory is *incorrect*. With the help of an impartial attitude and a little good will, it should not be hard to find the way to a further clarification of the subject.

The war neuroses, in so far as they are distinguished from the ordinary neuroses of peace-time by special characteristics, are to be regarded as traumatic neuroses whose occurrence has been made possible or has been promoted by a conflict in the ego. Abraham's paper affords good evidence for this conflict, which has also been recognized by the English and American writers quoted by Jones. The conflict is between the soldier's old peaceful ego and his new warlike one, and it becomes acute as soon as the peace-ego realizes what danger it runs of losing its life owing to the rashness of its newly formed, parasitic double. It would be equally true to say that the old ego is protecting itself from a mortal danger by taking flight into a traumatic neurosis or to say that it is defending itself against the new ego which it sees is threatening its life. Thus the precondition of the war neuroses, the soil that nourishes them, would seem to be a national [conscript] army; there would be no possibility of their arising in an army of professional soldiers or mercenaries.

Apart from this, the war neuroses are only traumatic neuroses, which, as we know, occur in peace-time too after frightening experiences or severe accidents, without any reference to a conflict in the ego.

The theory of the sexual aetiology of the neuroses, or, as we prefer to say, the libido theory of the neuroses, was originally put forward only in relation to the transference neuroses of peace-time and is easy to demonstrate in their case by the use of the technique of analysis. But its application to the other disorders which we later grouped together as the narcissistic neuroses already met with difficulties. An ordinary dementia praecox, a paranoia or a melancholia are essentially quite unsuitable material for demonstrating the validity of the libido theory or for serving as a first introduction to an understanding of it; and it is for that reason that psychiatrists, who neglect the transference neuroses, are unable to come to terms with it. But the traumatic neuroses of peace-time have always been regarded as the most refractory material of all in this respect; so that the emergence of the war neuroses could not introduce any new factor into the situation that already existed.

It only became possible to extend the libido theory to the narcissistic neuroses after the concept of a 'narcissistic libido' had been put forward and applied—a concept, that is, of an amount of sexual energy attached to the ego itself and finding satisfaction in the ego just as satisfaction is usually found only in objects. This entirely legitimate development of the concept of sexuality promises to accomplish as much for the severer neuroses and for the psychoses as can be expected of a theory which is feeling its way forwards on an empirical basis. The traumatic neuroses of peace will also fit into the scheme as soon as a successful outcome has been reached of our investigations into the relations which undoubtedly exist between fright, anxiety and narcissistic libido.

The traumatic neuroses and war neuroses may proclaim too loudly the effects of mortal danger and may be silent or speak only in muffled tones of the effects of frustration in love. But, on the other hand, the ordinary transference neuroses of peace-time set no aetiological store by the factor of mortal danger which, in the former class of neuroses, plays so mighty a part. It is even held that the peace-time neuroses are promoted by indulgence, good living and inactivity—which would afford an interesting contrast to the living-conditions under which the war neuroses develop. If they were to follow the example of their opponents, psycho-analysts, finding that their patients had fallen ill owing to frustration in love (owing to the claims of the libido being unsatisfied) would have to maintain that there can be no such things as danger-neuroses or that the disorders that appear after frightening experiences are not neuroses. They have, of course, no notion of maintaining any such thing. On the contrary, a convenient possibility occurs to them of bringing the two apparently divergent sets of facts together under a single hypothesis. In traumatic and war neuroses the human ego is defending itself from a danger which threatens it from without or which is embodied in a shape assumed by the ego itself. In the transference neuroses of peace the enemy from which the ego is defending itself is actually the libido, whose demands seem to it to be menacing. In both cases the ego is afraid of being damaged—in the latter case by the libido and in the former by external violence. It might, indeed, be said that in the case of the war neuroses, in contrast to the pure traumatic neuroses and in approximation to the transference neuroses, what is feared is nevertheless an internal enemy. The theoretical difficulties standing in the way of a unifying hypothesis of this kind do not seem insuperable: after all, we have a perfect right to describe repression, which lies at the basis of every neurosis, as a reaction to a trauma—as an elementary traumatic neurosis.

APPENDIX

Memorandum on the Electrical Treatment of War Neurotics[1]

(1955 [1920])

There were plenty of patients even in peace-time who, after traumas (that is, after frightening and dangerous experiences such as railway accidents, etc.) exhibited severe disturbances in their mental life and in their nervous activity, without physicians having reached an agreed judgement on these states. Some supposed that with such patients it was a question of severe injuries to the nervous system, similar to the haemorrhages and inflammations occurring in non-traumatic illnesses. And when anatomical examination failed to establish such processes, they nevertheless maintained their belief that finer changes in the tissues were the cause of the symptoms observed. They therefore classed these traumatic cases among the organic diseases. Other physicians maintained from the first that these

[1] [At the end of the first World War, after the break-up of the Austro-Hungarian Empire, many reports became current in Vienna that men suffering from war neuroses had been brutally treated by the army doctors. An enquiry into the matter was therefore instituted by the Austrian War Ministry, in the course of which Freud was called upon to give an expert opinion. He accordingly submitted a memorandum to the commission responsible for the enquiry, and subsequently appeared before them for oral examination. His memorandum was traced in the Archives of the War Ministry by Professor Josef Gicklhorn, of the University of Vienna, who has most generously put a photostat at our disposal. We are further indebted to Dr. K. R. Eissler, of New York (Secretary of the Sigmund Freud Archives), for having first drawn our attention to the document. The original MS occupies five and a half of the large foolscap sheets used habitually by Freud. The document is headed, in his handwriting: 'Gutachten über die elektrische Behandlung der Kriegsneurotiker von Prof. Dr. Sigm. Freud', and is dated by him: 'Wien, 23.2.20'. An official stamp at the top of the first page records that the memorandum was received by the 'Kommission zur Erhebung militärischer Pflichtverletzungen' (Commission for Enquiry into Violations of Military Duty) on February 25, 1920. Each page also bears the official stamp of the State Archives.—The English translation, which appears here for the first time, is by James Strachey; the original German has not yet (1955) been published.]

states could only be regarded as functional disturbances, and that the nervous system remained anatomically intact. But medical opinion had long found difficulty in explaining how such severe disturbances of function could occur without any gross injury to the organ.

The war that has recently ended produced and brought under observation an immense number of these traumatic cases. In the result, the controversy was decided in favour of the functional view. The great majority of physicians no longer believe that the so-called 'war neurotics' are ill as a result of tangible organic injuries to the nervous system, and the more clear-sighted among them have already decided, instead of using the indefinite description of a 'functional change', to introduce the unambiguous term 'mental change'.

Although the war neuroses manifested themselves for the most part as motor disturbances—tremors and paralyses—and although it was plausible to suppose that such a gross impact as that produced by the concussion due to the explosion of a shell near by or to being buried by a fall of earth would lead to gross mechanical effects, observations were nevertheless made which left no doubt as to the psychical nature of the causation of these so-called war neuroses. How could this be disputed when the same symptoms appeared behind the Front as well, far from the horrors of war, or immediately after a return from leave? The physicians were therefore led to regard war neurotics in a similar light to the nervous subjects of peace-time.

What is known as the psycho-analytic school of psychiatry, which was brought into being by me, had taught for the last twenty-five years that the neuroses of peace could be traced back to disturbances of emotional life. This explanation was now applied quite generally to war neurotics. We had further asserted that neurotic patients suffered from mental conflicts and that the wishes and inclinations which were expressed in the symptoms were unknown to the patients themselves—were, that is to say, unconscious. It was therefore easy to infer that the immediate cause of all war neuroses was an unconscious inclination in the soldier to withdraw from the demands, dangerous or outrageous to his feelings, made upon him by active service. Fear of losing his own life, opposition to the command to kill other people, rebellion against the ruthless suppression of his own personality by his superiors—these were the most important affective sources on which the inclination to escape from war was nourished.

A soldier in whom these affective motives were very powerful and clearly conscious would, if he was a healthy man, have been obliged to desert or pretend to be ill. Only the smallest proportion of war neurotics, however, were malingerers; the emotional impulses which rebelled in them against active service and drove them into illness were operative in them without becoming conscious to them. They remained unconscious because other motives, such as ambition, self-esteem, patriotism, the habit of obedience and the example of others, were to start with more powerful until, on some appropriate occasion, they were overwhelmed by the other, unconsciously-operating motives.

This insight into the causation of the war neuroses led to a method of treatment which seemed to be well-grounded and also proved highly effective in the first instance. It seemed expedient to treat the neurotic as a malingerer and to disregard the psychological distinction between conscious and unconscious intentions, although he was known not to be a malingerer. Since his illness served the purpose of withdrawing him from an intolerable situation, the roots of the illness would clearly be undermined if it was made even more intolerable to him than active service. Just as he had fled from the war into illness, means were now adopted which compelled him to flee back from illness into health, that is to say, into fitness for active service. For this purpose painful electrical treatment was employed, and with success. Physicians are glossing over the facts in retrospect when they assert that the strength of this electrical current was the same as had always been employed in functional disorders. This would only have been effective in the mildest cases; nor did it fit in with the underlying argument that a war neurotic's illness had to be made painful so that the balance of his motives would be tipped in favour of recovery.

This painful form of treatment introduced in the German army for therapeutic purposes could no doubt also be employed in a more moderate fashion. If it was used in the Vienna Clinics, I am personally convinced that it was never intensified to a cruel pitch by the initiative of Professor Wagner-Jauregg.[1]

[1] [Julius von Wagner-Jauregg was Professor of Psychiatry at the University of Vienna from 1893 to 1928.]

I cannot vouch for other physicians whom I did not know. The psychological education of medical men is in general decidedly deficient and more than one of them may have forgotten that the patient whom he was seeking to treat as a malingerer was, after all, not one.

This therapeutic procedure, however, bore a stigma from the very first. It did not aim at the patient's recovery, or not in the first instance; it aimed, above all, at restoring his fitness for service. Here Medicine was serving purposes foreign to its essence. The physician himself was under military command and had his own personal dangers to fear—loss of seniority or a charge of neglecting his duty—if he allowed himself to be led by considerations other than those prescribed for him. The insoluble conflict between the claims of humanity, which normally carry decisive weight for a physician, and the demands of a national war was bound to confuse his activity.

Moreover, the successes of treatment by a strong electric current, which were brilliant to begin with, turned out afterwards not to be lasting. A patient who, having been restored to health by it, was sent back to the Front, could repeat the business afresh and have a relapse, by means of which he at least gained time and escaped the danger which was at the moment the immediate one. If he was once more under fire his fear of the electric current receded, just as during the treatment his fear of active service had faded. In the course of the war years, too, a rapidly increasing fatigue in the popular spirit made itself felt more and more, and a growing dislike of fighting, so that the treatment I have described began to fail in its effects. In these circumstances some of the army doctors gave way to the inclination, characteristic of Germans, to carry through their intentions regardless of all else—which should never have happened. The strength of the current, as well as the severity of the rest of the treatment, were increased to an unbearable point in order to deprive war neurotics of the advantage they gained from their illness. The fact has never been contradicted that in German hospitals there were deaths at that time during treatment and suicides as a result of it. I am quite unable to say, however, whether the Vienna Clinics, too, passed through this phase of therapy.

I am in a position to bring forward conclusive evidence of the final break-down of the electrical treatment of the war neuroses. In 1918 Dr. Ernst Simmel, head of a hospital for war neuroses at Posen, published a pamphlet in which he reported the extraordinarily favourable results achieved in severe cases of war neurosis by the psychotherapeutic method introduced by me. As a result of this publication, the next Psycho-Analytical Congress, held in Budapest in September 1918,[1] was attended by official delegates of the German, Austrian and Hungarian Army Command, who promised that Centres should be set up for the purely psychological treatment of war neuroses. This promise was made although the delegates can have been left in no doubt that with this considerate, laborious and tedious kind of treatment it was impossible to count on the quickest restoration of these patients to fitness for service. Preparations for the establishment of Centres of this kind were actually under way, when the revolution broke out and put an end to the war and to the influence of the administrative offices which had hitherto been all-powerful. But with the end of the war the war neurotics, too, disappeared—a final but impressive proof of the psychical causation of their illnesses.

Vienna, 23.2.20.

[1] [In the original MS. this date is quite clearly written '1818'.]

THE 'UNCANNY'
(1919)

DAS UNHEIMLICHE

(*a*) German Editions:

1919 *Imago*, **5** (5–6), 297–324.
1922 *S.K.S.N.*, **5**, 229–73.
1924 *G.S.*, **10**, 369–408.
1924 *Dichtung und Kunst*, 99–138.
1947 *G.W.*, **12**, 229–68.

(*b*) English Translation:

'The "Uncanny" '

1925 *C.P.*, **4**, 368–407. (Tr. Alix Strachey.)

The present translation is a considerably modified version of the one published in 1925.

This paper, published in the autumn of 1919, is mentioned by Freud in a letter to Ferenczi of May 12 of the same year, in which he says he has dug an old paper out of a drawer and is re-writing it. Nothing is known as to when it was originally written or how much it was changed, though the footnote quoted from *Totem and Taboo* on p. 241 below shows that the subject was present in his mind as early as 1913. The passages dealing with the 'compulsion to repeat' (p. 234 ff.) must in any case have formed part of the revision. They include a summary of much of the contents of *Beyond the Pleasure Principle* (1920*g*) and speak of it as 'already completed'. The same letter to Ferenczi of May 12, 1919, announced that a draft of this latter work was finished, though it was not in fact published for another year. Further details will be found in the Editor's Note to *Beyond the Pleasure Principle*, *Standard Ed.*, **18**, 3.

The first section of the present paper, with its lengthy quotation from a German dictionary, raises special difficulties for the translator. It is to be hoped that readers will not allow themselves to be discouraged by this preliminary obstacle, for the paper is full of interesting and important material, and travels far beyond merely linguistic topics.

THE 'UNCANNY'

I

It is only rarely that a psycho-analyst feels impelled to investigate the subject of aesthetics, even when aesthetics is understood to mean not merely the theory of beauty but the theory of the qualities of feeling. He works in other strata of mental life and has little to do with the subdued emotional impulses which, inhibited in their aims and dependent on a host of concurrent factors, usually furnish the material for the study of aesthetics. But it does occasionally happen that he has to interest himself in some particular province of that subject; and this province usually proves to be a rather remote one, and one which has been neglected in the specialist literature of aesthetics.

The subject of the 'uncanny'[1] is a province of this kind. It is undoubtedly related to what is frightening—to what arouses dread and horror; equally certainly, too, the word is not always used in a clearly definable sense, so that it tends to coincide with what excites fear in general. Yet we may expect that a special core of feeling is present which justifies the use of a special conceptual term. One is curious to know what this common core is which allows us to distinguish as 'uncanny' certain things which lie within the field of what is frightening.

As good as nothing is to be found upon this subject in comprehensive treatises on aesthetics, which in general prefer to concern themselves with what is beautiful, attractive and sublime—that is, with feelings of a positive nature—and with the circumstances and the objects that call them forth, rather than with the opposite feelings of repulsion and distress. I know of only one attempt in medico-psychological literature, a fertile but not exhaustive paper by Jentsch (1906). But I must confess that I have not made a very thorough examination of the literature, especially the foreign literature, relating to this present modest contribution of mine, for reasons which, as may

[1] [The German word, translated throughout this paper by the English 'uncanny', is '*unheimlich*', literally 'unhomely'. The English term is not, of course, an exact equivalent of the German one.]

easily be guessed, lie in the times in which we live;[1] so that my paper is presented to the reader without any claim to priority.

In his study of the 'uncanny' Jentsch quite rightly lays stress on the obstacle presented by the fact that people vary so very greatly in their sensitivity to this quality of feeling. The writer of the present contribution, indeed, must himself plead guilty to a special obtuseness in the matter, where extreme delicacy of perception would be more in place. It is long since he has experienced or heard of anything which has given him an uncanny impression, and he must start by translating himself into that state of feeling, by awakening in himself the possibility of experiencing it. Still, such difficulties make themselves powerfully felt in many other branches of aesthetics; we need not on that account despair of finding instances in which the qnality in question will be unhesitatingly recognized by most people.

Two courses are open to us at the outset. Either we can find out what meaning has come to be attached to the word 'uncanny' in the course of its history; or we can collect all those properties of persons, things, sense-impressions, experiences and situations which arouse in us the feeling of uncanniness, and then infer the unknown nature of the uncanny from what all these examples have in common. I will say at once that both courses lead to the same result: the uncanny is that class of the frightening which leads back to what is known of old and long familiar. How this is possible, in what circumstances the familiar can become uncanny and frightening, I shall show in what follows. Let me also add that my investigation was actually begun by collecting a number of individual cases, and was only later confirmed by an examination of linguistic usage. In this discussion, however, I shall follow the reverse course.

The German word '*unheimlich*' is obviously the opposite of '*heimlich*' ['homely'], '*heimisch*' ['native']—the opposite of what is familiar; and we are tempted to conclude that what is 'uncanny' is frightening precisely because it is *not* known and familiar. Naturally not everything that is new and unfamiliar is frightening, however; the relation is not capable of inversion.

[1] [An allusion to the first World War only just concluded.]

We can only say that what is novel can easily become frightening and uncanny; some new things are frightening but not by any means all. Something has to be added to what is novel and unfamiliar in order to make it uncanny.

On the whole, Jentsch did not get beyond this relation of the uncanny to the novel and unfamiliar. He ascribes the essential factor in the production of the feeling of uncanniness to intellectual uncertainty; so that the uncanny would always, as it were, be something one does not know one's way about in. The better orientated in his environment a person is, the less readily will he get the impression of something uncanny in regard to the objects and events in it.

It is not difficult to see that this definition is incomplete, and we will therefore try to proceed beyond the equation 'uncanny' = 'unfamiliar'. We will first turn to other languages. But the dictionaries that we consult tell us nothing new, perhaps only because we ourselves speak a language that is foreign. Indeed, we get an impression that many languages are without a word for this particular shade of what is frightening.

I should like to express my indebtedness to Dr. Theodor Reik for the following excerpts:—

LATIN: (K. E. Georges, *Deutschlateinisches Wörterbuch*, 1898). An uncanny place: *locus suspectus*; at an uncanny time of night: *intempesta nocte*.

GREEK: (Rost's and Schenkl's Lexikons). ξένος (i.e. strange, foreign).

ENGLISH: (from the dictionaries of Lucas, Bellows, Flügel and Muret-Sanders). Uncomfortable, uneasy, gloomy, dismal, uncanny, ghastly; (of a house) haunted; (of a man) a repulsive fellow.

FRENCH: (Sachs-Villatte). *Inquiétant, sinistre, lugubre, mal à son aise.*

SPANISH: (Tollhausen, 1889). *Sospechoso, de mal aguëro, lúgubre, siniestro.*

The Italian and Portuguese languages seem to content themselves with words which we should describe as circumlocutions. In Arabic and Hebrew 'uncanny' means the same as 'daemonic', 'gruesome'.

Let us therefore return to the German language. In Daniel Sanders's *Wörterbuch der Deutschen Sprache* (1860, **1**, 729), the following entry, which I here reproduce in full, is to be found under the word '*heimlich*'. I have laid stress on one or two passages by italicizing them.[1]

Heimlich, adj., subst. *Heimlichkeit* (pl. *Heimlichkeiten*): I. Also *heimelich, heimelig*, belonging to the house, not strange, familiar, tame, intimate, friendly, etc.

(*a*) (Obsolete) belonging to the house or the family, or regarded as so belonging (cf. Latin *familiaris*, familiar): *Die Heimlichen*, the members of the household; *Der heimliche Rat* (Gen. xli, 45; 2 Sam. xxiii. 23; 1 Chron. xii. 25; Wisd. viii. 4), now more usually *Geheimer Rat* [Privy Councillor].

(*b*) Of animals: tame, companionable to man. As opposed to wild, e.g. 'Animals which are neither wild nor *heimlich*', etc. 'Wild animals . . . that are trained to be *heimlich* and accustomed to men.' 'If these young creatures are brought up from early days among men they become quite *heimlich*, friendly' etc. —So also: 'It (the lamb) is so *heimlich* and eats out of my hand.' 'Nevertheless, the stork is a beautiful, *heimelich* bird.'

(*c*) Intimate, friendlily comfortable; the enjoyment of quiet content, etc., arousing a sense of agreeable restfulness and security as in one within the four walls of his house.[2] 'Is it still *heimlich* to you in your country where strangers are felling your woods?' 'She did not feel too *heimlich* with him.' 'Along a high, *heimlich*, shady path . . ., beside a purling, gushing and babbling woodland brook.' 'To destroy the *Heimlichkeit* of the home.' 'I could not readily find another spot so intimate and *heimlich* as this.' 'We pictured it so comfortable, so nice, so cosy and *heimlich*.' 'In quiet *Heimlichkeit*, surrounded by close walls.' 'A careful housewife, who knows how to make a pleasing *Heimlichkeit* (*Häuslichkeit* [domesticity]) out of the smallest means.' 'The man who till recently had been so strange to him now seemed to him all the more *heimlich*.' 'The protestant land-owners do not feel . . . *heimlich* among their catholic inferiors.' 'When it grows *heimlich* and still, and the evening quiet alone watches

[1] [In the translation which follows in the text above, a few details, mainly giving the sources of the quotations, have been omitted. For purposes of reference, we reprint in an Appendix the entire extract from Sanders's Dictionary exactly as it is given in German in Freud's original paper except that a few minor misprints have been put right. (Cf. p. 253.)]

[2] [It may be remarked that the English 'canny', in addition to its more usual meaning of 'shrewd', can mean 'pleasant', 'cosy'.]

over your cell.' 'Quiet, lovely and *heimlich*, no place more fitted for their rest.' 'He did not feel at all *heimlich* about it.'—Also, [in compounds] 'The place was so peaceful, so lonely, so shadily-*heimlich*.' 'The in- and outflowing waves of the current, dreamy and lullaby-*heimlich*.' Cf. in especial *Unheimlich* [see below]. Among Swabian Swiss authors in especial, often as a trisyllable: 'How *heimelich* it seemed to Ivo again of an evening, when he was at home.' 'It was so *heimelig* in the house.' 'The warm room and the *heimelig* afternoon.' 'When a man feels in his heart that he is so small and the Lord so great—that is what is truly *heimelig*.' 'Little by little they grew at ease and *heimelig* among themselves.' 'Friendly *Heimeligkeit*.' 'I shall be nowhere more *heimelich* than I am here.' 'That which comes from afar . . . assuredly does not live quite *heimelig* (*heimatlich* [at home], *freundnachbarlich* [in a neighbourly way]) among the people.' 'The cottage where he had once sat so often among his own people, so *heimelig*, so happy.' 'The sentinel's horn sounds so *heimelig* from the tower, and his voice invites so hospitably.' 'You go to sleep there so soft and warm, so wonderfully *heim'lig*.' —*This form of the word deserves to become general in order to protect this perfectly good sense of the word from becoming obsolete through an easy confusion with* II [see below]. Cf: ' "*The Zecks* [a family name] *are all 'heimlich'*." (in sense II) " '*Heimlich*'? . . . *What do you understand by 'heimlich'?*" "*Well, . . . they are like a buried spring or a dried-up pond. One cannot walk over it without always having the feeling that water might come up there again.*" "*Oh, we call it 'unheimlich'; you call it 'heimlich'. Well, what makes you think that there is something secret and untrustworthy about this family?*" ' (Gutzkow).

(*d*) Especially in Silesia: gay, cheerful; also of the weather.

II. Concealed, kept from sight, so that others do not get to know of or about it, withheld from others. To do something *heimlich*, i.e. behind someone's back; to steal away *heimlich*; *heimlich* meetings and appointments; to look on with *heimlich* pleasure at someone's discomfiture; to sigh or weep *heimlich*; to behave *heimlich*, as though there was something to conceal; *heimlich* love-affair, love, sin; *heimlich* places (which good manners oblige us to conceal) (1 Sam. v. 6). 'The *heimlich* chamber' (privy) (2 Kings x. 27.). Also, 'the *heimlich* chair'. 'To throw into pits or *Heimlichkeiten*'.—'Led the steeds *heimlich* before Laomedon.'—'As secretive, *heimlich*, deceitful and malicious towards cruel masters . . . as frank, open, sympathetic and helpful towards a friend in misfortune.' 'You have still to learn what is *heimlich* holiest to me.' 'The *heimlich* art' (magic). 'Where public ventilation has to stop, there *heimlich* machinations begin.' 'Freedom is the whispered watchword of *heimlich* conspirators and the loud battle-cry of professed revolutionaries.' 'A holy, *heimlich* effect.' 'I have roots that are most *heimlich*. I am grown in the deep earth.' 'My *heimlich* pranks.' 'If he is not given it openly and scrupulously he may seize it *heimlich* and unscrupulously.' 'He had achromatic telescopes constructed *heimlich* and secretly.' 'Henceforth I desire that there should be nothing *heimlich* any longer between us.'—To discover, disclose, betray someone's *Heimlichkeiten*; 'to concoct *Heimlichkeiten* behind my back'. 'In my time we studied *Heimlichkeit*.' 'The hand of understanding can alone undo the powerless spell of the *Heimlichkeit* (of hidden gold).' 'Say, where is the place of concealment . . . in what place of hidden *Heimlichkeit*?' 'Bees, who make the lock of *Heimlichkeiten*' (i.e. sealing-wax). 'Learned in strange *Heimlichkeiten*' (magic arts).

For compounds see above, I*c*. Note especially the negative '*un-*': eerie, weird, arousing gruesome fear: 'Seeming quite *unheimlich* and ghostly to him.' 'The *unheimlich*, fearful hours of night.' 'I had already long since felt an *unheimlich*, even gruesome feeling.' 'Now I am beginning to have an *unheimlich* feeling.' . . . 'Feels an *unheimlich* horror.' '*Unheimlich* and motionless like a stone image.' 'The *unheimlich* mist called hill-fog.' 'These pale youths are *unheimlich* and are brewing heaven knows what mischief.' '"*Unheimlich*" *is the name for everything that ought to have remained . . . secret and hidden but has come to light*' (Schelling).—'To veil the divine, to surround it with a certain *Unheimlichkeit*.'—*Unheimlich* is not often used as opposite to meaning II (above).

What interests us most in this long extract is to find that among its different shades of meaning the word '*heimlich*' exhibits one which is identical with its opposite, '*unheimlich*'. What is *heimlich* thus comes to be *unheimlich*. (Cf. the quotation from Gutzkow: 'We call it "*unheimlich*"; you call it "*heimlich*".') In general we are reminded that the word '*heimlich*' is not unambiguous, but belongs to two sets of ideas, which, without being contradictory, are yet very different: on the one hand it means what is familiar and agreeable, and on the other, what is concealed and kept out of sight.[1] '*Unheimlich*' is customarily used, we are told, as the contrary only of the first signification of '*heimlich*', and not of the second. Sanders tells us nothing concerning a possible genetic connection between these two meanings of *heimlich*. On the other hand, we notice that Schelling says something which throws quite a new light on the concept of the *Unheimlich*, for which we were certainly not prepared. According to him, everything is *unheimlich* that ought to have remained secret and hidden but has come to light.

Some of the doubts that have thus arisen are removed if we consult Grimm's dictionary. (1877, **4**, Part 2, 873 ff.)

We read:

Heimlich; adj. and adv. *vernaculus, occultus*; MHG. heimelîch, heimlîch.

(P. 874.) In a slightly different sense: 'I feel *heimlich*, well, free from fear.' . . .

[3] (*b*) *Heimlich* is also used of a place free from ghostly influences . . . familiar, friendly, intimate.

(P. 875: *β*) Familiar, amicable, unreserved.

4. *From the idea of 'homelike', 'belonging to the house', the further idea is developed of something withdrawn from the eyes of strangers, something concealed, secret; and this idea is expanded in many ways* . . .

(P. 876.) 'On the left bank of the lake there lies a meadow *heimlich* in the wood.' (Schiller, *Wilhelm Tell*, I. 4.). . . Poetic licence, rarely so used in modern speech . . . *Heimlich* is used in conjunction with a verb expressing the act of concealing: 'In the secret of his tabernacle he shall hide me *heimlich*.' (Ps. xxvii. 5.) . . . *Heimlich* parts of the human body, *pudenda* . . . 'the men that died not were smitten on their *heimlich* parts.' (1 Samuel v. 12.) . . .

(*c*) Officials who give important advice which has to be kept secret in matters of state are called *heimlich* councillors; the adjective, according to modern usage, has been replaced by *geheim* [secret] . . . 'Pharaoh called Joseph's name "him to whom secrets are revealed" ' (*heimlich* councillor). (Gen. xli. 45.)

[1] [According to the Oxford English Dictionary, a similar ambiguity attaches to the English 'canny', which may mean not only 'cosy' but also 'endowed with occult or magical powers'.]

(P. 878.) 6. *Heimlich*, as used of knowledge—mystic, allegorical: a *heimlich* meaning, *mysticus, divinus, occultus, figuratus*.

(P. 878.) *Heimlich* in a different sense, as withdrawn from knowledge, unconscious . . . *Heimlich* also has the meaning of that which is obscure, inaccessible to knowledge . . . 'Do you not see? They do not trust us; they fear the *heimlich* face of the Duke of Friedland.' (Schiller, *Wallensteins Lager*, Scene 2.)

9. *The notion of something hidden and dangerous, which is expressed in the last paragraph, is still further developed, so that 'heimlich' comes to have the meaning usually ascribed to 'unheimlich'*. Thus: 'At times I feel like a man who walks in the night and believes in ghosts; every corner is *heimlich* and full of terrors for him'. (Klinger, *Theater*, 3. 298.)

Thus *heimlich* is a word the meaning of which develops in the direction of ambivalence, until it finally coincides with its opposite, *unheimlich*. *Unheimlich* is in some way or other a sub-species of *heimlich*. Let us bear this discovery in mind, though we cannot yet rightly understand it, alongside of Schelling's [1] definition of the *Unheimlich*. If we go on to examine individual instances of uncanniness, these hints will become intelligible to us.

II

When we proceed to review the things, persons, impressions, events and situations which are able to arouse in us a feeling of the uncanny in a particularly forcible and definite form, the first requirement is obviously to select a suitable example to start on. Jentsch has taken as a very good instance 'doubts whether an apparently animate being is really alive; or conversely, whether a lifeless object might not be in fact animate'; and he refers in this connection to the impression made by waxwork figures, ingeniously constructed dolls and automata. To these he adds the uncanny effect of epileptic fits, and of manifestations of insanity, because these excite in the spectator the impression of automatic, mechanical processes at work behind the ordinary appearance of mental activity. Without entirely accepting this author's view, we will take it as a starting-point for our own investigation because in what follows he reminds us

[1] [In the original version of the paper (1919) only, the name 'Schleiermacher' was printed here, evidently in error.]

of a writer who has succeeded in producing uncanny effects better than anyone else.

Jentsch writes: 'In telling a story, one of the most successful devices for easily creating uncanny effects is to leave the reader in uncertainty whether a particular figure in the story is a human being or an automaton, and to do it in such a way that his attention is not focused directly upon his uncertainty, so that he may not be led to go into the matter and clear it up immediately. That, as we have said, would quickly dissipate the peculiar emotional effect of the thing. E. T. A. Hoffmann has repeatedly employed this psychological artifice with success in his fantastic narratives.'

This observation, undoubtedly a correct one, refers primarily to the story of 'The Sand-Man' in Hoffmann's *Nachtstücken*,[1] which contains the original of Olympia, the doll that appears in the first act of Offenbach's opera, *Tales of Hoffmann*. But I cannot think—and I hope most readers of the story will agree with me—that the theme of the doll Olympia, who is to all appearances a living being, is by any means the only, or indeed the most important, element that must be held responsible for the quite unparalleled atmosphere of uncanniness evoked by the story. Nor is this atmosphere heightened by the fact that the author himself treats the episode of Olympia with a faint touch of satire and uses it to poke fun at the young man's idealization of his mistress. The main theme of the story is, on the contrary, something different, something which gives it its name, and which is always re-introduced at critical moments: it is the theme of the 'Sand-Man' who tears out children's eyes.

This fantastic tale opens with the childhood recollections of the student Nathaniel. In spite of his present happiness, he cannot banish the memories associated with the mysterious and terrifying death of his beloved father. On certain evenings his mother used to send the children to bed early, warning them that 'the Sand-Man was coming'; and, sure enough, Nathaniel would not fail to hear the heavy tread of a visitor, with whom his father would then be occupied for the evening. When questioned about the Sand-Man, his mother, it is true, denied

[1] Hoffmann's *Sämtliche Werke*, Grisebach Edition, 3. [A translation of 'The Sand-Man' is included in *Eight Tales of Hoffmann*, translated by J. M. Cohen, London, Pan Books, 1952.]

that such a person existed except as a figure of speech; but his nurse could give him more definite information: 'He's a wicked man who comes when children won't go to bed, and throws handfuls of sand in their eyes so that they jump out of their heads all bleeding. Then he puts the eyes in a sack and carries them off to the half-moon to feed his children. They sit up there in their nest, and their beaks are hooked like owls' beaks, and they use them to peck up naughty boys' and girls' eyes with.'

Although little Nathaniel was sensible and old enough not to credit the figure of the Sand-Man with such gruesome attributes, yet the dread of him became fixed in his heart. He determined to find out what the Sand-Man looked like; and one evening, when the Sand-Man was expected again, he hid in his father's study. He recognized the visitor as the lawyer Coppelius, a repulsive person whom the children were frightened of when he occasionally came to a meal; and he now identified this Coppelius with the dreaded Sand-Man. As regards the rest of the scene, Hoffmann already leaves us in doubt whether what we are witnessing is the first delirium of the panic-stricken boy, or a succession of events which are to be regarded in the story as being real. His father and the guest are at work at a brazier with glowing flames. The little eavesdropper hears Coppelius call out: 'Eyes here! Eyes here!' and betrays himself by screaming aloud. Coppelius seizes him and is on the point of dropping bits of red-hot coal from the fire into his eyes, and then of throwing them into the brazier, but his father begs him off and saves his eyes. After this the boy falls into a deep swoon; and a long illness brings his experience to an end. Those who decide in favour of the rationalistic interpretation of the Sand-Man will not fail to recognize in the child's phantasy the persisting influence of his nurse's story. The bits of sand that are to be thrown into the child's eyes turn into bits of red-hot coal from the flames; and in both cases they are intended to make his eyes jump out. In the course of another visit of the Sand-Man's, a year later, his father is killed in his study by an explosion. The lawyer Coppelius disappears from the place without leaving a trace behind.

Nathaniel, now a student, believes that he has recognized this phantom of horror from his childhood in an itinerant optician, an Italian called Giuseppe Coppola, who at his university town, offers him weather-glasses for sale. When Nathanile refuses, the man goes on: 'Not weather-glasses? not weather-glasses? also got fine eyes, fine eyes!' The student's terror is allayed when he finds that the proffered eyes are only harmless spectacles, and he buys a pocket spy-glass from Coppola. With its aid he looks across into Professor Spalanzani's house opposite and there spies Spalanzani's beautiful, but strangely silent and motionless daughter, Olympia. He soon falls in love with her so violently that, because of her, he quite forgets the clever and sensible girl to whom he is betrothed. But Olympia is an automaton whose clock-work has been made by Spalanzani, and whose eyes have been put in by Coppola, the Sand-Man. The student surprises the two Masters quarrelling over their handiwork. The optician carries off the wooden eyeless doll; and the mechanician, Spalanzani, picks up Olympia's bleeding eyes from the ground and throws them at Nathaniel's breast, saying that Coppola had stolen them from the student. Nathaniel succumbs to a fresh attack of madness, and in his delirium his recollection of his father's death is mingled with this new experience. 'Hurry up! hurry up! ring of fire!' he cries. 'Spin about, ring of fire—Hurrah! Hurry up, wooden doll! lovely wooden doll, spin about—.' He then falls upon the professor, Olympia's 'father', and tries to strangle him.

Rallying from a long and serious illness, Nathaniel seems at last to have recovered. He intends to marry his betrothed, with whom he has become reconciled. One day he and she are walking through the city market-place, over which the high tower of the Town Hall throws its huge shadow. On the girl's suggestion, they climb the tower, leaving her brother, who is walking with them, down below. From the top, Clara's attention is drawn to a curious object moving along the street. Nathaniel looks at this thing through Coppola's spy-glass, which he finds in his pocket, and falls into a new attack of madness. Shouting 'Spin about, wooden doll!' he tries to throw the girl into the gulf below. Her brother, brought to her side by her cries, rescues her and hastens down with her to safety. On the tower above, the madman rushes round, shrieking 'Ring of fire, spin about!'—and we know the origin of the words. Among the people who begin to gather below there comes forward the figure of the lawyer Coppelius, who has suddenly returned. We may suppose that it was his approach, seen through the spy-glass, which threw Nathaniel into his fit of madness. As the onlookers prepare to go up and overpower the madman, Coppelius laughs and says: 'Wait a bit; he'll come down of himself.' Nathaniel suddenly stands still, catches sight of Coppelius, and with a wild shriek 'Yes! "Fine eyes—fine eyes"!' flings himself over the parapet. While he lies on the paving-stones with a shattered skull the Sand-Man vanishes in the throng.

This short summary leaves no doubt, I think, that the feeling of something uncanny is directly attached to the figure of the Sand-Man, that is, to the idea of being robbed of one's eyes, and that Jentsch's point of an intellectual uncertainty has nothing to do with the effect. Uncertainty whether an object is living or inanimate, which admittedly applied to the doll Olympia, is quite irrelevant in connection with this other, more striking instance of uncanniness. It is true that the writer creates a kind of uncertainty in us in the beginning by not letting us know, no doubt purposely, whether he is taking us into the real world or into a purely fantastic one of his own creation. He has, of course, a right to do either; and if he chooses to stage his action in a world peopled with spirits, demons and ghosts, as Shakespeare does in *Hamlet*, in *Macbeth* and, in a different sense, in *The Tempest* and *A Midsummer-Night's Dream*, we must bow to his decision and treat his setting as though it were real for as long as we put ourselves into his hands. But this uncertainty disappears in the course of Hoffmann's story, and we perceive that he intends to make us, too, look through the demon optician's spectacles or spy-glass—perhaps, indeed, that the author in his very own person once peered through such an instrument. For the conclusion of the story makes it quite clear that Coppola the optician really *is* the lawyer Coppelius[1] and also, therefore, the Sand-Man.

There is no question therefore, of any intellectual uncertainty here: we know now that we are not supposed to be looking on at the products of a madman's imagination, behind which we, with the superiority of rational minds, are able to detect the sober truth; and yet this knowledge does not lessen the impression of uncanniness in the least degree. The theory of

[1] Frau Dr. Rank has pointed out the association of the name with '*coppella*' = crucible, connecting it with the chemical operations that caused the father's death; and also with '*coppo*' = eye-socket. [Except in the first (1919) edition this footnote was attached, it seems erroneously, to the first occurrence of the name Coppelius on this page.]

intellectual uncertainty is thus incapable of explaining that impression.

We know from psycho-analytic experience, however, that the fear of damaging or losing one's eyes is a terrible one in children. Many adults retain their apprehensiveness in this respect, and no physical injury is so much dreaded by them as an injury to the eye. We are accustomed to say, too, that we will treasure a thing as the apple of our eye. A study of dreams, phantasies and myths has taught us that anxiety about one's eyes, the fear of going blind, is often enough a substitute for the dread of being castrated. The self-blinding of the mythical criminal, Oedipus, was simply a mitigated form of the punishment of castration—the only punishment that was adequate for him by the *lex talionis*. We may try on rationalistic grounds to deny that fears about the eye are derived from the fear of castration, and may argue that it is very natural that so precious an organ as the eye should be guarded by a proportionate dread. Indeed, we might go further and say that the fear of castration itself contains no other significance and no deeper secret than a justifiable dread of this rational kind. But this view does not account adequately for the substitutive relation between the eye and the male organ which is seen to exist in dreams and myths and phantasies; nor can it dispel the impression that the threat of being castrated in especial excites a peculiarly violent and obscure emotion, and that this emotion is what first gives the idea of losing other organs its intense colouring. All further doubts are removed when we learn the details of their 'castration complex' from the analysis of neurotic patients, and realize its immense importance in their mental life.

Moreover, I would not recommend any opponent of the psycho-analytic view to select this particular story of the Sand-Man with which to support his argument that anxiety about the eyes has nothing to do with the castration complex. For why does Hoffmann bring the anxiety about eyes into such intimate connection with the father's death? And why does the Sand-Man always appear as a disturber of love? He separates the unfortunate Nathaniel from his betrothed and from her brother, his best friend; he destroys the second object of his love, Olympia, the lovely doll; and he drives him into suicide at the moment when he has won back his Clara and is about to be happily united to her. Elements in the story like these, and many others, seem arbitrary and meaningless so long as we deny all connection between fears about the eye and castration; but they become intelligible as soon as we replace the Sand-Man by the dreaded father at whose hands castration is expected.[1]

[1] In fact, Hoffmann's imaginative treatment of his material has not made such wild confusion of its elements that we cannot reconstruct their original arrangement. In the story of Nathaniel's childhood, the figures of his father and Coppelius represent the two opposites into which the father-imago is split by his ambivalence; whereas the one threatens to blind him—that is, to castrate him—, the other, the 'good' father, intercedes for his sight. The part of the complex which is most strongly repressed, the death-wish against the 'bad' father, finds expression in the death of the 'good' father, and Coppelius is made answerable for it. This pair of fathers is represented later, in his student days, by Professor Spalanzani and Coppola the optician. The Professor is in himself a member of the father-series, and Coppola is recognized as identical with Coppelius the lawyer. Just as they used before to work together over the secret brazier, so now they have jointly created the doll Olympia; the Professor is even called the father of Olympia. This double occurrence of activity in common betrays them as divisions of the father-imago: both the mechanician and the optician were the father of Nathaniel (and of Olympia as well). In the frightening scene in childhood, Coppelius, after sparing Nathaniel's eyes, had screwed off his arms and legs as an experiment; that is, he had worked on him as a mechanician would on a doll. This singular feature, which seems quite outside the picture of the Sand-Man, introduces a new castration equivalent; but it also points to the inner identity of Coppelius with his later counterpart, Spalanzani the mechanician, and prepares us for the interpretation of Olympia. This automatic doll can be nothing else than a materialization of Nathaniel's feminine attitude towards his father in his infancy. Her fathers, Spalanzani and Coppola, are, after all, nothing but new editions, reincarnations of Nathaniel's pair of fathers. Spalanzani's otherwise incomprehensible statement that the optician has stolen Nathaniel's eyes (see above, [p. 229]), so as to set them in the doll, now becomes significant as supplying evidence of the identity of Olympia and Nathaniel. Olympia is, as it were, a dissociated complex of Nathaniel's which confronts him as a person, and Nathaniel's enslavement to this complex is expressed in his senseless obsessive love for Olympia. We may with justice call love of this kind narcissistic, and we can understand why someone who has fallen victim to it should relinquish the real, external object of his love. The psychological truth of the situation in which the young man, fixated upon his father by his castration complex, becomes incapable of loving a woman, is amply proved by numerous analyses of patients whose story, though less fantastic, is hardly less tragic than that of the student Nathaniel.

Hoffmann was the child of an unhappy marriage. When he was

We shall venture, therefore, to refer the uncanny effect of the Sand-Man to the anxiety belonging to the castration complex of childhood. But having reached the idea that we can make an infantile factor such as this responsible for feelings of uncanniness, we are encouraged to see whether we can apply it to other instances of the uncanny. We find in the story of the Sand-Man the other theme on which Jentsch lays stress, of a doll which appears to be alive. Jentsch believes that a particularly favourable condition for awakening uncanny feelings is created when there is intellectual uncertainty whether an object is alive or not, and when an inanimate object becomes too much like an animate one. Now, dolls are of course rather closely connected with childhood life. We remember that in their early games children do not distinguish at all sharply between living and inanimate objects, and that they are especially fond of treating their dolls like live people. In fact, I have occasionally heard a woman patient declare that even at the age of eight she had still been convinced that her dolls would be certain to come to life if she were to look at them in a particular, extremely concentrated, way. So that here, too, it is not difficult to discover a factor from childhood. But, curiously enough, while the Sand-Man story deals with the arousing of an early childhood fear, the idea of a 'living doll' excites no fear at all; children have no fear of their dolls coming to life, they may even desire it. The source of uncanny feelings would not, therefore, be an infantile fear in this case, but rather an infantile wish or even merely an infantile belief. There seems to be a contradiction here; but perhaps it is only a complication, which may be helpful to us later on.

Hoffmann is the unrivalled master of the uncanny in literature. His novel, *Die Elixire des Teufels* [*The Devil's Elixir*], contains a whole mass of themes to which one is tempted to ascribe the uncanny effect of the narrative;[1] but it is too obscure and

three years old, his father left his small family, and was never united to them again. According to Grisebach, in his biographical introduction to Hoffmann's works, the writer's relation to his father was always a most sensitive subject with him.

[1] [Under the rubric 'Varia' in one of the issues of the *Internationale Zeitschrift für Psychoanalyse* for 1919 (**5**, 308), the year in which the present paper was first published, there appears over the initials 'S.F.' a short note which it is not unreasonable to attribute to Freud. Its insertion

intricate a story for us to venture upon a summary of it. Towards the end of the book the reader is told the facts, hitherto concealed from him, from which the action springs; with the result, not that he is at last enlightened, but that he falls into a state of complete bewilderment. The author has piled up too much material of the same kind. In consequence one's grasp of the story as a whole suffers, though not the impression it makes. We must content ourselves with selecting those themes of uncanniness which are most prominent, and with seeing whether they too can fairly be traced back to infantile sources. These themes are all concerned with the phenomenon of the 'double', which appears in every shape and in every degree of development. Thus we have characters who are to be considered identical because they look alike. This relation is accentuated by mental processes leaping from one of these characters to another—by what we should call telepathy—, so that the one possesses knowledge, feelings and experience in common with the other. Or it is marked by the fact that the subject identifies himself with someone else, so that he is in doubt as to which his self is, or substitutes the extraneous self for his own. In other words, there is a doubling, dividing and interchanging of the self. And finally there is the constant recurrence of the same thing [1]—the repetition of the same features or character-traits or vicissitudes, of the same crimes, or even the same names through several consecutive generations.

The theme of the 'double' has been very thoroughly treated by Otto Rank (1914). He has gone into the connections which

here, though strictly speaking irrelevant, may perhaps be excused. The note is headed: 'E. T. A. Hoffmann on the Function of Consciousness' and it proceeds: 'In *Die Elixire des Teufels* (Part II, p. 210, in Hesse's edition)—a novel rich in masterly descriptions of pathological mental states—Schönfeld comforts the hero, whose consciousness is temporarily disturbed, with the following words: "And what do you get out of it? I mean out of the particular mental function which we call consciousness, and which is nothing but the confounded activity of a damned toll-collector—excise-man—deputy-chief customs officer, who has set up his infamous bureau in our top storey and who exclaims, whenever any goods try to get out: 'Hi! hi! exports are prohibited . . . they must stay here . . . here, in this country. . . .' " ']

[1] [This phrase seems to be an echo from Nietzsche (e.g. from the last part of *Also Sprach Zarathustra*). In Chapter III of *Beyond the Pleasure Principle* (1920*g*), *Standard Ed.*, **18**, 22, Freud puts a similar phrase 'the perpetual recurrence of the same thing' into inverted commas.]

the 'double' has with reflections in mirrors, with shadows, with guardian spirits, with the belief in the soul and with the fear of death; but he also lets in a flood of light on the surprising evolution of the idea. For the 'double' was originally an insurance against the destruction of the ego, an 'energetic denial of the power of death', as Rank says; and probably the 'immortal' soul was the first 'double' of the body. This invention of doubling as a preservation against extinction has its counterpart in the language of dreams, which is fond of representing castration by a doubling or multiplication of a genital symbol.[1] The same desire led the Ancient Egyptians to develop the art of making images of the dead in lasting materials. Such ideas, however, have sprung from the soil of unbounded self-love, from the primary narcissism which dominates the mind of the child and of primitive man. But when this stage has been surmounted, the 'double' reverses its aspect. From having been an assurance of immortality, it becomes the uncanny harbinger of death.

The idea of the 'double' does not necessarily disappear with the passing of primary narcissism, for it can receive fresh meaning from the later stages of the ego's development. A special agency is slowly formed there, which is able to stand over against the rest of the ego, which has the function of observing and criticizing the self and of exercising a censorship within the mind, and which we become aware of as our 'conscience'. In the pathological case of delusions of being watched, this mental agency becomes isolated, dissociated from the ego, and discernible to the physician's eye. The fact that an agency of this kind exists, which is able to treat the rest of the ego like an object—the fact, that is, that man is capable of self-observation—renders it possible to invest the old idea of a 'double' with a new meaning and to ascribe a number of things to it—above all, those things which seem to self-criticism to belong to the old surmounted narcissism of earliest times.[2]

[1] [Cf. *The Interpretation of Dreams*, *Standard Ed.*, **5**, 357.]

[2] I believe that when poets complain that two souls dwell in the human breast, and when popular psychologists talk of the splitting of people's egos, what they are thinking of is this division (in the sphere of ego-psychology) between the critical agency and the rest of the ego, and not the antithesis discovered by psycho-analysis between the ego and what is unconscious and repressed. It is true that the distinction between these two antitheses is to some extent effaced by the circumstance that foremost among the things that are rejected by the criticism of the ego

But it is not only this latter material, offensive as it is to the criticism of the ego, which may be incorporated in the idea of a double. There are also all the unfulfilled but possible futures to which we still like to cling in phantasy, all the strivings of the ego which adverse external circumstances have crushed, and all our suppressed acts of volition which nourish in us the illusion of Free Will.[1] [Cf. Freud, 1901*b*, Chapter XII (B).]

But after having thus considered the *manifest* motivation of the figure of a 'double', we have to admit that none of this helps us to understand the extraordinarily strong feeling of something uncanny that pervades the conception; and our knowledge of pathological mental processes enables us to add that nothing in this more superficial material could account for the urge towards defence which has caused the ego to project that material outward as something foreign to itself. When all is said and done, the quality of uncanniness can only come from the fact of the 'double' being a creation dating back to a very early mental stage, long since surmounted—a stage, incidentally, at which it wore a more friendly aspect. The 'double' has become a thing of terror, just as, after the collapse of their religion, the gods turned into demons.[2]

The other forms of ego-disturbance exploited by Hoffmann can easily be estimated along the same lines as the theme of the 'double'. They are a harking-back to particular phases in the evolution of the self-regarding feeling, a regression to a time when the ego had not yet marked itself off sharply from the external world and from other people. I believe that these factors are partly responsible for the impression of uncanniness, although it is not easy to isolate and determine exactly their share of it.

The factor of the repetition of the same thing will perhaps not appeal to everyone as a source of uncanny feeling. From

are derivatives of the repressed.—[Freud had already discussed this critical agency at length in Section III of his paper on narcissism (1914*c*), and is was soon to be further expanded into the 'ego-ideal' and 'super-ego' in Chapter XI of his *Group Psychology* (1921*c*) and Chapter III of *The Ego and the Id* (1923*b*) respectively.]

[1] In Ewers's *Der Student von Prag*, which serves as the starting-point of Rank's study on the 'double', the hero has promised his beloved not to kill his antagonist in a duel. But on his way to the duelling-ground he meets his 'double', who has already killed his rival.

[2] Heine, *Die Götter im Exil*.

what I have observed, this phenomenon does undoubtedly, subject to certain conditions and combined with certain circumstances, arouse an uncanny feeling, which, furthermore, recalls the sense of helplessness experienced in some dream-states. As I was walking, one hot summer afternoon, through the deserted streets of a provincial town in Italy which was unknown to me, I found myself in a quarter of whose character I could not long remain in doubt. Nothing but painted women were to be seen at the windows of the small houses, and I hastened to leave the narrow street at the next turning. But after having wandered about for a time without enquiring my way, I suddenly found myself back in the same street, where my presence was now beginning to excite attention. I hurried away once more, only to arrive by another *détour* at the same place yet a third time. Now, however, a feeling overcame me which I can only describe as uncanny, and I was glad enough to find myself back at the piazza I had left a short while before, without any further voyages of discovery. Other situations which have in common with my adventure an unintended recurrence of the same situation, but which differ radically from it in other respects, also result in the same feeling of helplessness and of uncanniness. So, for instance, when, caught in a mist perhaps, one has lost one's way in a mountain forest, every attempt to find the marked or familiar path may bring one back again and again to one and the same spot, which one can identify by some particular landmark. Or one may wander about in a dark, strange room, looking for the door or the electric switch, and collide time after time with the same piece of furniture—though it is true that Mark Twain succeeded by wild exaggeration in turning this latter situation into something irresistibly comic.[1]

If we take another class of things, it is easy to see that there, too, it is only this factor of involuntary repetition which surrounds what would otherwise be innocent enough with an uncanny atmosphere, and forces upon us the idea of something fateful and inescapable when otherwise we should have spoken only of 'chance'. For instance, we naturally attach no importance to the event when we hand in an overcoat and get a cloak-room ticket with the number, let us say, 62; or when we find that our cabin on a ship bears that number. But the impression is altered if two such events, each in itself indifferent, happen

[1] [Mark Twain, *A Tramp Abroad*, London, 1880, **1**, 107.]

close together—if we come across the number 62 several times in a single day, or if we begin to notice that everything which has a number—addresses, hotel rooms, compartments in railway trains—invariably has the same one, or at all events one which contains the same figures. We do feel this to be uncanny. And unless a man is utterly hardened and proof against the lure of superstition, he will be tempted to ascribe a secret meaning to this obstinate recurrence of a number; he will take it, perhaps, as an indication of the span of life allotted to him.[1] Or suppose one is engaged in reading the works of the famous physiologist, Hering, and within the space of a few days receives two letters from two different countries, each from a person called Hering, though one has never before had any dealings with anyone of that name. Not long ago an ingenious scientist (Kammerer, 1919) attempted to reduce coincidences of this kind to certain laws, and so deprive them of their uncanny effect. I will not venture to decide whether he has succeeded or not.

How exactly we can trace back to infantile psychology the uncanny effect of such similar recurrences is a question I can only lightly touch on in these pages; and I must refer the reader instead to another work,[2] already completed, in which this has been gone into in detail, but in a different connection. For it is possible to recognize the dominance in the unconscious mind of a 'compulsion to repeat' proceeding from the instinctual impulses and probably inherent in the very nature of the instincts—a compulsion powerful enough to overrule the pleasure principle, lending to certain aspects of the mind their daemonic character, and still very clearly expressed in the impulses of small children; a compulsion, too, which is responsible for a part of the course taken by the analyses of neurotic patients. All these considerations prepare us for the discovery that whatever reminds us of this inner 'compulsion to repeat' is perceived as uncanny.

Now, however, it is time to turn from these aspects of the matter, which are in any case difficult to judge, and look for some undeniable instances of the uncanny, in the hope that

[1] [Freud had himself reached the age of 62 a year earlier, in 1918.]

[2] [This was published a year later as *Beyond the Pleasure Principle* (1920*g*). The various manifestations of the 'compulsion to repeat' enumerated here are enlarged upon in Chapters II and III of that

an analysis of them will decide whether our hypothesis is a valid one.

In the story of 'The Ring of Polycrates',[1] the King of Egypt turns away in horror from his host, Polycrates, because he sees that his friend's every wish is at once fulfilled, his every care promptly removed by kindly fate. His host has become 'uncanny' to him. His own explanation, that the too fortunate man has to fear the envy of the gods, seems obscure to us; its meaning is veiled in mythological language. We will therefore turn to another example in a less grandiose setting. In the case history of an obsessional neurotic,[2] I have described how the patient once stayed in a hydropathic establishment and benefited greatly by it. He had the good sense, however, to attribute his improvement not to the therapeutic properties of the water, but to the situation of his room, which immediately adjoined that of a very accommodating nurse. So on his second visit to the establishment he asked for the same room, but was told that it was already occupied by an old gentleman, whereupon he gave vent to his annoyance in the words: 'I wish he may be struck dead for it.' A fortnight later the old gentleman really did have a stroke. My patient thought this an 'uncanny' experience. The impression of uncanniness would have been stronger still if less time had elapsed between his words and the untoward event, or if he had been able to report innumerable similar coincidences. As a matter of fact, he had no difficulty in producing coincidences of this sort; but then not only he but every obsessional neurotic I have observed has been able to relate analogous experiences. They are never surprised at their invariably running up against someone they have just been thinking of, perhaps for the first time for a long while. If they say one day 'I haven't had any news of so-and-so for a long time', they will be sure to get a letter from him the next morning, and an accident or a death will rarely take place without having passed through their mind a little while before. They are in the habit of referring to this state of affairs in the most

work. The 'compulsion to repeat' had already been described by Freud as a clinical phenomenon, in a technical paper published five years earlier (1914*g*).]

[1] [Schiller's poem based on Herodotus.]

[2] 'Notes upon a Case of Obsessional Neurosis' (1909*d*) [*Standard Ed.*, **10**, 234].

modest manner, saying that they have 'presentiments' which 'usually' come true.

One of the most uncanny and wide-spread forms of superstition is the dread of the evil eye, which has been exhaustively studied by the Hamburg oculist Seligmann (1910–11). There never seems to have been any doubt about the source of this dread. Whoever possesses something that is at once valuable and fragile is afraid of other people's envy, in so far as he projects on to them the envy he would have felt in their place. A feeling like this betrays itself by a look[1] even though it is not put into words; and when a man is prominent owing to noticeable, and particularly owing to unattractive, attributes, other people are ready to believe that his envy is rising to a more than usual degree of intensity and that this intensity will convert it into effective action. What is feared is thus a secret intention of doing harm, and certain signs are taken to mean that that intention has the necessary power at its command.

These last examples of the uncanny are to be referred to the principle which I have called 'omnipotence of thoughts', taking the name from an expression used by one of my patients.[2] And now we find ourselves on familiar ground. Our analysis of instances of the uncanny has led us back to the old, animistic conception of the universe. This was characterized by the idea that the world was peopled with the spirits of human beings; by the subject's narcissistic overvaluation of his own mental processes; by the belief in the omnipotence of thoughts and the technique of magic based on that belief; by the attribution to various outside persons and things of carefully graded magical powers, or '*mana*'; as well as by all the other creations with the help of which man, in the unrestricted narcissism of that stage of development, strove to fend off the manifest prohibitions of reality. It seems as if each one of us has been through a phase of individual development corresponding to this animistic stage in primitive men, that none of us has passed through it without preserving certain residues and traces of it which are still capable of manifesting themselves, and that everything which now strikes us as 'uncanny' fulfils the condition of touching

[1] ['The evil eye' in German is '*der böse Blick*', literally 'the evil look'.]

[2] [The obsessional patient referred to just above—the 'Rat Man' (1909*d*), *Standard Ed.*, **10**, 233f.]

those residues of animistic mental activity within us and bringing them to expression.[1]

At this point I will put forward two considerations which, I think, contain the gist of this short study. In the first place, if psycho-analytic theory is correct in maintaining that every affect belonging to an emotional impulse, whatever its kind, is transformed, if it is repressed, into anxiety, then among instances of frightening things there must be one class in which the frightening element can be shown to be something repressed which *recurs*. This class of frightening things would then constitute the uncanny; and it must be a matter of indifference whether what is uncanny was itself originally frightening or whether it carried some *other* affect. In the second place, if this is indeed the secret nature of the uncanny, we can understand why linguistic usage has extended *das Heimliche* ['homely'] into its opposite, *das Unheimliche* (p. 226); for this uncanny is in reality nothing new or alien, but something which is familiar and old-established in the mind and which has become alienated from it only through the process of repression. This reference to the factor of repression enables us, furthermore, to understand Schelling's definition [p. 224] of the uncanny as something which ought to have remained hidden but has come to light.

It only remains for us to test our new hypothesis on one or two more examples of the uncanny.

Many people experience the feeling in the highest degree in relation to death and dead bodies, to the return of the dead, and to spirits and ghosts. As we have seen [p. 221] some languages in use to-day can only render the German expression 'an *unheimlich* house' by 'a *haunted* house'. We might indeed have begun our investigation with this example, perhaps the most striking of all, of something uncanny, but we refrained from doing so because the uncanny in it is too much intermixed with what is purely gruesome and is in part overlaid by it. There is scarcely any other matter, however, upon which our

[1] Cf. my book *Totem and Taboo* (1912–13), Essay III, 'Animism, Magic and the Omnipotence of Thoughts', where the following footnote will be found: 'We appear to attribute an "uncanny" quality to impressions that seek to confirm the omnipotence of thoughts and the animistic mode of thinking in general, after we have reached a stage at which, in our *judgement*, we have abandoned such beliefs.' [*Standard Ed.*, **13**, 86.]

thoughts and feelings have changed so little since the very earliest times, and in which discarded forms have been so completely preserved under a thin disguise, as our relation to death. Two things account for our conservatism: the strength of our original emotional reaction to death and the insufficiency of our scientific knowledge about it. Biology has not yet been able to decide whether death is the inevitable fate of every living being or whether it is only a regular but yet perhaps avoidable event in life.[1] It is true that the statement 'All men are mortal' is paraded in text-books of logic as an example of a general proposition; but no human being really grasps it, and our unconscious has as little use now as it ever had for the idea of its own mortality.[2] Religions continue to dispute the importance of the undeniable fact of individual death and to postulate a life after death; civil governments still believe that they cannot maintain moral order among the living if they do not uphold the prospect of a better life hereafter as a recompense for mundane existence. In our great cities, placards announce lectures that undertake to tell us how to get into touch with the souls of the departed; and it cannot be denied that not a few of the most able and penetrating minds among our men of science have come to the conclusion, especially towards the close of their own lives, that a contact of this kind is not impossible. Since almost all of us still think as savages do on this topic, it is no matter for surprise that the primitive fear of the dead is still so strong within us and always ready to come to the surface on any provocation. Most likely our fear still implies the old belief that the dead man becomes the enemy of his survivor and seeks to carry him off to share his new life with him. Considering our unchanged attitude towards death, we might rather enquire what has become of the repression, which is the necessary condition of a primitive feeling recurring in the shape of something uncanny. But repression is there, too. All supposedly educated people have ceased to believe officially that the dead can become visible as spirits, and have made any such appearances

[1] [This problem figures prominently in *Beyond the Pleasure Principle* (1920*g*), on which Freud was engaged while writing the present paper. See *Standard Ed.*, **18**, 44 ff.]

[2] [Freud had discussed the individual's attitude to death at greater length in the second part of his paper 'Thoughts for the Times on War and Death' (1915*b*).]

dependent on improbable and remote conditions; their emotional attitude towards their dead, moreover, once a highly ambiguous and ambivalent one, has been toned down in the higher strata of the mind into an unambiguous feeling of piety.[1]

We have now only a few remarks to add—for animism, magic and sorcery, the omnipotence of thoughts, man's attitude to death, involuntary repetition and the castration complex comprise practically all the factors which turn something frightening into something uncanny.

We can also speak of a living person as uncanny, and we do so when we ascribe evil intentions to him. But that is not all; in addition to this we must feel that his intentions to harm us are going to be carried out with the help of special powers. A good instance of this is the '*Gettatore*',[2] that uncanny figure of Romanic superstition which Schaeffer, with intuitive poetic feeling and profound psycho-analytic understanding, has transformed into a sympathetic character in his *Josef Montfort*. But the question of these secret powers brings us back again to the realm of animism. It was the pious Gretchen's intuition that Mephistopheles possessed secret powers of this kind that made him so uncanny to her.

> Sie fühlt dass ich ganz sicher ein Genie,
> Vielleicht sogar der Teufel bin.[3]

The uncanny effect of epilepsy and of madness has the same origin. The layman sees in them the working of forces hitherto unsuspected in his fellow-men, but at the same time he is dimly aware of them in remote corners of his own being. The Middle Ages quite consistently ascribed all such maladies to the influence of demons, and in this their psychology was almost correct. Indeed, I should not be surprised to hear that psychoanalysis, which is concerned with laying bare these hidden forces, has itself become uncanny to many people for that very reason. In one case, after I had succeeded—though none too rapidly—in effecting a cure in a girl who had been an invalid

[1] Cf. *Totem and Taboo* [*Standard Ed.*, **13**, 66].

[2] [Literally 'thrower' (of bad luck), or 'one who casts' (the evil eye).—Schaeffer's novel was published in 1918.]

[3] [She feels that surely I'm a genius now,—
Perhaps the very Devil indeed!
Goethe, *Faust*, Part I (Scene 16),
(Bayard Taylor's translation).]

for many years, I myself heard this view expressed by the patient's mother long after her recovery.

Dismembered limbs, a severed head, a hand cut off at the wrist, as in a fairy tale of Hauff's,[1] feet which dance by themselves, as in the book by Schaeffer which I mentioned above—all these have something peculiarly uncanny about them, especially when, as in the last instance, they prove capable of independent activity in addition. As we already know, this kind of uncanniness springs from its proximity to the castration complex. To some people the idea of being buried alive by mistake is the most uncanny thing of all. And yet psycho-analysis has taught us that this terrifying phantasy is only a transformation of another phantasy which had originally nothing terrifying about it at all, but was qualified by a certain lasciviousness—the phantasy, I mean, of intra-uterine existence.[2]

There is one more point of general application which I should like to add, though, strictly speaking, it has been included in what has already been said about animism and modes of working of the mental apparatus that have been surmounted; for I think it deserves special emphasis. This is that an uncanny effect is often and easily produced when the distinction between imagination and reality is effaced, as when something that we have hitherto regarded as imaginary appears before us in reality, or when a symbol takes over the full functions of the thing it symbolizes, and so on. It is this factor which contributes not a little to the uncanny effect attaching to magical practices. The infantile element in this, which also dominates the minds of neurotics, is the over-accentuation of psychical reality in comparison with material reality—a feature closely allied to the belief in the omnipotence of thoughts. In the middle of the isolation of war-time a number of the English *Strand Magazine* fell into my hands; and, among other somewhat redundant matter, I read a story about a young married couple who move into a furnished house in which there is a curiously shaped table with carvings of crocodiles on it. Towards evening an intolerable and very specific smell begins to pervade the house; they

[1] [*Die Geschichte von der abgehauenen Hand* ('The Story of the Severed Hand').]

[2] [See Section VIII of Freud's analysis of the 'Wolf Man' (1918*b*), above p. 101 ff.]

stumble over something in the dark; they seem to see a vague form gliding over the stairs—in short, we are given to understand that the presence of the table causes ghostly crocodiles to haunt the place, or that the wooden monsters come to life in the dark, or something of the sort. It was a naïve enough story, but the uncanny feeling it produced was quite remarkable.

To conclude this collection of examples, which is certainly not complete, I will relate an instance taken from psycho-analytic experience; if it does not rest upon mere coincidence, it furnishes a beautiful confirmation of our theory of the uncanny. It often happens that neurotic men declare that they feel there is something uncanny about the female genital organs. This *unheimlich* place, however, is the entrance to the former *Heim* [home] of all human beings, to the place where each one of us lived once upon a time and in the beginning. There is a joking saying that 'Love is home-sickness'; and whenever a man dreams of a place or a country and says to himself, while he is still dreaming: 'this place is familiar to me, I've been here before', we may interpret the place as being his mother's genitals or her body.[1] In this case too, then, the *unheimlich* is what was once *heimisch*, familiar; the prefix '*un*' ['un-'] is the token of repression.[2]

III

In the course of this discussion the reader will have felt certain doubts arising in his mind; and he must now have an opportunity of collecting them and bringing them forward.

It may be true that the uncanny [*unheimlich*] is something which is secretly familiar [*heimlich-heimisch*], which has undergone repression and then returned from it, and that everything that is uncanny fulfils this condition. But the selection of material on this basis does not enable us to solve the problem of the uncanny. For our proposition is clearly not convertible. Not everything that fulfils this condition—not everything that recalls repressed desires and surmounted modes of thinking belonging to the prehistory of the individual and of the race—is on that account uncanny.

Nor shall we conceal the fact that for almost every example

[1] [Cf. *The Interpretation of Dreams* (1900*a*), *Standard Ed.*, **5**, 399.]

[2] [See Freud's paper on 'Negation' (1925*h*).]

adduced in support of our hypothesis one may be found which rebuts it. The story of the severed hand in Hauff's fairy tale [p. 244] certainly has an uncanny effect, and we have traced that effect back to the castration complex; but most readers will probably agree with me in judging that no trace of uncanniness is provoked by Herodotus's story of the treasure of Rhampsinitus, in which the master-thief, whom the princess tries to hold fast by the hand, leaves his brother's severed hand behind with her instead. Again, the prompt fulfilment of the wishes of Polycrates [p. 239] undoubtedly affects us in the same uncanny way as it did the king of Egypt; yet our own fairy stories are crammed with instantaneous wish-fulfilments which produce no uncanny effect whatever. In the story of 'The Three Wishes', the woman is tempted by the savoury smell of a sausage to wish that she might have one too, and in an instant it lies on a plate before her. In his annoyance at her hastiness her husband wishes it may hang on her nose. And there it is, dangling from her nose. All this is very striking but not in the least uncanny. Fairy tales quite frankly adopt the animistic standpoint of the omnipotence of thoughts and wishes, and yet I cannot think of any genuine fairy story which has anything uncanny about it. We have heard that it is in the highest degree uncanny when an inanimate object—a picture or a doll—comes to life; nevertheless in Hans Andersen's stories the household utensils, furniture and tin soldiers are alive, yet nothing could well be more remote from the uncanny. And we should hardly call it uncanny when Pygmalion's beautiful statue comes to life.

Apparent death and the re-animation of the dead have been represented as most uncanny themes. But things of this sort too are very common in fairy stories. Who would be so bold as to call it uncanny, for instance, when Snow-White opens her eyes once more? And the resuscitation of the dead in accounts of miracles, as in the New Testament, elicits feelings quite unrelated to the uncanny. Then, too, the theme that achieves such an indubitably uncanny effect, the unintended recurrence of the same thing, serves other and quite different purposes in another class of cases. We have already come across one example [p. 237] in which it is employed to call up a feeling of the comic; and we could multiply instances of this kind. Or again, it works as a means of emphasis, and so on. And once more: what is the origin of the uncanny effect of silence, darkness and solitude?

Do not these factors point to the part played by danger in the genesis of what is uncanny, notwithstanding that in children these same factors are the most frequent determinants of the expression of fear [rather than of the uncanny]? And are we after all justified in entirely ignoring intellectual uncertainty as a factor, seeing that we have admitted its importance in relation to death [p. 242]?

It is evident therefore, that we must be prepared to admit that there are other elements besides those which we have so far laid down as determining the production of uncanny feelings. We might say that these preliminary results have satisfied *psycho-analytic* interest in the problem of the uncanny, and that what remains probably calls for an *aesthetic* enquiry. But that would be to open the door to doubts about what exactly is the value of our general contention that the uncanny proceeds from something familiar which has been repressed.

We have noticed one point which may help us to resolve these uncertainties: nearly all the instances that contradict our hypothesis are taken from the realm of fiction, of imaginative writing. This suggests that we should differentiate between the uncanny that we actually experience and the uncanny that we merely picture or read about.

What is *experienced* as uncanny is much more simply conditioned but comprises far fewer instances. We shall find, I think, that it fits in perfectly with our attempt at a solution, and can be traced back without exception to something familiar that has been repressed. But here, too, we must make a certain important and psychologically significant differentiation in our material, which is best illustrated by turning to suitable examples.

Let us take the uncanny associated with the omnipotence of thoughts, with the prompt fulfilment of wishes, with secret injurious powers and with the return of the dead. The condition under which the feeling of uncanniness arises here is unmistakable. We—or our primitive forefathers—once believed that these possibilities were realities, and were convinced that they actually happened. Nowadays we no longer believe in them, we have *surmounted* these modes of thought; but we do not feel quite sure of our new beliefs, and the old ones still exist within us ready to seize upon any confirmation. As soon as something *actually happens* in our lives which seems to confirm the old, discarded beliefs we get a feeling of the uncanny; it is as though we were making a judgement something like this: 'So, after all, it is *true* that one can kill a person by the mere wish!' or, 'So the dead *do* live on and appear on the scene of their former activities!' and so on. Conversely, anyone who has completely and finally rid himself of animistic beliefs will be insensible to this type of the uncanny. The most remarkable coincidences of wish and fulfilment, the most mysterious repetition of similar experiences in a particular place or on a particular date, the most deceptive sights and suspicious noises—none of these things will disconcert him or raise the kind of fear which can be described as 'a fear of something uncanny'. The whole thing is purely an affair of 'reality-testing', a question of the material reality of the phenomena.[1]

The state of affairs is different when the uncanny proceeds from repressed infantile complexes, from the castration complex, womb-phantasies, etc.; but experiences which arouse this kind of uncanny feeling are not of very frequent occurrence in real life. The uncanny which proceeds from actual experience belongs for the most part to the first group [the group dealt with in the previous paragraph]. Nevertheless the distinction between the two is theoretically very important. Where the

[1] Since the uncanny effect of a 'double' also belongs to this same group it is interesting to observe what the effect is of meeting one's own image unbidden and unexpected. Ernst Mach has related two such observations in his *Analyse der Empfindungen* (1900, 3). On the first occasion he was not a little startled when he realized that the face before him was his own. The second time he formed a very unfavourable opinion about the supposed stranger who entered the omnibus, and thought 'What a shabby-looking school-master that man is who is getting in!'—I can report a similar adventure. I was sitting alone in my *wagon-lit* compartment when a more than usually violent jolt of the train swung back the door of the adjoining washing-cabinet, and an elderly gentleman in a dressing-gown and a travelling cap came in. I assumed that in leaving the washing-cabinet, which lay between the two compartments, he had taken the wrong direction and come into my compartment by mistake. Jumping up with the intention of putting him right, I at once realized to my dismay that the intruder was nothing but my own reflection in the looking-glass on the open door. I can still recollect that I thoroughly disliked his appearance. Instead, therefore, of being *frightened* by our 'doubles', both Mach and I simply failed to recognize them as such. Is it not possible, though, that our dislike of them was a vestigial trace of the archaic reaction which feels the 'double' to be something uncanny?

uncanny comes from infantile complexes the question of material reality does not arise; its place is taken by psychical reality. What is involved is an actual repression of some content of thought and a return of this repressed content, not a cessation of *belief in the reality* of such a content. We might say that in the one case what had been repressed is a particular ideational content, and in the other the belief in its (material) reality. But this last phrase no doubt extends the term 'repression' beyond its legitimate meaning. It would be more correct to take into account a psychological distinction which can be detected here, and to say that the animistic beliefs of civilized people are in a state of having been (to a greater or lesser extent) *surmounted* [rather than repressed]. Our conclusion could then be stated thus: an uncanny experience occurs either when infantile complexes which have been repressed are once more revived by some impression, or when primitive beliefs which have been surmounted seem once more to be confirmed. Finally, we must not let our predilection for smooth solutions and lucid exposition blind us to the fact that these two classes of uncanny experience are not always sharply distinguishable. When we consider that primitive beliefs are most intimately connected with infantile complexes, and are, in fact, based on them, we shall not be greatly astonished to find that the distinction is often a hazy one.

The uncanny as it is depicted in *literature*, in stories and imaginative productions, merits in truth a separate discussion. Above all, it is a much more fertile province than the uncanny in real life, for it contains the whole of the latter and something more besides, something that cannot be found in real life. The contrast between what has been repressed and what has been surmounted cannot be transposed on to the uncanny in fiction without profound modification; for the realm of phantasy depends for its effect on the fact that its content is not submitted to reality-testing. The somewhat paradoxical result is that *in the first place a great deal that is not uncanny in fiction would be so if it happened in real life; and in the second place that there are many more means of creating uncanny effects in fiction than there are in real life.*

The imaginative writer has this licence among many others, that he can select his world of representation so that it either coincides with the realities we are familiar with or departs from them in what particulars he pleases. We accept his ruling in every case. In fairy tales, for instance, the world of reality is left behind from the very start, and the animistic system of beliefs is frankly adopted. Wish-fulfilments, secret powers, omnipotence of thoughts, animation of inanimate objects, all the elements so common in fairy stories, can exert no uncanny influence here; for, as we have learnt, that feeling cannot arise unless there is a conflict of judgement as to whether things which have been 'surmounted' and are regarded as incredible may not, after all, be possible; and this problem is eliminated from the outset by the postulates of the world of fairy tales. Thus we see that fairy stories, which have furnished us with most of the contradictions to our hypothesis of the uncanny, confirm the first part of our proposition—that in the realm of fiction many things are not uncanny which would be so if they happened in real life. In the case of these stories there are other contributory factors, which we shall briefly touch upon later.

The creative writer can also choose a setting which though less imaginary than the world of fairy tales, does yet differ from the real world by admitting superior spiritual beings such as daemonic spirits or ghosts of the dead. So long as they remain within their setting of poetic reality, such figures lose any uncanniness which they might possess. The souls in Dante's *Inferno*, or the supernatural apparitions in Shakespeare's *Hamlet*, *Macbeth* or *Julius Caesar*, may be gloomy and terrible enough, but they are no more really uncanny than Homer's jovial world of gods. We adapt our judgement to the imaginary reality imposed on us by the writer, and regard souls, spirits and ghosts as though their existence had the same validity as our own has in material reality. In this case too we avoid all trace of the uncanny.

The situation is altered as soon as the writer pretends to move in the world of common reality. In this case he accepts as well all the conditions operating to produce uncanny feelings in real life; and everything that would have an uncanny effect in reality has it in his story. But in this case he can even increase his effect and multiply it far beyond what could happen in reality, by bringing about events which never or very rarely happen in fact. In doing this he is in a sense betraying us to the superstitiousness which we have ostensibly surmounted; he deceives us by promising to give us the sober truth, and then after all overstepping it. We react to his inventions as we would have reacted to real experiences; by the time we have seen through his trick it is already too late and the author has achieved his object. But it must be added that his success is not unalloyed. We retain a feeling of dissatisfaction, a kind of grudge against the attempted deceit. I have noticed this particularly after reading Schnitzler's *Die Weissagung* [*The Prophecy*] and similar stories which flirt with the supernatural. However, the writer has one more means which he can use in order to avoid our recalcitrance and at the same time to improve his chances of success. He can keep us in the dark for a long time about the precise nature of the presuppositions on which the world he writes about is based, or he can cunningly and ingeniously avoid any definite information on the point to the last. Speaking generally, however, we find a confirmation of the second part of our proposition—that fiction presents more opportunities for creating uncanny feelings than are possible in real life.

Strictly speaking, all these complications relate only to that class of the uncanny which proceeds from forms of thought that have been surmounted. The class which proceeds from repressed complexes is more resistant and remains as powerful in fiction as in real experience, subject to one exception [see p. 252]. The uncanny belonging to the first class—that proceeding from forms of thought that have been surmounted—retains its character not only in experience but in fiction as well, so long as the setting is one of material reality; but where it is given an arbitrary and artificial setting in fiction, it is apt to lose that character.

We have clearly not exhausted the possibilities of poetic licence and the privileges enjoyed by story-writers in evoking or in excluding an uncanny feeling. In the main we adopt an unvarying passive attitude towards real experience and are subject to the influence of our physical environment. But the storyteller has a *peculiarly* directive power over us; by means of the moods he can put us into, he is able to guide the current of our emotions, to dam it up in one direction and make it flow in another, and he often obtains a great variety of effects from the same material. All this is nothing new, and has doubtless long since been fully taken into account by students of aesthetics. We have drifted into this field of research half involuntarily, through the temptation to explain certain instances which contradicted our theory of the causes of the uncanny. Accordingly we will now return to the examination of a few of those instances.

We have already asked [p. 246] why it is that the severed hand in the story of the treasure of Rhampsinitus has no uncanny effect in the way that the severed hand has in Hauff's story. The question seems to have gained in importance now that we have recognized that the class of the uncanny which proceeds from repressed complexes is the more resistant of the two. The answer is easy. In the Herodotus story our thoughts are concentrated much more on the superior cunning of the master-thief than on the feelings of the princess. The princess may very well have had an uncanny feeling, indeed she very probably fell into a swoon; but *we* have no such sensations, for we put ourselves in the thief's place, not in hers. In Nestroy's farce, *Der Zerrissene* [*The Torn Man*], another means is used to avoid any impression of the uncanny in the scene in which the fleeing man, convinced that he is a murderer, lifts up one trapdoor after another and each time sees what he takes to be the ghost of his victim rising up out of it. He calls out in despair, 'But I've only killed *one* man. Why this ghastly multiplication?' We know what went before this scene and do not share his error, so what must be uncanny to him has an irresistibly comic effect on us. Even a 'real' ghost, as in Oscar Wilde's *Canterville Ghost*, loses all power of at least arousing *gruesome* feelings in us as soon as the author begins to amuse himself by being ironical about it and allows liberties to be taken with it. Thus we see how independent emotional effects can be of the actual subject-matter in the world of fiction. In fairy stories feelings of fear—including therefore uncanny feelings—are ruled out altogether. We understand this, and that is why we ignore any opportunities we find in them for developing such feelings.

Concerning the factors of silence, solitude and darkness [pp. 246–7], we can only say that they are actually elements in the production of the infantile anxiety from which the majority of human beings have never become quite free. This problem has been discussed from a psycho-analytic point of view elsewhere.[1]

[1] [See the discussion of children's fear of the dark in Section V of the third of Freud's *Three Essays* (1905*d*), *Standard Ed.*, **7**, 224 *n.*]

APPENDIX

Extract from Daniel Sanders's *Wörterbuch der Deutschen Sprache* [1]

Heimlich, a. (-keit, f. -en): **1.** auch Heimelich, heimelig, zum Hause gehörig, nicht fremd, vertraut, zahm, traut und traulich, anheimelnd etc. (*a*) (veralt.) zum Haus, zur Familie gehörig oder: wie dazu gehörig betrachtet, vgl. lat. familiaris, vertraut: Die Heimlichen, die Hausgenossen; Der heimliche Rath. 1. Mos. 41, 45; 2. Sam. 23, 23. 1 Chr. 12, 25. Weish. 8, 4., wofür jetzt: Geheimer (s. *d* **1.**) Rath üblich ist, s. Heimlicher—(*b*) von Thieren zahm, sich den Menschen traulich anschließend. Ggstz. wild, z. B.: Thier, die weder wild noch heimlich sind, etc. Eppendorf. 88; Wilde Thier . . . so man sie h. und gewohnsam um die Leute aufzeucht. 92. So diese Thierle von Jugend bei den Menschen erzogen, werden sie ganz h., freundlich etc., Stumpf 608a etc.—So noch: So h. ist's (das Lamm) und frißt aus meiner Hand. Hölty; Ein schöner, heimelicher (s. *c*) Vogel bleibt der Storch immerhin. Linck, Schl. 146. s. Häuslich **1** etc.—(*c*) traut, traulich anheimelnd; das Wohlgefühl stiller Befriedigung etc., behaglicher Ruhe u. sichern Schutzes, wie das umschlossne, wohnliche Haus erregend (vgl. Geheuer): Ist dir's h. noch im Lande, wo die Fremden deine Wälder roden? Alexis H. 1, 1, 289; Es war ihr nicht allzu h. bei ihm. Brentano Wehm. 92; Auf einem hohen h—en Schattenpfade . . ., längs dem rieselnden rauschenden und plätschernden Waldbach. Forster B. 1, 417. Die H—keit der Heimath zerstören. Gervinus Lit. 5, 375. So vertraulich und h. habe ich nicht leicht ein Plätzchen gefunden. G[oethe], 14, 14; Wir dachten es uns so bequem, so artig, so gemüthlich und h. 15, 9; In stiller H—keit, umzielt von engen Schranken. Haller; Einer sorglichen Hausfrau, die mit dem Wenigsten eine vergnügliche H—keit (Häuslichkeit) zu schaffen versteht. Hartmann Unst. 1, 188; Desto h—er kam ihm jetzt der ihm erst kurz noch so fremde Mann vor. Kerner 540; Die protestantischen Besitzer fühlen sich . . . nicht h. unter ihren katholischen Unterthanen. Kohl. Irl. 1, 172; Wenns h. wird und leise/die Abendstille nur

[1] [Cf. p. 222.]

an deiner Zelle lauscht. Tiedge 2, 39; Still und lieb und h., als sie sich/zum Ruhen einen Platz nur wünschen möchten. W[ieland], 11, 144; Es war ihm garnicht h. dabei 27. 170, etc.—Auch: Der Platz war so still, so einsam, so schatten-h. Scherr Pilg. 1, 170; Die ab- und zuströmenden Fluthwellen, träumend und wiegenlied-h. Körner, Sch. 3, 320, etc.—Vgl. namentl. Un-h.—Namentl. bei schwäb., schwzr. Schriftst. oft dreisilbig: Wie 'heimelich' war es dann Ivo Abends wieder, als er zu Hause lag. Auerbach, D. 1, 249; In dem Haus ist mir's so heimelig gewesen. 4. 307; Die warme Stube, der heimelige Nachmittag. Gotthelf, Sch. 127, 148; Das ist das wahre Heimelig, wenn der Mensch so von Herzen fühlt, wie wenig er ist, wie groß der Herr ist. 147; Wurde man nach und nach recht gemüthlich und heimelig mit einander. U. 1, 297; Die trauliche Heimeligkeit. 380, 2, 86; Heimelicher wird es mir wohl nirgends werden als hier. 327; Pestalozzi 4, 240; Was von ferne herkommt . . . lebt gw. nicht ganz heimelig (heimatlich, freundnachbarlich) mit den Leuten. 325; Die Hütte, wo/er sonst so heimelig, so froh/ . . . im Kreis der Seinen oft gesessen. Reithard 20; Da klingt das Horn des Wächters so heimelig vom Thurm/da ladet seine Stimme so gastlich. 49; Es schläft sich da so lind und warm/so wunderheim'lig ein. 23, etc.—Diese Weise verdiente allgemein zu werden, um das gute Wort vor dem Veralten wegen nahe liegender Verwechslung mit **2** zu bewahren. vgl.: 'Die Zecks sind alle h. (**2**)' H.? . . Was verstehen sie unter h.? . .—'Nun . . . es kommt mir mit ihnen vor, wie mit einem zugegrabenen Brunnen oder einem ausgetrockneten Teich. Man kann nicht darüber gehen, ohne daß es Einem immer ist, als könnte da wieder einmal Wasser zum Vorschein kommen.' Wir nennen das un-h.; Sie nennen's h. Worin finden Sie denn, daß diese Familie etwas Verstecktes und Unzuverlässiges hat? etc. Gutzkow R. 2, 61.[1]—(*d*) (s. *c*) namentl. schles.: fröhlich, heiter, auch vom Wetter, s. Adelung und Weinhold.

2. versteckt, verborgen gehalten, so daß man Andre nicht davon oder darum wissen lassen, es ihnen verbergen will, vgl. Geheim (**2**), von welchem erst nhd. Ew. es doch zumal in der älteren Sprache, z. B. in der Bibel, wie Hiob 11, 6; 15, 8;

[1] [Spaced type, here and below, is introduced by Freud.]

Weish. 2, 22; 1. Kor. 2, 7 etc., und so auch H—keit statt Geheimnis. Math. 13, 35 etc., nicht immer genau geschieden wird: H. (hinter Jemandes Rücken) Etwas thun, treiben; Sich h. davon schleichen; H—e Zusammenkünfte, Verabredungen; Mit h—er Schadenfreude zusehen; H. seufzen, weinen; H. thun, als ob man etwas zu verbergen hätte; H—e Liebschaft, Liebe, Sünde; H—e Orte (die der Wohlstand zu verhüllen gebietet). 1. Sam. 5, 6; Das h—e Gemach (Abtritt). 2. Kön. 10, 27; W[ieland], 5, 256 etc., auch: Der h—e Stuhl. Zinkgräf 1, 249; In Graben, in H—keiten werfen. 3, 75; Rollenhagen Fr. 83 etc.—Führte h. vor Laomedon/die Stuten vor. B[ürger], 161 b etc.—Ebenso versteckt, h., hinterlistig und boshaft gegen grausame Herren . . . wie offen, frei, theilnehmend und dienstwillig gegen den leidenden Freund. Burmeister gB 2, 157; Du sollst mein h. Heiligstes noch wissen. Chamisso 4, 56; Die h—e Kunst (der Zauberei). 3, 224; Wo die öffentliche Ventilation aufhören muß, fängt die h—e Machination an. Forster, Br. 2, 135; Freiheit ist die leise Parole h. Verschworener, das laute Feldgeschrei der öffentlich Umwälzenden. G[oethe], 4, 222; Ein heilig, h. Wirken. 15; Ich habe Wurzeln/die sind gar h., /im tiefen Boden/bin ich gegründet. 2, 109; Meine h—e Tücke (vgl. Heimtücke). 30, 344; Empfängt er es nicht offenbar und gewissenhaft, so mag er es h. und gewissenlos ergreifen. 39, 33; Ließ h. und geheimnisvoll achromatische Fernröhre zusammensetzen. 375; Von nun an, will ich, sei nichts H—es/ mehr unter uns. Sch[iller], 369 b.—Jemandes H—keiten entdecken, offenbaren, verrathen; H—keiten hinter meinem Rücken zu brauen. Alexis. H. 2, 3, 168; Zu meiner Zeit/befliß man sich der H—keit. Hagedorn 3, 92; Die H—keit und das Gepuschele unter der Hand. Immermann, M. 3, 289; Der H—keit (des verborgnen Golds) unmächtigen Bann/kann nur die Hand der Einsicht lösen. Novalis. 1, 69; /Sag'an, wo du sie . . . verbirgst, in welches Ortes verschwiegener H. Sch[iller], 495 b; Ihr Bienen, die ihr knetet/der H—keiten Schloß (Wachs zum Siegeln). Tieck, Cymb. 3, 2; Erfahren in seltnen H—keiten (Zauberkünsten). Schlegel Sh. 6, 102 etc., vgl. Geheimnis L[essing], 10: 291 ff.

Zsstzg. s. 1 *c*, so auch nam. der Ggstz.: Un-: unbehagliches, banges Grauen erregend: Der schier ihm un-h., gespenstisch erschien. Chamisso 3, 238; Der Nacht un-h., bange Stunden. 4, 148; Mir war schon lang' un-h., ja graulich zu Muthe. 242;

Nun fängts mir an, un-h. zu werden. G[oethe], 6, 330; . . . Empfindet ein u—es Grauen. Heine, Verm. 1, 51; Un-h. und starr wie ein Steinbild. Reis, 1, 10; Den u—en Nebel, Haarrauch geheißen. Immermann M., 3, 299; Diese blassen Jungen sind un-h. und brauen Gott weiß was Schlimmes. Laube, Band. 1, 119; Un-h. nennt man Alles, was im Geheimnis, im Verborgnen . . . bleiben sollte und hervorgetreten ist. Schelling, 2, 2, 649 etc.—Das Göttliche zu verhüllen, mit einer gewissen U—keit zu umgeben 658, etc.—Unüblich als Ggstz. von (2), wie es Campe ohne Beleg anführt.

PREFACE TO REIK'S *RITUAL: PSYCHO-ANALYTIC STUDIES*
(1919)

PREFACE TO REIK'S *PROBLEME DER RELIGIONSPSYCHOLOGIE*

(*a*) German Editions:

1919 In T. Reik, *Probleme der Religionspsychologie*, I Teil: 'Das Ritual', vii–xii, Leipzig and Vienna: Internationaler Psychoanalytischer Verlag.

1928 2nd ed., published under the title *Das Ritual: Psychoanalytische Studien*. Same publishers.

1928 *G.S.*, **11**, 256–60.

1947 *G.W.*, **12**, 325–9.

(*b*) English Translations:

Preface to Reik's *Ritual: Psycho-Analytic Studies*

1931 In Reik, *Ritual: Psycho-Analytic Studies*, 5–10, London: Hogarth Press and Institute of Psycho-Analysis; New York: Norton. (Tr. D. Bryan.)

1950 *C.P.*, **5**, 92–7. (Under the title 'Psycho-Analysis and Religious Origins'.) (Tr. J. Strachey.)

The present translation is the one published in 1950, slightly revised. No second volume of Reik's original book was ever issued.

PREFACE TO REIK'S *RITUAL: PSYCHO-ANALYTIC STUDIES*

Psycho-analysis was born out of medical necessity. It sprang from the need for bringing help to neurotic patients, who had found no relief through rest-cures, through the arts of hydropathy or through electricity. A most remarkable observation made by Josef Breuer had excited a hope that the more one understood of the hitherto unexplored origin of their symptoms the more extensive would be the help one could afford them. Thus it came about that psycho-analysis, being originally a purely medical technique, was from the first directed towards research, towards the discovery of causal chains at once far-reaching and recondite.

Its further course led it away from the study of the somatic determinants of nervous disease to an extent that was bewildering to physicians. Instead, it was brought into contact with the mental substance of human lives—the lives not only of the sick, but of the healthy, the normal and the supernormal. It had to deal with emotions and passions, and most of all with those which the poets never tire of depicting and celebrating—the emotions of love. It learnt to recognize the power of memories, the unsuspected importance of the years of childhood in shaping the adult, and the strength of wishes, which falsify human judgements and lay down fixed lines for human endeavour.

For a time psycho-analysis seemed fated to merge into psychology without being able to show why the psychology of the sick differed from that of the normal. In the course of its advance, however, it came up against the problem of dreams, which are abnormal products of the mind created by normal men under regularly recurrent physiological conditions. When psycho-analysis had solved the problem of dreams, it had discovered in *unconscious* psychical processes the common ground in which the highest and the lowest of mental impulses have their roots and from which spring the most normal as well as the most morbid and erratic of mental productions. The new picture of the workings of the mind began to grow ever clearer and more complete. It was a picture of obscure instinctual forces, organic in origin, striving towards inborn aims, and, above them, of an agency comprising more highly organized mental structures—acquisitions of human evolution made under the impact of human history—, an agency which has taken over portions of the instinctual impulses, has developed them further or has even directed them towards higher aims, but which in any case binds them firmly and manipulates their energy to suit its own purposes. This higher organization, however, which is known to us as the ego, has rejected another portion of these same elementary instinctual impulses as being unserviceable because they cannot be fitted into the organic unity of the individual or because they rebel against the individual's cultural aims. The ego is not in a position to exterminate these unsubdued mental powers, but it turns its back on them, lets them remain at the lowest psychological level, defends itself from their demands by the energetic erection of protective and antithetical barriers or seeks to come to terms with them by means of substitutive satisfactions. These instincts which have fallen victim to repression—untamed and indestructible, yet inhibited from any kind of activity—together with their primitive mental representatives, constitute the mental underworld, the nucleus of the true unconscious, and are at every moment ready to assert their demands and, by hook or by crook, to force their way forward to satisfaction. To this is due the instability of the proud superstructure of the mind, the emergence at night of the proscribed and repressed material in the form of dreams, and the tendency to fall ill with neuroses and psychoses as soon as the balance of power between the ego and the repressed shifts to the disadvantage of the ego.

A little reflection was bound to show that it would be impossible to restrict to the provinces of dreams and nervous disorders a view such as this of the life of the human mind. If that view has hit upon a truth, it must apply equally to *normal* mental events, and even the highest achievements of the human spirit must bear a demonstrable relation to the factors found in pathology—to repression, to the efforts at mastering the unconscious and to the possibilities of satisfying the primitive instincts. There was thus an irresistible temptation and, indeed, a scientific duty, to apply the research methods of psycho-analysis, in regions far remote from its native soil, to the various mental sciences. And indeed psycho-analytic work upon patients itself pointed persistently in the direction of this new task, for it was obvious that the forms assumed by the different neuroses echoed the most highly admired productions of our culture. Thus hysterics are undoubtedly imaginative artists, even if they express their phantasies *mimetically* in the main and without considering their intelligibility to other people; the ceremonials and prohibitions of obsessional neurotics drive us to suppose that they have created a private religion of their own; and the delusions of paranoics have an unpalatable external similarity and internal kinship to the systems of our philosophers. It is impossible to escape the conclusion that these patients are, in an *asocial* fashion, making the very attempts at solving their conflicts and appeasing their pressing needs which, when those attempts are carried out in a fashion that is acceptable to the majority, are known as poetry, religion and philosophy.

In 1913 Otto Rank and Hanns Sachs, in an extremely interesting work, brought together the results which had been achieved up to that time in the application of psycho-analysis to the mental sciences.[1] The most easily accessible branches of those sciences seem to be mythology and the history of literature and religion. No final formula has yet been found enabling us to give an appropriate place to myths in this connection. Otto Rank, in a large volume on the incest complex (1912), has produced evidence of the surprising fact that the choice of subject-matter, especially for dramatic works, is principally determined by the ambit of what psycho-analysis has termed the 'Oedipus complex'. By working it over with the greatest variety of modifications, distortions and disguises, the dramatist seeks to deal with his own most personal relations to this emotional theme. It is in attempting to master the Oedipus complex—that is to say, a person's emotional attitude towards his family, or in a narrower sense towards his father and mother—that individual neurotics come to grief, and for this reason that complex habitually forms the nucleus of their neuroses. It does not owe its importance to any unintelligible conjunction; the emphasis laid upon the relation of children to their parents is an expression of the biological facts that the young of the human race pass through a long period of dependence and are slow in reaching maturity, as well as that their capacity for love undergoes a

[1] [Freud himself had made a similar attempt in an article which he contributed to *Scientia* (1913*j*).]

complicated course of development. Consequently, the overcoming of the Oedipus complex coincides with the most efficient way of mastering the archaic, animal heritage of humanity. It is true that that heritage comprises all the forces that are required for the subsequent cultural development of the individual, but they must first be sorted out and worked over. This archaic heirloom is not fit to be used for the purposes of civilized social life in the form in which it is inherited by the individual.

To find the starting-point for the psycho-analytic view of religious life we must go a step further. What is to-day the heritage of the individual was once a new acquisition and has been handed on from one to another of a long series of generations. Thus the Oedipus complex too may have had stages of development, and the study of prehistory may enable us to trace them out. Investigation suggests that life in the human family took a quite different form in those remote days from that with which we are now familiar. And this idea is supported by findings based on observations of contemporary primitive races. If the prehistoric and ethnological material on this subject is worked over psycho-analytically, we arrive at an unexpectedly precise result: namely that God the Father once walked upon earth in bodily form and exercised his sovereignty as chieftain of the primal human horde until his sons united to slay him. It emerges further that this crime of liberation and the reactions to it had as their result the appearance of the first social ties, the basic moral restrictions and the oldest form of religion, totemism. But the later religions too have the same content, and on the one hand they are concerned with obliterating the traces of that crime or with expiating it by bringing forward other solutions of the struggle between the father and sons, while on the other hand they cannot avoid repeating once more the elimination of the father. Incidentally, an echo of this monstrous event, which overshadowed the whole course of human development, is also to be found in myths.

This hypothesis, which is founded on the observations of Robertson Smith [1889] and was developed by me in *Totem and Taboo* [1912–13], has been taken by Theodor Reik as the basis of his studies on the problems of the psychology of religion, of which this is the first volume.[1] In accordance with psycho-analytic technique these studies start out from hitherto

[1] [See p. 258 above.]

unexplained details of religious life, and by means of their elucidation gain access to the fundamental postulates and ultimate aims of religions; moreover they keep steadily in view the relation between prehistoric man and contemporary primitive societies as well as the connection between the products of civilization and the substitutive structures of neurotics. In conclusion, I would draw attention to the author's own introduction and express my belief that his work will recommend itself to the notice of specialists in the branch of knowledge with which it deals.

SHORTER WRITINGS
(1919)

A NOTE ON PSYCHO-ANALYTIC PUBLICATIONS AND PRIZES[1]

(1919)

In the Autumn of 1918 a member of the Budapest Psycho-Analytical Society informed me that a Fund had been set aside for cultural purposes from the profits made by industrial undertakings during the war. The decision as to its use lay jointly with himself and the Chief Burgermaster of the city of Budapest, Dr. Stephan Bárczy. They had agreed to devote the considerable sum of money concerned to the purposes of the psycho-analytic movement and to hand over its administration to me. I accepted this commission, and I now fulfil my duty of offering public thanks to the Chief Burgermaster (who soon afterwards received the Psycho-Analytical Congress in Budapest with so much honour) as well as to the anonymous member who has performed such a high service to the cause of psycho-analysis.[2]

The Fund thus placed at my disposal, which was given my name, was allotted by me to the foundation of an international psycho-analytic publishing business [the '*Internationaler Psycho-analytischer Verlag*']. I considered that in the present circumstances this was our most important need.

Unlike many other scientific undertakings, our two periodical publications, the *Internationale Zeitschrift für ärztliche Psychoanalyse* and *Imago*, did not come to an end during the war. We succeeded in keeping them in existence, but in consequence of the increasing difficulties, closing of frontiers and rise in prices which accompanied the war, it became necessary to reduce them considerably in size and to allow undesirably long intervals to elapse between the publication of successive issues. Of the four editors of the two journals (Ferenczi, Jones, Rank and Sachs) one, being a subject of an enemy State, was cut off from

[1] ['Internationaler psychoanalytischer Verlag und Preiszuteilungen für psychoanalytische Arbeiten', *Int. Z. Psychoanal.*, **5**, (1919), 137; *G.W.*, **12** (1947), 333. The present translation, the first into English, is by James Strachey.]

[2] [This was Dr. Anton von Freund. See Freud's obituary of him (1920*c*). The Fifth International Psycho-Analytical Congress was held in Budapest in September, 1918.]

us; two others had joined the forces and were fully engaged in their military duties; only Dr. Sachs was left at work, and he self-sacrificingly assumed the whole burden. A few of the local psycho-analytical societies found it necessary to suspend their meetings entirely; the number of contributors shrank, as did that of the subscribers. It was easy to foresee that the publisher's natural dissatisfaction would soon put in question the continuance of the journals to which we attached so much importance. Yet numerous indications, which reached us even from the front-line trenches, pointed to the fact that contemporary interest in psycho-analysis had not diminished. I think I was justified in my intention to put an end to these difficulties and dangers by the foundation of an international psycho-analytic publishing business. This publishing house is already in existence to-day, as a limited liability company; it is under the direction of Dr. Otto Rank, who has been for so many years secretary of the Vienna Society and co-editor of the two psycho-analytic journals, and who has returned after many years' absence on active service to his earlier work in the service of psycho-analysis.

The new publishing house, supported by the funds of the Budapest endowment, has assumed the task of ensuring the regular appearance and reliable distribution of the two journals. As soon as the difficulties of external circumstances permit, it is intended that they shall be restored to their former dimensions, and that these dimensions may if necessary be increased, without any extra charge to the subscribers. But in addition to this, and without waiting for an improvement, the publishing house will proceed to print books and pamphlets dealing with the field of medical and applied psycho-analysis; and since it is not a profit-making concern, it will be able to pay better heed to the interests of authors than is usually done by commercial publishers.

Simultaneously with the establishment of the psycho-analytic publishing house it was decided to award annual prizes out of the interest on the Budapest endowment, to two outstanding pieces of work, one each in the field of medical and of applied psycho-analysis. These prizes—to the amount of 1,000 Austrian *Kronen* [1]—are intended to be awarded, not to authors, but to individual works, so that there will be a possibility of the same author winning a prize repeatedly. The decision on the question

[1] [This was equivalent at the time to £50 or $250.]

of which among the writings published during a particular period are to receive prizes has not been transferred to a committee but will be kept in the hands of a single person, the Administrator of the fund for the time being; otherwise, if a committee of adjudicators were to be formed of the most experienced and discerning analysts, their own writings would have to be excluded from consideration, and the scheme might easily fail in its intention of distinguishing exemplary achievements in psycho-analytic literature. If the adjudicator finds himself hesitating between two works of almost equal value, he will be empowered to divide the prize between them, without the award of a half-prize implying any less appreciation of the work in question.

It is intended that these prizes shall in general be awarded every year and that the choice should lie between the whole of the psycho-analytically important literature published during that period, irrespectively of whether the author of the work in question is a Member of the International Psycho-Analytical Association.

The first prizes have already been awarded and relate to papers published during the period of the war, from 1914 to 1918. The prize for medical psycho-analysis has been divided between Karl Abraham's paper 'The First Pregenital Stage of the Libido' (1916) and Ernst Simmel's pamphlet *Kriegsneurosen und psychisches Trauma* [*War Neuroses and Psychical Trauma*] (1918). The prize for applied psycho-analysis has been awarded to Theodor Reik's paper 'Die Pubertätsriten der Wilden' ['Puberty Rites among Savages'] (1915).

FREUD.

EDITOR'S NOTE

Two further announcements on the same subject, both of them printed over Freud's signature, appeared subsequently: 'Preiszuteilungen' (*Int. Z. Psychoanal.*, **7**, 381), and 'Preisausschreibung' (ibid., **8**, 527). The first was published late in 1921:

'AWARD OF PRIZES

'A recent gift made by Dr. Max Eitingon, the director of the Berlin Clinic, has made it possible for me to revive the award of prizes (first made in 1919) for psycho-analytic writings of peculiar merit. The prize for *medical* psycho-analysis has been awarded to A. Stärcke (of Den Dolder, Holland) for his two publications "Der Kastrationskomplex" [1920] and "Psychoanalyse und Psychiatrie" [1921] (both of them Congress papers), of which the first appeared in the current volume of this periodical and the second as a supplementary issue. The prize for *applied* psycho-analysis has gone to Dr. G. Róheim (of Budapest) for his paper "Das Selbst" [1921] and his Congress paper on Australian Totemism [1920]. The amount of each prize was one thousand marks. [About £50.]

FREUD.'

The second of these announcements was published at the end of 1922:

'PRIZE OFFER

'At the Seventh International Psycho-Analytical Congress, in Berlin, I laid down as the subject for a prize: "The Relation between Analytic Technique and Analytic Theory." The questions to be discussed are how far the technique has influenced the theory and how far they assist or hinder each other at the present time.

'Works dealing with this subject should be sent to me at the address given below before May 1, 1923. They should be legibly typewritten. They should have a motto attached and should be accompanied by a sealed envelope enclosing the author's name. They must be written either in German or English. In judging the works submitted I shall have the assistance of Dr. K. Abraham and Dr. M. Eitingon.

'The prize amounts to 20,000 marks[1] at the value current at the time of the Congress.

'Berggasse 19, Vienna IX.

FREUD.'

According to an official statement in *Int. Z. Psychoanal.*, **10**, 106, no entries were submitted for this prize; but the subject was discussed in a symposium at the Eighth (Salzburg) Congress in 1924.

[1] [Owing to the collapse of the exchanges at this date it is impossible to give any estimate of the equivalent values of this sum.]

JAMES J. PUTNAM[1]

(1919)

Among the first pieces of news to reach us after the raising of the barrier separating us from the Anglo-Saxon countries comes the painful report of the death of Putnam, the President of the great pan-American psycho-analytic group. He lived to be over seventy-two years old, remained intellectually active to the end, and died peacefully of heart-failure during his sleep in November 1918. Putnam, who was until a few years ago Professor of Neuropathology at Harvard University, was the great support of psycho-analysis in America. His numerous theoretical works (a few of which made their first appearance in the *Internationale Zeitschrift*) have, by their clarity and wealth of ideas, and by the decisively favourable line they took, contributed immensely towards creating the high esteem which psycho-analysis now enjoys in America both in psychiatric teaching and in public opinion. His example may have been no less effective. He was universally respected for his unimpeachable character, and it was recognized that he was influenced only by the highest ethical considerations. His closer personal acquaintances could not escape the conclusion that he was one of those happily compensated people of the obsessional type for whom what is noble is second nature and for whom any concession to unworthiness has become an impossibility.

J. J. Putnam's personal appearance was made familiar to European analysts through the part he took in the Weimar Congress of 1911. The editor of the *Zeitschrift* hopes to include in its next issue a portrait of our honoured friend and a detailed appreciation of his scientific achievements.[2]

[1] [*Int. Z. Psychoanal.*, **5** (1919), 136 (signed 'Der Herausgeber' ['The Director']); *G.S.*, **11** (1928), 276; *G.W.*, **12** (1947), 315. The present translation, the first into English, is by James Strachey.]

[2] [This was contributed by Ernest Jones (1919). A fuller discussion of Putnam's work by Freud himself was published some two years later as a preface to a collection of Putnam's writings (Freud 1921*a*). Freud also translated one of Putnam's papers (1910) anonymously and added the following footnote to the translation (*Zbl. Psychoan.*, **1** (1911), 137): 'This lecture delivered by the Professor of Neurology at Boston

[Harvard] University is offered to our readers as an offset to the many unjust and uncomprehending attacks that are levelled against psycho-analysis, in place of counter-criticisms which might easily lead to embittered feelings. J. Putnam is not only one of the most eminent neurologists in America but also a man everywhere greatly respected for his unimpeachable character and high moral standards. Although he has left his youth far behind him, he took his open stand last year in the front rank of the champions of psycho-analysis.'

The last sentence of this footnote was commented on by Freud soon afterwards in a short paper on the forgetting of proper names (1911*i*) which was also included in the 1911 edition of *The Psychopathology of Everyday Life* (1901*b*), Chapter III, No. 11. See also Jones (1955), 82–3.

VICTOR TAUSK[1]

(1919)

AMONG the sacrifices, fortunately few in number, claimed by the war from the ranks of psycho-analysis, we must count Dr. Victor Tausk. This rarely-gifted man, a Vienna specialist in nervous diseases, took his own life before peace was signed.

Dr. Tausk, who was only in his forty-second year, had for more than ten years been one of the closer circle of Freud's followers. Originally a lawyer by profession, he had for some considerable time been acting as a magistrate in Bosnia when, under the stress of severe personal troubles, he abandoned his career and turned to journalism, for which he was peculiarly suited by his wide general education. After working for some time as a journalist in Berlin, he came to Vienna in the same capacity. Here he became acquainted with psycho-analysis and soon decided to devote himself to it entirely. Although he was no longer a young man and was the father of a family, he was not deterred by the great difficulties and sacrifices involved in yet another change in profession, and one which must necessitate an interruption of several years before he could once more earn his living. For he embarked on the tedious study of medicine only as a means to enable him to carry on a psycho-analytic practice.

Shortly before the outbreak of the [first] World War, Tausk had obtained his second doctor's degree [2] and set up in Vienna as a nerve-specialist. Here, after a relatively short time, he had begun building up a considerable practice and had achieved some excellent results. These activities promised the rising young doctor full satisfaction as well as a means of support; but he was all at once violently torn from them by the war. He was called up immediately for active service and soon promoted to senior rank. He carried out his medical duties with devotion in the various theatres of war in the North and in the Balkans

[1] [*Int. Z. Psychoanal.*, **5** (1919), 225 (signed 'Die Redaktion' ['The Editorial Committee']); *G.S.*, **11** (1928), 277; *G.W.*, **12** (1947), 316. The present translation, the first into English, is by James Strachey.]

[2] [I.e. in medicine. He already had a doctor's degree in Law.]

(finally in Belgrade), and received official commendation. It is also greatly to his honour that during the war he threw himself wholeheartedly, and with complete disregard of the consequences, into exposing the numerous abuses which so many doctors unfortunately tolerated in silence or for which they even shared the responsibility. [Cf. above, pp. 213–14.]

The stresses of many years' service in the field could not fail to exercise a severely damaging psychological effect on so intensely conscientious a man. At the last Psycho-Analytical Congress, which we held in Budapest in September 1918 and which brought analysts together once more after many years of separation, Dr. Tausk, who had long been suffering from physical ill-health, was already showing signs of unusual nervous irritability. When, soon afterwards, in the late autumn of last year, he came to the end of his military service and returned to Vienna, he was faced for the third time, in his state of mental exhaustion, with the hard task of building up a new existence—this time under the most unfavourable internal and external conditions. In addition to this, Dr. Tausk, who has left two grown-up sons to whom he was a devoted father, was on the brink of contracting a new marriage. He was no longer able to cope with the many demands imposed on him in his ailing state by harsh reality. On the morning of July 3rd [1919] he put an end to his life.

Dr. Tausk had been a member of the Vienna Psycho-Analytical Society since the autumn of 1909. He was well known to the readers of this journal [1] from his numerous contributions, which were distinguished by sharp observation, sound judgement and a particular clearness of expression. These writings exhibit plainly the philosophical training which the author was able so happily to combine with the exact methods of science. His strong need to establish things on a philosophical foundation and to achieve epistemological clarity compelled him to formulate, and seek as well to master, the whole profundity and comprehensive meaning of the very difficult problems involved. Perhaps he sometimes went too far in this direction, in his impetuous urge for investigation. Perhaps the time was not yet ripe for laying such general foundations as these for the young science of psycho-analysis. The psycho-analytic consideration of philosophical problems, for which Tausk showed special apti-

[1] [The *Internationale Zeitschrift für Psychoanalyse.*]

tude, promises to become more and more fruitful. One of his last works, on the psycho-analysis of the function of judgement, which was delivered at the Budapest Congress and has not yet been published,[1] gives evidence of this direction taken by his interest.

In addition to his gift for philosophy and attraction towards it, Tausk possessed a quite exceptional medico-psychological capacity and produced some excellent work in that field too. His clinical activities, to which we owe valuable researches into various psychoses (e.g. melancholia and schizophrenia) justified the fairest hopes and gave him the prospective appointment to a University Lectureship [*Dozentur*] for which he had applied.

Psycho-analysis was particularly indebted to Dr. Tausk, who was a brilliant speaker, for the courses of lectures which he gave over a period of many years to large audiences of both sexes and in which he introduced them to the principles and problems of psycho-analysis. His audiences were able to admire the clarity and didactic skill of his lectures no less than the profundity with which he handled individual topics.

All those who knew him well valued his straightforward character, his honesty towards himself and towards others and the superiority of a nature which was distinguished by a striving for nobility and perfection. His passionate temperament found expression in sharp, and sometimes too sharp, criticisms, which however were combined with a brilliant gift for exposition. These personal qualities exercised a great attraction on many people, and some, too, may have been repelled by them. No one, however, could escape the impression that here was a man of importance.

How much psycho-analysis meant for him, even up to his last moments, is shown by letters which he left behind, in which he expressed his unreserved belief in it and his hope that it will find recognition at a not too distant date. There is no doubt that this man, of whom our science and his friends in Vienna have been prematurely robbed, has contributed to that aim. He is sure of an honourable memory in the history of psycho-analysis and its earliest struggles.

[1] [It seems never to have appeared in print.]

BIBLIOGRAPHY
AND AUTHOR INDEX

[Titles of books and periodicals are in italics; titles of papers are in inverted commas. Abbreviations are in accordance with the *World List of Scientific Periodicals* (London, 1952). Further abbreviations used in this volume will be found in the List at the end of this bibliography. Numerals in thick type refer to volumes; ordinary numerals refer to pages. The figures in round brackets at the end of each entry indicate the page or pages of this volume on which the work in question is mentioned. In the case of the Freud entries, the letters attached to the dates of publication are in accordance with the corresponding entries in the complete bibliography of Freud's writings to be included in the last volume of the *Standard Edition.*

For non-technical authors, and for technical authors where no specific work is mentioned, see the General Index.]

ABRAHAM, K. (1916) 'Untersuchungen über die früheste prägenitale Entwicklungsstufe der Libido', *Int. Z. Psychoan.*, **4**, 71. (269)
[*Trans.:* 'The First Pregenital Stage of the Libido', *Selected Papers on Psycho-Analysis*, London, 1927, Chap. XII.]

ANDREAS-SALOMÉ, L. (1916) ' "Anal" und "Sexual" ', *Imago*, **4**, 249. (133)

BINET, A. (1888) *Études de psychologie expérimentale: le fétichisme dans l'amour*, Paris. (182)

BREUER, J., and FREUD, S. (1895) *see* FREUD, S. (1895*d*)

BRUNSWICK, R. MACK. (1928) 'A Supplement to Freud's "History of an Infantile Neurosis" ', *Int. J. Psycho-Anal.*, **9**, 439. Reprinted with an addition in *The Psycho-Analytic Reader*, ed. R. Fliess, London and New York, 1950. (122)

FERENCZI, S. (1912) 'Über passagere Symptombildung während der Analyse', *Zbl. Psychoan.*, **2**, 588. (40, 153)
[*Trans.:* 'Transitory Symptom-Constructions during the Analysis', *First Contributions to Psycho-Analysis*, London, 1952, Chap. VII.]

(1919) 'Technische Schwierigkeiten einer Hysterieanalyse', *Int. Z. Psychoan.*, **5**, 34. (162)
[*Trans.:* 'Technical Difficulties in an Analysis of Hysteria', *Further Contributions to the Theory and Technique of Psycho-Analysis*, London, 1926, Chap. XV.]

(1921) 'Weitere Ausbau der "aktiven Technik" in der Psychoanalyse', *Int. Z. Psychoan.*, **7**, 233. (162)
[*Trans.:* 'The Further Development of an Active Therapy in Psycho-Analysis', *Further Contributions to the Theory and Technique of Psycho-Analysis*, London, 1926, Chap. XVI.]

(1927) 'Zur Kritik der Rankschen "Technik der Psychoanalyse" ', *Int. Z. Psychoan.*, **13**, 1. (47)

[*Trans.:* Review of Rank's *Technik der Psychoanalyse, Int. J. Psycho-Anal.*, 8 (1927), 93.]

FREUD, S. (1895*d*) With BREUER, J., *Studien über Hysterie*, Vienna. *G.S.*, **1**, 3; *G.W.*, **1**, 99. Omitting Breuer's contributions. (45, 76, 123)
[*Trans.: Studies on Hysteria, Standard Ed.*, **2**. Including Breuer's contributions.]

(1896*b*) 'Weitere Bemerkungen über die Abwehr-Neuropsychosen', *G.S.*, **1**, 363; *G.W.*, **1**, 379. (75)
[*Trans.:* 'Further Remarks on the Neuro-sychoses of Defence', *C.P.*, **1**, 155; *Standard Ed.*, **3**.]

(1900*a*) *Die Traumdeutung*, Vienna. *G.S.*, **2–3**; *G.W.*, **2–3**. (33, 35, 51–2, 102, 103, 128, 152, 156, 235, 245)
[*Trans.: The Interpretation of Dreams*, London and New York, 1955; *Standard Ed.*, **4–5**.]

(1901*b*) *Zur Psychopathologie des Alltagslebens*, Berlin, 1904. *G.S.*, **4**; *G.W.*, **4**. (148, 236, 272)
[*Trans.: The Psychopathology of Everyday Life, Standard Ed.*, **6**.]

(1905*d*) *Drei Abhandlungen zur Sexualtheorie*, Vienna. *G.S.*, **5**, 3; *G.W.*, **5**, 29. (5, 81, 106, 115, 126, 133, 177, 182, 252)
[*Trans.: Three Essays on the Theory of Sexuality*, London, 1949; *Standard Ed.*, **7**, 125.]

(1905*e* [1901]) 'Bruchstück einer Hysterie-Analyse', *G.S.*, **8**, 3; *G.W.*, **5**, 163. (42, 92, 123)
[*Trans.:* 'Fragment of an Analysis of a Case of Hysteria', *C.P.*, **3**, 13; *Standard Ed.*, **7**, 3.]

(1906*a*) 'Meine Ansichten über die Rolle der Sexualität in der Ätiologie der Neurosen', *G.S.*, **5**, 123; *G.W.*, **5**, 149. (95)
[*Trans.:* 'My Views on the Part played by Sexuality in the Aetiology of the Neuroses', *C.P.*, **1**, 272; *Standard Ed.*, **7**, 271.]

(1908*b*) 'Charakter und Analerotik', *G.S.*, **5**, 261; *G.W.*, **7**, 203. (72, 127, 128)
[*Trans.:* 'Character and Anal Erotism', *C.P.*, **2**, 45; *Standard Ed.*, **9**,]

(1908*c*) 'Über infantile Sexualtheorien', *G.S.*, **5**, 168; *G.W.*, **7**, 171. (131)
[*Trans.:* 'On the Sexual Theories of Children', *C.P.*, **2**, 59; *Standard Ed.*, **9**.]

(1909*b*) 'Analyse der Phobie eines fünfjährigen Knaben', *G.S.*, **8**, 129; *G.W.*, **7**, 243. (5, 9, 123, 130, 155)
[*Trans.:* 'Analysis of a Phobia in a Five-Year-Old Boy', *C.P.*, **3**, 148; *Standard Ed.*, **10**, 3.]

(1909*d*) 'Bemerkungen über einen Fall von Zwangsneurose', *G.S.*, **8**, 269; *G.W.*, **7**, 381. (75, 103, 123, 149, 195, 239, 240)
[*Trans.:* 'Notes upon a Case of Obsessional Neurosis', *C.P.*, **3**, 293; *Standard Ed.*, **10**, 155.]

(1910*c*) *Eine Kindheitserinnerung des Leonardo da Vinci*, Vienna. *G.S.*, **9**, 371; *G.W.*, **8**, 128. (20, 146)
[*Trans.: Leonardo da Vinci and a Memory of His Childhood, Standard Ed.*, **11**.]

(1910*d*) 'Die zukünftigen Chancen der psychoanalytischen Therapie', *G.S.*, **6**, 25; *G.W.*, **8**, 104. (158)
[*Trans.:* 'The Future Prospects of Psycho-Analytic Therapy', *C.P.*, **2**, 285; *Standard Ed.*, **11**.]

(1911*b*) 'Formulierungen über die zwei Prinzipien des psychischen Geschehens', *G.S.*, **5**, 409; *G.W.*, **8**, 230. (204)
[*Trans.:* 'Formulations on the Two Principles of Mental Functioning', *C.P.*, **4**, 13; *Standard Ed.*, **12**.]

(1911*c*) 'Psychoanalytische Bemerkungen über einen autobiographisch beschriebenen Fall von Paranoia (Dementia Paranoides)', *G.S.*, **8**, 355; *G.W.*, **8**, 240. (84, 123)
[*Trans.:* 'Psycho-Analytic Notes on an Autobiographical Account of a Case of Paranoia (Dementia Paranoides)', *C.P.*, **3**, 387; *Standard Ed.*, **12**.]

(1911*i*) 'Ein Beitrag zum Vergessen von Eigennamen' [in 1901*b* from 4th ed. onwards], *Zbl, Psychoan.*, **1**, 407; *G.S.*, **4**, 37; *G.W.*, **4**, 37. (272)
[*Trans.:* In 1901*b*, *Standard Ed.*, **6**.]

(1911*j*) Translation with footnote of James J. Putnam's 'On the Etiology and Treatment of the Psychoneuroses', 1910, under the title 'Über Ätiologie und Behandlung der Psychoneurosen', *Zbl. Psychoan.*, **1**, Nr. 4, 137.
[*Trans.:* ootnote to James J. Putnam's 'Über Ätiologie und Behandlung der Psychoneurosen', incorporated in Editor's Footnote to 1919*b*, *Standard Ed.*, **17**, 271.]

(1912*a*) 'Nachtrag zu dem autobiographisch beschriebenen Fall von Paranoia (Dementia Paranoides)', *G.S.*, **8**, 432; *G.W.*, **8**, 317. (123)
[*Trans.:* '"Postscript" to the Case of Paranoia', *C.P.*, **3**, 467; *Standard Ed.*, **12**.]

(1912*c*) 'Über neurotische Erkrankungstypen', *G.S.*, **5**, 400; *G.W.*, **8**, 322. (118, 163)
[*Trans.:* 'Types of Onset of Neurosis', *C.P.*, **2**, 113; *Standard Ed.*, **12**.]

(1912*h*) Nachfrage des Herausgebers über Kindheitsträume, *Zbl. Psychoan.*, **2**, 680.
[*Trans.:* Request for Examples of Childhood Dreams, included in 1918*b*, *Standard Ed.*, **17**, **4**.]

(1912–13) *Totem und Tabu*, Vienna, 1913. *G.S.*, **10**, 3; *G.W.*, **9**. (6, 59, 114, 218, 241, 243, 262)
[*Trans.: Totem and Taboo*, London, 1950; New York, 1952; *Standard Ed.*, **13**, 1.]

(1913*c*) 'Weitere Ratschläge zur Technik der Psychoanalyse: [1] Zur Einleitung der Behandlung', *G.S.*, **6**, 84; *G.W.*, **8**, 454. (167)
[*Trans.:* 'On Beginning the Treatment (Further Recommendations on the Technique of Psycho-Analysis, I)', *C.P.*, **2**, 342; *Standard Ed.*, **12**.]

(1913*d*) 'Märchenstoffe in Träumen', *G.S.*, **3**, 259; *G.W.*, **10**, 2. (4, 29, 85)

[*Trans.:* 'The Occurrence in Dreams of Material from Fairy Tales', *C.P.*, **4**, 236; *Standard Ed.*, **12**.]

(1913*i*) 'Die Disposition zur Zwangsneurose', *G.S.*, **5**, 277; *G.W.*, **8**, 442. (64, 117, 127, 182)

[*Trans.:* 'The Predisposition to Obsessional Neurosis', *C.P.*, **2**, 122; *Standard Ed.*, **12**.]

(1913*j*) 'Das Interesse an der Psychoanalyse', *G.S.*, **4**, 313; *G.W.*, **8**, 390. (261)

[*Trans.* 'The Claims of Psycho-Analysis to Scientific Interest', *Standard Ed.*, **13**, 165.]

(1913*l*) 'Kindheitsträume mit spezieller Bedeutung', *Int. Z. Psychoan.*, **1**, 79.

[*Trans.:* 'Childhood Dreams with a Particular Meaning', included in 1918*b*, *Standard Ed.*, **17**, 4.]

(1914*a*) 'Über fausse reconnaissance ("déjà raconté") während der psychoanalytischen Arbeit', *G.S.*, **6**, 76; *G.W.*, **10**, 116. (5, 85)

[*Trans.:* 'Fausse Reconnaissance ("déjà raconté") in Psycho-Analytic Treatment', *C.P.*, **2**, 334; *Standard Ed.*, **13**, 201.]

(1914*c*) 'Zur Einführung des Narzissmus', *G.S.*, **6**, 155; *G.W.*, **10**, 138. (6, 53, 129, 136, 194, 236)

[*Trans.:* 'On Narcissism: an Introduction', *C.P.*, **4**, 30; *Standard Ed.*, **14**.]

(1914*d*) 'Zur Geschichte der psychoanalytischen Bewegung', *G.S.*, **4**, 411; *G.W.*, **10**, 44. (7, 23, 164)

[*Trans.:* 'On the History of the Psycho-Analytic Movement', *C.P.*, **1**, 287; *Standard Ed.*, **14**.]

(1914*g*) 'Weitere Ratschläge zur Technik der Psychoanalyse: II. Erinnern, Wiederholen und Durcharbeiten', *G.S.*, **6**, 109; *G.W.*, **10**, 126. (159, 239)

[*Trans.:* 'Recollecting, Repeating and Working Through (Further Recommendations on the Technique of Psycho-Analysis, II)', *C.P.*, **2**, 366; *Standard Ed.*, **12**.]

(1915*a* 'Weitere Ratschläge zur Technik der Psychoanalyse: III. Bemerkugen über die Übertragungsliebe', *G.S.*, **6**, 120; *G.W.*, **10**, 306. (162)

[*Trans.:* 'Observations on Transference-Love (Further Recommendations on the Technique of Psycho-Analysis, III)', *C.P.*, **2**, 377; *Standard Ed.*, **12**.]

(1915*b*) 'Zeitgemässes über Krieg und Tod', *G.S.*, **10**, 315; *G.W.*, **10**, 324. (242)

[*Trans.:* 'Thoughts for the Times on War and Death', *C.P.*, **4**, 288; *Standard Ed.*, **14**.]

(1915*c*) 'Triebe und Triebschicksale', *G.S.*, **5**, 443; *G.W.*, **10**, 210. (26, 106, 194)

[*Trans.:* 'Instincts and their Vicissitudes', *C.P.*, **4**, 60; *Standard Ed.*, **14**.]

(1915*d*) 'Die Verdrängung', *G.S.*, **5**, 466; *G.W.*, **10**, 248. (5, 178)

[*Trans.:* 'Repression', *C.P.*, **4**, 84; *Standard Ed.*, **14**.]

(1915*e*) 'Das Unbewusste', *G.S.*, **5**, 480; *G.W.*, **10**, 264. (10, 81, 178)

[*Trans.*: 'The Unconscious', *C.P.*, **4**, 98; *Standard Ed.*, **14.**]

(1915*f*) 'Mitteilung eines der psychoanalytischen Theorie widersprechenden Falles von Paranoia', *G.S.*, **5**, 288; *G.W.*, **10**, 234. (116, 123)

[*Trans.*: 'A Case of Paranoia Running Counter to the Psycho-Analytic Theory of the Disease', *C.P.*, **2**, 150; *Standard Ed.*, **14.**]

(1916*d*) 'Einige Charaktertypen aus der psychoanalytischen Arbeit', *G.S.*, **10**, 287; *G.W.*, **10**, 364. (28)

[*Trans.*: 'Some Character-Types Met with in Psycho-Analytic Work', *C.P.*, **4**, 318; *Standard Ed.*, **14.**]

(1916–17) *Vorlesungen zur Einführung in die Psychoanalyse*, Vienna. *G.S.*, **7**; *G.W.*, **11.** (5, 7, 57, 60, 97, 136, 159, 193)

[*Trans.*: *Introductory Lectures on Psycho-Analysis*, revised ed., London, 1929 (*A General Introduction to Psychoanalysis*, New York, 1935); *Standard Ed.*, **15–16.**]

(1917*a*) 'Eine Schwierigkeit der Psychoanalyse', *G.S.*, **10**, 347; *G.W.*, **12**, 3. (98)

[*Trans.*: 'A Difficulty in the Path of Psycho-Analysis', *C.P.*, **4**, 347; *Standard Ed.*, **17**, 137.]

(1917*b*) 'Eine Kindheitserinnerung aus *Dichtung und Wahrheit*', *G.S.*, **10**, 357; *G.W.*, **12**, 15.

[*Trans.*: 'A Childhood Recollection from *Dichtung und Wahrheit*' *C.P.*, **4**, 357; *Standard Ed.*, **17**, 147.]

(1917*c*) 'Über Triebumsetzungen insbesondere der Analerotik', *G.S.*, **5**, 268; *G.W.*, **10**, 402. (5, 80)

[*Trans.*: 'On Transformations of Instinct, as Exemplified in Anal Erotism', *C.P.*, **2**, 164; *Standard Ed.*, **17**, 127.]

(1917*e*) 'Trauer und Melancholie', *G.S.*, **5**, 535; *G.W.*, **10**, 428. (6)

[*Trans.*: 'Mourning and Melancholia', *C.P.*, **4**, 152; *Standard Ed.*, **14.**]

(1918*b* [1914]) 'Aus der Geschichte einer infantilen Neurose', *G.S.*, **8**, 439; *G.W.*, **12**, 29. (123, 126, 166, 178, 198, 201, 244)

[*Trans.*: 'From the History of an Infantile Neurosis', *C.P.*, **3**, 473; *Standard Ed.*, **17**, 3.]

(1919*a* [1918]) 'Wege der psychoanalytischen Therapie', *G.S.*, **6**, 136; *G.W.*, **12**, 183.

[*Trans.*: 'Lines of Advance in Psycho-Analytic Therapy', *C.P.*, **2**, 392; *Standard Ed.*, **17**, 159.]

(1919*b*) 'James J. Putnam', *G.S.*, **11**, 276; *G.W.*, **12**, 315.

[*Trans.*: 'James J. Putnam', *Standard Ed.*, **17**, 271.]

(1919*c*) 'Internationaler psychoanalytischer Verlag und Preiszuteilungen für psychoanalytische Arbeiten', *G W* , **12**, 333.

[*Trans* : 'A Note on Psycho-Analytic Publications and Prizes', *Standard Ed.*, **17**, 267.]

(1919*d*) Einleitung zu *Zur Psychoanalyse der Kriegsneurosen*, Vienna. *G.S.*, **11**, 252; *G.W.*, **12**, 321.

[*Trans.*: Introduction to *Psycho-Analysis and the War Neuroses*, London and New York, 1921. *C.P.*, **5**, 83; *Standard Ed.*, **17**, 207.]

(1919*e*) ' "Ein Kind wird geschlagen" ', *G.S.*, **5**, 344; *G.W.*, **12**, 197. (6, 26, 111)
[*Trans.:* ' "A Child is Being Beaten" ', *C.P.*, **2**, 172; *Standard Ed.*, **17**, 177.]
(1919*f*) 'Victor Tausk', *G.S.*, **11**, 277; *G.W.*, **12**, 316.
[*Trans.:* 'Victor Tausk', *Standard Ed.*, **17**, 273.]
(1919*g*) Vorrede zu Reik *Probleme der Religionspsychologie*, Vienna. *G.S.*, **11**, 256; *G.W.*, **12**, 325.
[*Trans.:* Preface to Reik's *Ritual: Psycho-Analytic Studies*, London and New York, 1931. *C.P.*, **5**, 92; *Standard Ed.*, **17**, 259.]
(1919*h*) 'Das Unheimliche', *G.S.*, **10**, 369; *G.W.*, **12**, 229.
[*Trans.:* 'The "Uncanny" ', *C.P.*, **4**, 368; *Standard Ed.*, **17**, 219.]
(1919*j* [1918]) 'Kell-e az egyetemen a psychoanalysist tanitani?', *Gyógyászat* (Budapest), **59**, Nr. 13, 192.
[*Trans.:* 'On the Teaching of Psycho-Analysis in Universities', *Standard Ed.*, **17**, 171.]
(1919*k*) 'E. T. A. Hoffmann über die Bewusstseinsfunktion', *Int. Z. Psychoan.*, **5**, Nr. 4, 308.
[*Trans.:* in 1919*h*, *Standard Ed.*, **17**, 233*n*.]
(1920*a*) 'Über die Psychogenese eines Falles von weiblicher Homosexualität', *G.S.*, **5**, 312; *G.W.*, **12**, 271. (123)
[*Trans.:* 'The Psychogenesis of a Case of Female Homosexuality', *C.P.*, **2**, 202; *Standard Ed.*, **18**, 147.]
(1920*c*) 'Dr. Anton von Freund', *G.S.*, **11**, 280; *G.W.*, **13**, 435. (267)
[*Trans.:* 'Dr. Anton von Freund', *Standard Ed.*, **18**, 267.]
(1920*g*) *Jenseits des Lustprinzips*, Vienna. *G.S.*, **6**, 191; *G.W.*, **13**, 3. (86, 194, 218, 234, 238, 242)
[*Trans.:* *Beyond the Pleasure Principle*, London, 1950; *Standard Ed.*, **18**, 7.]
(1921*a*) Preface [in English] to J. J. Putnam's *Addresses on Psycho-Analysis*, London and New York. *G.S.*, **11**, 262; *G.W.*, **13**, 437; *Standard Ed.*, **18**, 269. (165, 271)
(1921*c*) *Massenpsychologie und Ich-Analyse*, Vienna. *G.S.*, **6**, 261; *G.W.* **13**, 73. (27, 236)
[*Trans.:* *Group Psychology and the Analysis of the Ego*, London, 1922; New York, 1940; *Standard Ed.*, **18**, 69.]
(1921*d*) 'Preiszuteilungen', *Int. Z. Psychoan.*, **7**, 38.
[*Trans.:* 'Award of Prizes', included in 1919*c*, *Standard Ed.*, **17**, 269.]
(1922*c*) 'Nachschrift zur Analyse des kleinen Hans', *G.S.*, **8**, 264; *G.W.*, **13**, 431. (123)
[*Trans.:* 'Postscript to the "Analysis of a Phobia in a Five-Year-Old Boy" ', *C.P.*, **3**, 288; *Standard Ed.*, **10**, 148.]
(1922*d*) 'Preisausschreibung', *Int. Z. Psychoan.*, **8**, 527.
[*Trans.:* 'Prize Offer', included in 1919*c*, *Standard Ed.*, **17**, 269.]
(1923*b*) *Das Ich und das Es*, Vienna. *G.S.*, **6**, 353; *G.W.*, **13**, 237. (6, 102, 182, 194, 236)
[*Trans.:* *The Ego and the Id*, London, 1927; *Standard Ed.*, **19**.]

(1923*c*) 'Bemerkungen zur Theorie und Praxis der Traumdeutung', *G.S.*, **3**, 305; *G.W.*, **13**, 301. (52)
[*Trans.*: 'Remarks on the Theory and Practice of Dream-Interpretation', *C.P.*, **5**, 136; *Standard Ed.*, **19**.]

(1924*c*) 'Das ökonomische Problem des Masochismus', *G.S.*, **5**, 374; *G.W.*, **13**, 371. (197)
[*Trans.*: 'The Economic Problem of Masochism', *C.P.*, **2**, 255; *Standard Ed.*, **19**.]

(1924*d*) 'Der Untergang des Ödipuskomplexes', *G.S.*, **5**, 423; *G.W.*, **13**, 395. (188)
[*Trans.*: 'The Dissolution of the Oedipus Complex', *C.P.*, **2**, 269; *Standard Ed.*, **19**.]

(1925*e*) 'Die Widerstände gegen die Psychoanalyse', *G.S.*, **11**, 224; *G.W.*, **14**, 99. (136)
[*Trans.*: 'The Resistances to Psycho-Analysis', *C.P.*, **5**, 163; *Standard Ed.*, **19**.]

(1925*h*) 'Die Verneinung', *G.S.*, **11**, 3; *G.W.*, **14**, 11. (81, 245)
[*Trans.*: 'Negation', *C.P.*, **5**, 181; *Standard Ed.*, **19**.]

(1926*d*) *Hemmung, Symptom und Angst*, Vienna. *G.S.*, **11**, 23; *G.W.*, **14**, 133. (5, 75, 111, 113, 161)
[*Trans.*: *Inhibitions, Symptoms and Anxiety*, London, 1936 (*The Problem of Anxiety*, New York, 1936); *Standard Ed.*, **20**.]

(1927*c*) *Die Zukunft einer Illusion*, Vienna. *G.S.*, **11**, 411; *G.W.*, **14**, 325. (115)
[*Trans.*: *The Future of an Illusion*, London, 1928; *Standard Ed.*, **21**.]

(1930*a*) *Das Unbehagen in der Kultur*, Vienna. *G.S.*, **12**, 29; *G.W.*, **14**, 421. (92)
[*Trans.*: *Civilization and its Discontents*, London and New York, 1930; *Standard Ed.*, **21**.]

(1932*a*) 'Zur Gewinnung des Feuers', *G.S.*, **12**, 141; *G.W.*, **16**, 3. (92)
[*Trans.*: 'The Acquisition and Control of Fire', *C.P.*, **5**, 288; *Standard Ed.*, **22**.]

(1937*c*) 'Die endliche und die unendliche Analyse', *G.W.*, **16**, 59. (5, 11, 122, 158, 178, 200)
[*Trans.*: 'Analysis Terminable and Interminable', *C.P.*, **5**, 316; *Standard Ed.*, **23**.]

(1937*d*) 'Konstruktionen in der Analyse', *G.W.*, **16**, 43. (19, 51, 158)
[*Trans.*: 'Constructions in Analysis', *C.P.*, **5**, 358; *Standard Ed.*, **23**.]

(1950*a* [1887–1902]) *Aus den Anfängen der Psychoanalyse*, London. Includes 'Entwurf einer Psychologie' (1895). (39, 45, 111, 178)
[*Trans.*: *The Origins of Psycho-Analysis*, London and New York, 1954. (Partly, including 'A Project for a Scientific Psychology', in *Standard Ed.*, **1**.)]

(1955*a* [1907–8]) Original Record of the Case of Obsessional Neurosis (the 'Rat Man'), *Standard Ed.*, **10**, 259. German text unpublished. (123)

(1955*c* [1920]) 'Memorandum on the Electrical Treatment of War Neuroses', *Standard Ed.*, **17**, 211. (206)
[*German Text* (unpublished): 'Gutachten über die elektrische Behandlung der Kriegsneurotiker.']

GARDINER, M. (1952) 'Meetings with the Wolf-Man', *Bull. Philad. Ass. Psychoan.*, **2**, 32; reprinted in *Bull. Menninger Clin.*, **17** (1953), 41. (122)

GRIMM, J. and W. (1877) *Deutsches Wörterbuch*, **4**, Leipzig. (225–6)

HALL, G. S. (1914) 'A Synthetic Genetic Study of Fear', *Amer. J. Psychol.*, **25**, 149. (113)

HITSCHMANN, E. (1913) 'Weitere Mitteilung von Kindheitsträumen mit spezieller Bedeutung', *Int. Z. Psychoan.*, **1**, 476. (4)

JENTSCH, E. (1906) 'Zur Psychologie des Unheimlichen', *Psychiat.-neurol. Wschr.*, **8**, 195. (219–21, 226–7)

JONES, ERNEST (1914) 'Die Stellungnahme des psychoanalytischen Arztes zu den aktuellen Konflikten', *Int. Z. Psychoan.*, **2**, 6. (165)
[*English Text:* 'The Attitude of the Psycho-Analytic Physician towards Current Conflicts', *Papers on Psycho-Analysis*, 2nd ed., London, 1918, Chap. XVII.]

(1919) 'Professor Dr. James Jackson Putnam', *Int. Z. Psychoan.*, **5**, 233. (271)
[*English Text:* 'Dr. James Jackson Putnam', *Int. J. Psycho-Anal.*, **1** (1920), 6.]

(1955) *Sigmund Freud: Life and Work*, Vol. 2, London and New York. (3, 6, 122, 272)

JUNG, C. G. (1917) *Die Psychologie der unbewussten Prozesse*, Zurich. (97)

KAMMERER, P. (1919) *Das Gesetz der Serie*, Vienna. (238)

MACH, E. (1900) *Die Analyse der Empfindung*, 2nd ed., Jena. (248)

MARCINOWSKI, J. (1918) 'Erotische Quellen der Minderwertigkeitsgefühle', *Z. Sexualwiss. Bonn*, **4**, 313. (193)

OPHUIJSEN, J. H. W. VAN (1917) 'Beiträge zum Männlichkeitskomplex der Frau', *Int. Z. Psychoan.*, **4**, 241. (191)
Trans.: 'Contributions to the Masculinity Complex in Women', *Int. J. Psycho-Anal.*, **5** (1924), 39.]

PUTNAM, J. J. (1910) 'On the Etiology and Treatment of the Psychoneuroses', *Boston med. surg. J.*, **163**, 75; *Addresses on Psycho-Analysis*, London and New York, 1921, Chap. III. (271)

RANK, O. (1912*a*) 'Völkerpsychologische Parallelen zu den infantilen Sexualtheorien', *Zbl. Psychoan.*, **2**, 372 and 425. (32)

(1912*b*) *Das Inzestmotiv in Dichtung und Sage*, Vienna. (261)

(1914) 'Der Doppelgänger', *Imago*, **3**, 97. (234–6)

(1926) *Technik der Psvchoanalyse I. Die analytische Situation*, Vienna. (47)

RANK, O., and SACHS, H. (1913) *Die Bedeutung der Psychoanalyse für die Geisteswissenschaften, Wiesbaden.* (261)
[*Trans.: The Significance of Psychoanalysis for the Mental Sciences*, New York, 1916.]

REIK, T. (1915–16) 'Die Pubertätsriten der Wilden', *Imago*, **4**, 125 and 189. (269)

SACHS, H., and RANK, O. (1913) *See* RANK, O., and SACHS, H. (1913)

SANDERS, D. (1860) *Wörterbuch der Deutschen Sprache*, Leipzig. (221–5, 253–6)

SELIGMANN, S. (1910–11) *Der böse Blick und Verwandtes*, Berlin. (240)

SIMMEL, E. (1918) *Kriegsneurosen und psychisches Trauma*, Munich. (269)

SMITH, W. ROBERTSON (1889) *Lectures on the Religion of the Semites*, London. (262)

LIST OF ABBREVIATIONS

G.S. = Freud, *Gesammelte Schriften* (12 vols.), Vienna, 1924–34
G.W. = Freud, *Gesammelte Werke* (18 vols.), London, from 1940
C.P. = Freud, *Collected Papers* (5 vols.), London, 1924–50
Standard Ed. = Freud, *Standard Edition* (24 vols.), London, from 1953
S.K.S.N. = Freud, *Sammlung kleiner Schriften zur Neurosenlehre* (5 vols.), Vienna, 1906–22
Dichtung und Kunst = Freud, *Psychoanalytische Studien an Werken der Dichtung und Kunst*, Vienna, 1924
Neurosenlehre und Technik = Freud, *Schriten zur Neurosenlehre und zur psychoanalytischen Technik (1913–1926)*, Vienna, 1931
Psychoanalyse der Neurosen = Freud, *Studien zur Psychoanalyse der Neurosen aus den Jahren 1913–1925*, Vienna, 1926
Sexualtheorie und Traumlehre = Freud, *Kleine Schriften zur Sexualtheorie und zur Traumlehre*, Vienna, 1931
Technik und Metapsychol. = Freud, *Zur Technik der Psvchoanalyse und zur Metapsychologie*, Vienna, 1924

GENERAL INDEX

This index includes the names of non-technical authors. It also includes the names of technical authors where no reference is made in the text to specific works. For references to specific technical works, the Bibliography should be consulted.—The compilation of the index was undertaken by Mrs. R. S. Partridge.